About the Autho

Among the best known and most respected gardening experts on the prairies, Hugh Skinner and Sara Williams bring decades of gardening experience to *Best Trees and Shrubs for the Prairies.*

Hugh Skinner holds a B.S.A. in horticulture from the University of Manitoba and has been active in the nursery industry for thirty years. He grows a wide variety of hardy plants and maintains a large collection of trees in the Frank Skinner Arboretum near Roblin, Manitoba, the result of ninety years of plant collecting, testing, and breeding, first started by his father, Frank Skinner. In the fall of 2001,

Hugh travelled to China to observe many hardy Asian tree and shrub species, his special interest, growing in botanical gardens and in their native habitat.

Sara Williams has recently retired as the horticultural specialist at the University of Saskatchewan. She is the co-author of *Perennials for the Plains and Prairies*, author of the award-winning *Creating the Prairie Xeriscape*, and holds a B.Sc. and M.Sc. in horticulture from the University of Saskatchewan. Sara has led garden tours to England, Scotland, Ireland, and elsewhere, and now spends much of her time in her five-acre garden near Saskatoon.

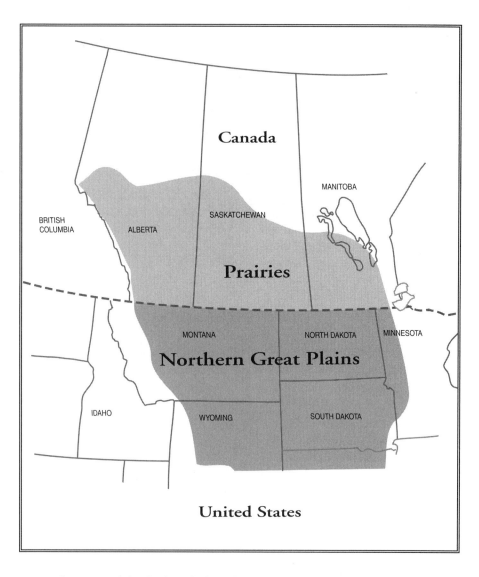

The trees and shrubs described in this book are recommended for gardens in the Canadian prairies and the northern Great Plains of the United States.

Best Trees and Shrubs for the Prairies

HUGH SKINNER AND
SARA WILLIAMS

FOREWORD BY DAVID TARRANT

FIFTH
HOUSE

Cover photos (left to right): top row, *Betula*, John Luckhurst; *Spiraea* and *Pinus*, Liesbeth Leatherbarrow; Assiniboine Park Gardens, Winnipeg, Manitoba, Lesley Reynolds; second row, *Rosa* 'William Baffin,' Lesley Reynolds; *Cotoneaster lucidus*, Brian Baldwin; *Malus baccata* 'Thunderchild,' Liesbeth Leatherbarrow; third row, *Berberis thunbergii* 'Rose Glow,' Sara Williams; evergreens, Lesley Reynolds; *Potentilla fruticosa* 'Pink Beauty,' Jeffries Nurseries Ltd.
Cover and interior design by John Luckhurst / GDL
Map by Articulate Eye
Edited by Roberta Coulter
Copyedited by Geri Rowlatt
Proofread by Meaghan Craven

The publisher gratefully acknowledges the support of The Canada Council for the Arts and the Department of Canadian Heritage. We acknowledge the financial support of the Government of Canada through the Book Publishing Industry Development Program (BPIDP) for our publishing activities.

THE CANADA COUNCIL | LE CONSEIL DES ARTS
FOR THE ARTS | DU CANADA
SINCE 1957 | DEPUIS 1957

Printed in Canada by Friesens

05 06 07 08/ 5 4 3

First published in the United States in 2004

National Library of Canada Cataloguing in Publication

Skinner, Hugh, 1951-
    Best trees and shrubs for the Prairies /
    Hugh Skinner and Sara Williams.

Includes bibliographical references and index.
ISBN 1-894004-95-7

1. Ornamental trees—Prairie Provinces. 2. Ornamental shrubs—Prairie Provinces. I. Williams, Sara, 1941- II. Title.

SB435.6.C32P73 2004   635.9'77'09712   C2003-907134-0

Fifth House Ltd.   Fitzhenry & Whiteside
A Fitzhenry & Whiteside Company   121 Harvard Avenue, Suite 2
1511-1800 4 St. SW   Allston, MA 02134
Calgary, Alberta, Canada
T2S 2S5
1-800-387-9776
www.fitzhenry.ca

Contents

✦

Dedication

✤

This book is dedicated to the pioneer prairie plant breeders who made it all possible:

W. J. Boughen, Georges Bugnet, W. A. (Bill) Cumming, Robert Erskine, Les Kerr, Henry Marshall, C. F. Patterson, A. J. (Bert) Porter, Robert Simonet, Frank L. Skinner, Percy Wright, John Walker, and John Wallace

And on a more personal level, Hugh wishes to dedicate this book to his father, Frank Skinner, who aroused his interest in plants, and to his mother, Helen, who patiently encouraged it.

Sara wishes to dedicate this book to her parents, Robert Shosteck and Dora Rabinovitz, who made her possible.

Acknowledgements

✤

Many people contributed to this book, and we thank them heartily for their expertise, generosity, support, and encouragement. For allowing us to use their fine photographs, we thank Lesley Reynolds, Liesbeth Leatherbarrow, Bailey Nurseries, Jeffries Nurseries, Brian Baldwin, John Davidson, Barbara Kam, and the Agriculture and Agri-Food Canada Research Centre, Morden, Manitoba. We also thank Erl Svendsen for the authors-in-a-tree photo.

Bill Schroeder, Rick Durand, Campbell Davidson, Paddy Tutty, and Catherine Miller answered questions and supplied sometimes esoteric information, while Brian Baldwin of the University of Saskatchewan College of Agriculture provided an exceptionally thorough (and opinionated) technical review.

Thanks also to the editorial/production team: Lesley Reynolds at Fifth House, for overseeing this project and negotiating the curves and roadblocks with patience and good humor; Roberta Coulter, for exceptional substantive editing (as always); Geri Rowlatt, for copy-editing; Meaghan Craven, for proofreading; and John Luckhurst, for design. As well, Rick Durand kindly and conscientiously reviewed the final proof and made several helpful suggestions.

Foreword

✤

Trees and shrubs are key components of any landscape, be it natural or cultivated, and as prairie gardeners well know, many of them are a challenge to establish in home gardens. Fortunately, thanks to plant introductions from similar climates and the dedication and success of prairie plant breeders, there are now countless beautiful and reliably hardy trees and shrubs available to grace prairie gardens.

Hugh Skinner and Sara Williams have combined their considerable expertise to select the best available trees and shrubs and provide complete and reliable information on how to grow them successfully. Between them they have left no stone unturned. Every suitable species is included, as well as an intriguing selection of borderline-hardy, challenging plants to tempt the adventurous gardener.

The recommendations and advice in *Best Trees and Shrubs for the Prairies* are based on the authors' many years of down-to-earth, hands-on experience cultivating almost all of the trees and shrubs that will grow on the prairies. I particularly like the detailed descriptions of important basics such as hardiness, placement, pruning, and the all-important soil preparation. The helpful, correct pronunciation of botanical names ensures that gardeners will be able to confidently and accurately request specific trees and shrubs when they visit the garden center.

Written in an easy-to-understand style, this comprehensive book will undoubtedly have great appeal to novice and expert prairie gardeners alike. Anyone who follows the valuable advice found within these pages will end up with a prize collection of beautiful, well-placed trees and shrubs that will give years of satisfaction and is sure to turn the heads of gardeners everywhere.

David Tarrant
Public Relations and Program Coordinator for the University of British Columbia Botanical Garden and Centre for Plant Research

Preface

❦

Planting a small tree or shrub is a leap of faith, reaffirmed every time we observe the landscapes developed by our parents and grandparents. Given time and nurturing, our saplings, too, will mature to provide shelter, privacy, shade, and beauty. They will become the "bones" of our garden, the structure upon which it depends.

Choosing the right tree or shrub for an individual landscape is difficult on the prairies, where hardiness is a major concern. Yet it is hardly impossible, and there are more choices available to prairie gardeners than ever before, thanks to the efforts of modern-day plant explorers and plant breeders. This book provides prairie gardeners with a palette of plant material for use in a variety of situations: a condominium courtyard, an urban lot, an acreage, or a farmyard. You'll find information on the best trees and shrubs for the plains and prairies, including both positive and, if warranted, negative characteristics.

Writing *Best Trees and Shrubs for the Prairies* forced us to organize our knowledge and defend our opinions, gained over many years of gardening in the prairie climate. The fact that we are separated by about 500 km (310 mi.) and deal with different soil and moisture conditions ensured that our opinions and experiences with these plants would differ. Still, the overlap of our experiences both surprised and pleased us.

Setting the plant selection criteria also posed a challenge. In the end, we chose to include trees and shrubs that are generally reliably hardy, widely available, have good landscape value, and are relatively pest and disease free. For the most part, we stuck to the tried and true of the woody prairie landscape, but some of our selections verge on the edge. These "edgy" plants may not be reliably hardy in all regions of the prairies, but have done very well in sheltered locations. Others, such as 'Depressa Aurea' common juniper, although worthy, are difficult to obtain at present. However, they will eventually show up in nurseries and garden centers if customers ask for them.

We have also included enough of the unusual to satisfy a gardener's need for diversity. For instance, rose daphne is notorious for suddenly giving up the ghost, but it is much too lovely to exclude. As well, some new introductions, such as the recent barberry cultivars, have not yet been thoroughly tested. Still, if there are disappointments—a 'Sensation' Manitoba maple killed to ground level—there are also pleasant surprises—a 'Golden Nugget' barberry coming unscathed through a winter with little snow cover.

We hope that you will share our passion for the trees and shrubs that give beauty to our landscape and pleasure to our souls and that you will find *Best Trees and Shrubs for the Prairies* helpful, informative, and enjoyable.

Introduction

✦

This book consists of two major parts. The first part begins with a chapter on landscaping and an examination of the functions that trees and shrubs perform in the landscape, such as providing shade, shelter, privacy, screening, and defining and delineating space. When selecting a tree or shrub, gardeners should consider its form, foliage, flowers, fruit, and bark. Placement of a plant is discussed from both the plant's and the gardener's perspective.

In the second chapter, you'll find information on the differences between trees and shrubs and on the critical importance of hardiness—where genetics, microclimate, and care interact. This chapter also tells you what you need to know about purchasing and planting trees and shrubs.

Maintenance is crucial to plant health. The third chapter covers information on pruning, including diagrams, as well as on environmental stresses, chemical injury, and insect and disease problems that may affect your trees and shrubs.

Part I includes several lists of trees and shrubs, ranging from those that are native to the prairies to those that have silver foliage, provide songbird habitat, are poisonous, sucker, or are drought tolerant, as well as several others. All of them are designed to help you select trees or shrubs for your landscape.

Part II covers the plants themselves, which are arranged alphabetically by botanical name (*Abies* to *Weigela*). Each entry includes the botanical name (and its pronunciation so you can ask for it with confidence at the garden center) and the common names. The Plant at a Glance section encapsulates important information: plant type, size, light requirements, soil preference, distinguishing features, and landscape use. In Plant at a Glance, the heading Height/Spread is used for plants that have differing measurements for the height and spread; the heading Height and Spread is used where those measurements are the same.

Along with the somewhat quirky information about its history, the folklore around it, or the origin of its name, the major portion of each entry centers on the plant's description, care, and culture and its recommended cultivars. The How to Grow section tells you what the plant needs to grow and to thrive. The name of the nursery or research station that introduced the plant may also be included. For example, Morden refers to the Agriculture and Agri-Food Canada Research centre in Morden, Manitoba.

Look for the heading On the Edge, which introduces short descriptions of unusual or less-used trees and shrubs. These include plants that will appeal to adventurous gardeners not afraid to push prairie gardening limits. We also include under this heading native species that are not always readily available, but well worth seeking out.

Finally, interesting and informative sidebars are found throughout the book and include everything from the relationship between willow and aspirin to the cause of variegated foliage.

🍁

Why Do We Use Latin Names?

Common names can be confusing for a number of reasons: the same plant often has more than one common name (*e.g.*, European mountain ash and rowan tree); the same common name may refer to more than one plant (cranberry refers to species of both *Viburnum* and *Vaccinium*); and common names may imply a close affinity between plants that does not exist (such as between mountain ash and ash). Latin names, however, give us a universal language for identifying plants, which allows botanists and horticulturists around the world to communicate about and to exchange plants.

Scientists give plants Latin names according to the international system of binomial nomenclature developed by Swedish botanist Carolus Linnaeus in the eighteenth century. The name of each plant species has two parts: the generic term (the genus) and the specific epithet. Together, these identify the species. In the name *Betula papyrifera*, *Betula* is the name of the genus and *papyrifera* is the specific epithet. A species is a group of plants occurring in nature that are similar in certain essential characteristics. A group of plants within a species can be assigned to a subordinate group that is a subspecies or botanical variety. These groups have either inheritable characteristics that are reasonably stable or a geographical distribution that is distinct. For example, *Pseudotsuga menziesii* var. *glauca* (Rocky Mountain Douglas fir) is more compact and bluish than the coastal subspecies *Pseudotsuga menziesii* var. *menziesii*.

Cultivars—cultivated varieties—are improved selections that have been developed by horticulturists and gardeners. Cultivars can be reproduced vegetatively by cloning from a single plant (*e.g.*, *Cornus alba* 'Bud's Yellow') or reproduced from a stable seed population (*e.g.*, *Acer ginnala* 'Flame').

Interspecific hybrids are the result of a hybrid between two related species. For example, *Syringa* x *prestoniae* is a hybrid between *S. villosa* and *S. reflexa*, of which there are many cultivars. The small "x" in front of the specific epithet indicates that it is an interspecific hybrid.

CHAPTER ONE

Landscaping with Trees and Shrubs

❦

FUNCTION FOLLOWS FORM: WHAT THEY DO AND WHY

The landscapes we work with as individual gardeners can be as small as a courtyard in a condominium or as expansive as a farmyard. But within each landscape, no matter what its size, trees and shrubs play many of the same roles. The major difference is in scale and proportion.

Trees and shrubs can provide shade, shelter from wind and dust, noise abatement, privacy, screening, enframement, or groundcover. In the process, many of them attract birds and wildlife, providing both habitat and food. And, through all of these roles, they soften and enhance our living space with their subtle beauty.

More than any other attribute, the form or shape of a tree or shrub determines its function. A horizontal juniper will never provide shade; an elm will never act as a groundcover. When you want "something tall and narrow" to give year-round privacy in the narrow space between your deck and your neighbor's, you choose a conical 'Brandon' cedar or a Rocky

Mountain juniper rather than a pine or spruce. Function indeed follows form.

SHADE

Shade trees are those we sit beneath to avoid the heat of the summer sun. They should be sufficiently "high headed" so we don't bump our heads while walking beneath them, their canopy should be wide enough to accommodate a number of people, and their foliage should be dense enough to filter out light.

But there's more to choosing a shade tree than the quality of the shade it casts. You should consider its attractiveness to insects, as you may not appreciate cankerworms trapezing down silken threads in the middle of a picnic supper, or aphid honeydew splatting on your burgers. Falling or fermenting fruit can also be a nuisance and attract wasps. And don't forget to think about scale—the tree should be in proportion to the size of your landscape. A large yard can accommodate a willow or basswood, while a low-headed flowering crabapple is better suited to a smaller space.

1

SHELTER

Farm shelterbelts are wide. They are made up of several rows of trees and shrubs, which are triangular in cross-section so that the wind is deflected up and over them. City and town lots lack sufficient space for a traditional shelterbelt, but the principle remains the same. In urban areas, noise is a more significant problem than wind and dust, unless you live in a newer subdivision, where dust and soil from nearby fields or construction sites may blow into your yard.

To deflect wind and dust and—to some degree—noise, plants must be dense enough to redirect the wind up and over your property. Try untrimmed cotoneaster, the larger purple barberries, or 'Sutherland' caragana. Evergreens will perform this function effectively through four seasons. Select a large evergreen shrub, such as Rocky Mountain juniper, 'Techny' cedar, or mugo pine. If you have enough space, try Colorado spruce.

PRIVACY AND SCREENING

City and town dwellers live cheek by jowl, with restrictive bylaws that limit the height of fences, and with little space for plants to do their job. Although trees always take up more space than a fence or a vine-covered trellis, some take up very little space, and there are no height restrictions on trees. If your neighbor's deck overlooks yours and space is limited, think tall and narrow: 'Brandon' or 'Skybound' cedar, 'Medora' or 'Gray Ice' juniper, 'Sutherland' caragana, or Swedish columnar aspen.

HIDING AND ENFRAMEMENT

Hiding and enframement are actually two sides of the same coin. We want to conceal objects we find distasteful and enhance those we find pleasing. In all likelihood, both belong to a neighbor. To hide a neighbor's old garage, for instance, try an informal shrub border of sufficient height to block your sight line, and composed mainly of evergreens so it is effective year-round.

Enframement involves planting a tree that will eventually accentuate a view you find pleasing. Ideally, it should be placed with its trunk on one side of the view, with an enframing branch overhead, and be as close to the property line as possible, so that its canopy acts as a "ceiling." A large flowering crabapple is a good choice. Dark purple foliage is much better for accentuating the predominantly green view beyond. Existing trees can be judiciously pruned to better enframe the view.

DEFINING AND DELINEATING SPACE

Like animals defining their territories, humans seem to need to define the spaces they inhabit as a way to establish boundaries. These can vary from the culturally based "comfort zone" between two people speaking to each other to an international border.

Property Lines

In terms of our landscapes, property lines are the most obvious definition of space. Although backyards are generally fenced, front-yard boundaries vary, depending on neighborhood conventions, bylaws, individual relationships, and personal preferences. They might be undefined with continuous lawn, have a token shrub or tree, be totally enclosed by a manicured hedge or fence, or be set off with an informal mixed tree and shrub border or a bed of woody and herbaceous plant material.

Transition Plantings
On larger rural properties, transition plantings separate the well-maintained yard from the fields, bush, or bunch-grass area beyond. Where natural bush exists, transition plantings can reflect native plants in the bush. Depending on the region, these might include some of those listed in the accompanying sidebar.

Native Shrubs for Rural Transition Plantings

Amelanchier alnifolia (saskatoon berry)
Artemisia cana (hoary sagebrush)
Artemisia tridentata (big sagebrush)
Cornus sericea (red osier dogwood)
Corylus spp. (hazelnut)
Eleagnus commutata (wolfwillow)
Juniperus communis (common juniper)
Juniperus horizontalis (creeping juniper)
Potentilla fruticosa (potentilla, shrubby cinquefoil)
Prunus pensylvanica (pincherry)
Prunus virginiana (chokecherry)
Rhus spp. (sumac)
Rosa acicularis (prickly rose)
Rosa arkansana (prairie rose)
Rosa woodsii (Wood's rose)
Shepherdia spp. (buffaloberry)
Symphoricarpos albus (snowberry)
Viburnum trilobum (American highbush cranberry)

Defining Internal Spaces
Informal tree and shrub borders delineate and separate spaces within a yard, for example, a vegetable plot from a children's play area, a dog run from a lawn, or a barbecue pit and picnic area from a fruit garden. They not only separate but also screen the less-attractive utility areas of our yards. Scale is particularly important here, so select plants of appropriate size and proportion.

Directing Traffic Flow and Barrier Plantings
The direction of human traffic within the landscape can be guided by woody plantings. In some situations, they may be the same as those that define spaces, for instance, low groundcovers, such as junipers, planted in a bed wide enough to deter jumping over.

Other situations might call for more proactive barrier plantings. Shortcuts across corner lots can be discouraged by plants such as shrub roses, pygmy caragana, or barberry. In addition to attractive flowers and foliage, these plants come well armed with spines or prickles to discourage human traffic. To discourage graffiti or vandalism in back lanes, try using the thorniest of prickly shrub roses, such as 'Jens Munk,' 'Hazeldean,' or 'Prairie Dawn.' Hawthorn, sea buckthorn, barberry, pygmy caragana, and cherry prinsepia have also been known to leave their mark on would-be intruders.

Barrier Plantings

Berberis spp. (barberry)
Caragana frutex 'Globosa' (globe caragana)
Caragana pygmaea (pygmy caragana)
Crataegus spp. (hawthorn)
Hippophae rhamnoides (common sea buckthorn)
Prinsepia sinensis (cherry prinsepia)
Pyrus spp. (pear)
Rosa spp. (rose)

WOODY GROUNDCOVERS

Groundcovers are moderately low-growing (up to 1m/3 ft.) plants that cover the soil, preventing soil and water loss and reducing or eliminating weed growth. Usually, their foliage is dense enough to exclude light from the plants beneath them, and their vigorous root systems spread horizontally by suckers, rhizomes, or stolons. This allows them to compete effectively for soil moisture and nutrients, and within two or three years, depending on the species and their initial spacing, they fill the space available. Once established, they require little maintenance.

Tough, aggressive, and durable, groundcovers exclude weeds because they act like weeds in terms of their assertive nature, their competitiveness, and often their drought tolerance. They are also useful for stabilizing soil, especially on a bank or slope where it's difficult to establish and maintain a lawn.

Groundcovers serve a number of design functions, while providing interest through color and texture. Lower groundcovers can unify shrub borders or island beds by weaving through them, especially when other plantings are young. Others can be used as lawn alternatives in small, awkwardly shaped, or inaccessible areas that are difficult to maintain or where a lawn is not needed. On smaller properties, informal islands or borders of groundcovers, such as pygmy caragana, dwarf dogwoods, bumalda spireas, smaller potentillas, 'Dart's Gold' ninebark, or dwarf barberries, can delineate space or define property lines, replacing more obtrusive hedges or fences. In farmyards or acreages, groundcovers can be used as transition plantings between high-maintenance lawns and outlying field, bush, or bunch-grass areas.

Low, horizontal groundcovers can emphasize and accent a vertical focal point like an especially nice tree, a sculpture, or yard art, such as a sundial. Depending on the height of the focal point, the groundcover can be almost prostrate, such as creeping juniper or cliff green, or it can be a taller grouping of dwarf spireas, dogwoods, barberries, or mugo pines. The contrast with the horizontal groundcover accentuates the vertical focal point.

❧

Planting a Slope

To establish shrubs as groundcovers on a slope, work from the top down, with staggered rows of planting holes. Groupings of different cultivars and species should be irregular and should cross these rows, so the rows "disappear" as the plants mature. The planting holes should be deep enough to be "diked" after planting in order to hold water when it rains or when the plants are irrigated. The soil within the holes should be well amended with organic matter, such as peat moss, well-rotted manure, or compost. After planting, water thoroughly and cover any exposed soil between the plants with 10 cm (4 in.) of organic mulch, such as post peelings, weed-free straw or hay, grass clippings, or leaves.

Acer ginnala (Amur or ginnala maple)
Amelanchier alnifolia (saskatoon berry)
Artemesia tridentata (big sagebrush)
Berberis spp. (barberry)
Caragana frutex 'Globosa' (globe caragana)
Caragana pygmaea (pygmy caragana)
Eleagnus commutata (wolfwillow)
Juniperus communis (common juniper)

Juniperus horizontalis (creeping juniper)
Juniperus sabina (savin juniper)
Prinsepia sinensis (cherry prinsepia)
Prunus pensylvanica (pincherry)
Prunus tenella (Russian almond)
Rhus spp. (sumac)
Rosa rugosa (rugosa rose)
Sorbaria sorbifolia (Ural false spirea)
Spiraea (spirea)
Symphoricarpos albus (snowberry)

NATURALIZATION AND WILDLIFE PLANTINGS

Naturalization can refer to plants introduced from another region that have "naturalized" in their new home, establishing themselves in wild or disturbed areas. It also refers to a landscape style in which plants are allowed to spread or otherwise procreate in a manner that appears "wild" or "natural." Here, we use the term to refer to tough and aggressive plants that are used on difficult sites.

Wildlife plantings are trees and shrubs that provide shelter, nesting sites, or food for wildlife, particularly songbirds.

Trees and Shrubs for Bird Habitat

Abies lasiocarpa (subalpine fir)
Acer ginnala (Amur or ginnala maple)
Acer negundo (Manitoba maple, box elder)
Amelanchier alnifolia (saskatoon berry)
Arctostaphylos uva-ursi (bearberry)
Aronia melanocarpa (chokeberry)
Berberis thunbergii (Japanese barberry)
Caragana arborescens (common caragana, Siberian pea shrub)
Celtis occidentalis (common hackberry)
Cotoneaster spp. (cotoneaster)
Crataegus spp. (hawthorn)
Diervilla lonicera (dwarf bush honeysuckle, diervilla)
Eleagnus angustifolia (Russian olive)
Eleagnus commutata (wolfwillow)

Fraxinus mandshurica (Manchurian ash)
Fraxinus pennsylvanica var. *subintegerrima* (green ash)
Juniperus spp. (juniper)
Larix sibirica (Siberian larch)
Lonicera tatarica (Tartarian honeysuckle)
Malus baccata (Siberian crabapple) and some cultivars
Ostrya virginiana (American hop hornbeam)
Picea spp. (spruce)
Pinus spp. (pine)
Populus spp. (poplar)
Prinsepia sinensis (cherry prinsepia)
Prunus spp. (plum, cherry, almond)
Pseudotsuga menziesii var. *glauca* (Rocky Mountain Douglas fir)
Pyrus ussuriensis (Ussurian pear, Manchurian pear)
Quercus macrocarpa (bur oak)
Rhus glabra (smooth sumac)
Sambucus racemosa (European red elder)
Shepherdia spp. (buffaloberry)
*Sorbu*s spp. (mountain ash, rowan)
Syringa spp. (lilac)
Thuja occidentalis (cedar)
Tilia spp. (linden, basswood)
Viburnum lantana (wayfaring tree)
Viburnum lentago (nannyberry)
Viburnum trilobum (American highbush cranberry)

Trees and Shrubs for Rural Naturalization Projects

Amorpha fruticosa (false indigo bush)
Aronia melanocarpa (chokeberry)
Artemisia tridentata (big sagebrush)
Corylus spp. (hazelnut)
Diervilla lonicera (dwarf bush honeysuckle, diervilla)
Eleagnus commutata (wolfwillow)
Fraxinus pennsylvanica var. *subintegerrima* (green ash)
Hippophae rhamnoides (common sea buckthorn)
Juniperus communis (common juniper)
Juniperus horizontalis (creeping juniper)
Prunus pensylvanica (pincherry)
Prunus virginiana (chokecherry)
Rhus spp. (sumac)
Sambucus racemosa (European red elder)
Shepherdia argentea (silverleaf buffaloberry)
Sorbaria sorbifolia (Ural false spirea)
Symphoricarpos albus (snowberry)

THE ROOT OF THE MATTER

The roots of trees and shrubs are crucial to them, but some cause problems in our landscapes. You can avoid such problems by selecting the right plant for the right place.

Suckers are shoots that originate from the root system. From the plant's point of view, they are simply a means of carrying on life (sometimes in the fast lane), reproducing, and spreading horizontally.

Plants that sucker more than modestly can quickly assume the role of garden thugs in a confined situation. They have no place in a manicured border or a small landscape. But some situations desperately need plants that sucker and cover ground as quickly as possible. In the wide-open space of a rural acreage or farmyard, for example, these characteristics are welcome.

Usually, trees with wide-spreading root systems that are close to the soil surface have a competitive edge over other nearby plants. Their efficiency at sucking up all of the available soil moisture (along with the dissolved nutrients in the soil water) stunts the growth of their neighbors. If you are considering developing a shade garden or a layered border below a canopy tree, select your canopy tree carefully. Choose one with a deep, rather than a shallow and spreading, root system.

Canopy Trees

Deep Root Systems

Acer saccharinum (silver maple)
Aesculus glabra (Ohio buckeye)
Celtis occidentalis (common hackberry)
Malus spp. (crabapple)
Pinus spp. (pine)
Pyrus spp. (pear)
Quercus macrocarpa (bur oak)
Tilia spp. (linden, basswood)

Shallow, Spreading Root Systems

Acer negundo (Manitoba maple, box elder)
Betula spp. (birch)
Picea spp. (spruce)
Populus spp. (poplar)
Syringa spp. (lilac)
Ulmus spp. (elm)

Suckering Trees and Shrubs

Amelanchier alnifolia (saskatoon berry)
Aronia melanocarpa (chokeberry)
Diervilla lonicera (dwarf bush honeysuckle, diervilla)
Eleagnus commutata (wolfwillow)
Halimodendron halodendron (Siberian salt tree)
Hippophae rhamnoides (common sea buckthorn)
Populus tremuloides (trembling aspen)
Prunus pensylvanica (pincherry)
Prunus tenella (Russian almond)
Prunus virginiana (chokecherry)
Rhus spp. (sumac)
Rosa pimpinellifolia var. *altaica* (Altai Scotch rose)
Salix exigua (coyote willow)
Syringa vulgaris (common lilac)

BEAUTY: IN THE EYE OF THE BEHOLDER

Besides what they do, trees and shrubs are valued for what they are. We plant them for aesthetic reasons—their beauty, as we perceive it. Beauty has many facets. Form or shape, foliage, flowers, fruit, and the color of stems and bark combine, both collectively and as individual specimens, to subtly soften and enhance our outdoor living space.

FORM

Some trees and shrubs are defined by their form or shape. A narrow, conical Rocky Mountain juniper is a sharp exclamation point in the landscape. 'Jumping Pound' pincherry is a small tree with a unique weeping form and four-season landscape value: white flowers in spring; red, edible fruit in late summer; orange foliage in fall; and a gnarled silhouette against the winter snow. Dwarf cedars such as 'Little Gem' and 'Little Giant' are almost globular. Other shrubs such as pygmy caragana or spike broom have a distinctly spiky form.

FOLIAGE

Foliage contributes to a plant's beauty. Besides the myriad shades of green, leaves can be red to purple, silver or gray, golden or blue, or one of the many variations of variegation. On evergreens, these colors have year-round beauty. On deciduous trees and shrubs, the golds, oranges, and reds of the autumn foliage are an important factor in plant selection.

The texture of leaves also adds to their aesthetic qualities. Some are compound, that is, they are composed of a number of individual leaflets that, depending on their size, can lend a leaf an almost tropical appearance, as in the large, compound leaves of elders and mountain ash, or can give it a very dense look, as in globe caragana.

Leaves can also be very finely cut or dissected, giving them a light and airy appearance such as those of fern-leafed caragana or the 'Dropmore Fernleaf' elder. In an oriental-style garden, these plants are respectable substitutes for the Japanese maples that are too tender to survive our prairie winters.

Summer Foliage Colors

Purple-red
Berberis cultivars (barberry)
Physocarpus opulifolius 'Monlo' (Diabolo® ninebark)
Prunus x *cistena* (purpleleafed sandcherry, cistena cherry)
Prunus virginiana selections (chokecherry)
Rosa rubrifolia (redleaf rose)

Blue
Juniperus scopulorum cultivars (Rocky Mountain juniper)
Picea pungens cultivars (Colorado spruce)

Silver-gray
Artemisia spp. (sagebrush)
Eleagnus spp. (wolfwillow, Russian olive)
Hippophae rhamnoides (common sea buckthorn)
Juniperus cultivars (juniper)
Populus alba (white poplar, silver-leafed poplar)
Shepherdia spp. (buffaloberry)

Yellow-gold
Berberis cultivars (barberry)
Juniperus cultivars (juniper)
Philadelphus coronarius 'Aureus' (golden mockorange)
Physocarpus opulifolius 'Nugget,' 'Luteus,' 'Dart's Gold' (golden ninebark)
Sambucus racemosa 'Goldenlocks,' 'Sutherland Golden' (golden elder)

Variegated
Cornus cultivars (dogwood)
Daphne burkwoodii (burkwood daphne)
Juniperus cultivars (juniper)
Syringa 'Dappled Dawn' (lilac)

Notable Fall Foliage Colors

Yellow-golden
Acer negundo (Manitoba maple, box elder)
Acer saccharinum (silver maple)
Betula spp. (birch)
Corylus spp. (hazelnut)
Fraxinus spp. (ash)
Juglans spp. (walnut, butternut)
Larix spp. (larch)
Ostrya virginiana (American hop hornbeam)
Phellodendron amurense (Amur cork tree)
Populus (poplar)
Quercus macrocarpa (bur oak)
Ribes alpinum (alpine currant)
Rosa spp. (rose)
Syringa villosa (late lilac)
Tilia spp. (linden, basswood)

Orange

Aesculus glabra (Ohio buckeye)
Cotoneaster lucidus (hedge cotoneaster)
Prunus pensylvanica (pincherry)
Rosa spp. (rose)
Sorbus spp. (mountain ash, rowan)

Red

Acer ginnala (Amur or ginnala maple)
Aronia melanocarpa (chokeberry)
Cornus sericea (red osier dogwood)
Diervilla lonicera (dwarf bush
    honeysuckle, diervilla)
Euonymus spp. (burning bush,
    spindle tree)
Prunus padus (mayday tree, European
    bird cherry)
Prunus tenella (Russian almond)
Rhus spp. (sumac)
Viburnum lentago (nannyberry)
Viburnum trilobum (American
    highbush cranberry)

FLOWERS, FRUIT, AND BARK

Many shrubs and some trees have conspicuous flowers. Ornamental flowering crabapple, plum, cherry, and pear trees come to mind immediately, but there are also the less well known but equally deserving Ohio buckeye, Japanese tree lilac, hawthorn, viburnum, mayday, and mountain ash.

Earliest to flower in the first half of May are the pears, plums, cherries, and forsythia, followed by the crabapples, hawthorns, and Ohio buckeye. By early June, the viburnums, mountain ash, and lilacs are in full glory. Potentillas, spireas, roses, and lindens are among the last to flower.

Flowers are fleeting, but fruit retained into winter not only make a striking contrast against the snow, but attract birds into our gardens through the late summer, fall, and winter. Trees with conspicuous fruit include mountain ash, crabapple, and the many viburnums, as well as cotoneaster, hawthorn, roses, and honeysuckle.

Bark is another important landscape feature. Many trees and shrubs have conspicuous bark or stem color or texture. Most birches have peeling or exfoliating white or bronze bark. The rich bronze of the Amur cherry is outstanding. The red, green, or golden stems of many dogwoods come into their own in late winter and early spring, as does the yellow, orange, or red new growth of willows in spring.

Trees and Shrubs with Conspicuous Flowers

Aesculus glabra (Ohio buckeye)
Amelanchier alnifolia (saskatoon berry)
Caragana spp. (caragana)
Cornus spp. (dogwood)
Crataegus spp. (hawthorn)
Cytisus spp. (broom)
Daphne spp. (daphne)
Diervilla lonicera (dwarf bush
    honeysuckle, diervilla)
Forsythia spp. (forsythia)
Genista spp. (broom, woadwaxen)
Halimodendron halodendron
    (Siberian salt tree)
Hydrangea spp. (hydrangea)
Lonicera spp. (honeysuckle)
Malus spp. (crabapple)

10

Philadelphus lewisii (Lewis mockorange)

Physocarpus opulifolius (common ninebark)

Potentilla fruticosa (potentilla, shrubby cinquefoil)

Prinsepia sinensis (cherry prinsepia)

Prunus maackii (Amur cherry)

Prunus nigra (Canada plum)

Prunus padus (mayday tree, European bird cherry)

Prunus pensylvanica (pincherry)

Prunus tenella (Russian almond)

Prunus tomentosa (Nanking cherry)

Prunus triloba var. *multiplex* (double flowering plum, double-flowering almond)

Prunus virginiana (chokecherry)

Pyrus ussuriensis (Ussurian pear, Manchurian pear)

Rhododendron spp. (rhododendron)

Rosa spp. (rose)

Sambucus racemosa (European red elder)

Sorbaria sorbifolia (Ural false spirea)

Sorbus spp. (mountain ash, rowan)

Spiraea spp. (spirea)

Syringa spp. (lilac)

Viburnum lantana (wayfaring tree)

Viburnum lentago (nannyberry)

Viburnum trilobum (American highbush cranberry)

Viburnum opulus (European cranberry)

Viburnum sargentii (Sargent's viburnum)

Viburnum rafinesquianum (arrowwood)

Weigela florida (weigela)

Trees and Shrubs with Conspicuous Fruit

Abies balsamea (balsam fir)–cones

Aesculus glabra (Ohio buckeye)–nuts

Amelanchier alnifolia (saskatoon berry)–blue berries

Arctostaphylos uva-ursi (bearberry)–red berries

Aronia melanocarpa (chokeberry)–black berries

Berberis spp. (barberry)–red berries

Cornus spp. (dogwood)–white berries

Cotoneaster spp. (cotoneaster)–red, black berries

Crataegus spp. (hawthorn)–red, black berries

Daphne spp. (daphne)–red berries

Eleagnus spp. (wolfwillow, Russian olive)–silver fruit

Euonymus spp. (burning bush, spindle tree)–orange-pink seed capsules

Hippophae rhamnoides (common sea buckthorn)–yellow-orange berries

Juglans spp. (walnut, butternut)–nuts

Juniperus spp. (juniper)–blue, berry-like cones

Larix spp. (larch)–cones

Malus spp. (crabapple)–yellow to red apples

Physocarpus spp. (ninebark)–pink seed capsules

Picea spp. (spruce)–cones

Pinus spp. (pine)–cones

Prinsepia sinensis (cherry prinsepia)–red berries

Prunus maackii (Amur cherry)–black cherries

Prunus padus (mayday tree, European bird cherry)–black cherries

Prunus pensylvanica (pincherry)–red cherries

Prunus tomentosa (Nanking cherry)–red cherries

Prunus virginiana (chokecherry)–black, red, yellow cherries

Quercus spp. (oak)–acorns

Rosa spp. (rose)–red, black, orange, or yellow hips

Shepherdia spp. (buffaloberry)–red berries

Sorbus spp. (mountain ash, rowan)–orange-red fruit

Symphoricarpos albus (snowberry)–white fruit

Viburnum spp. (cranberry)–red, black fruit

Trees and Shrubs with Interesting Stems and Bark

Betula spp. (birch)–white or bronze, exfoliating bark

Cornus spp. (dogwood)–red, yellow, green stems

Crataegus 'Toba' ('Toba' hawthorn)–twisting bark

Genista spp. (broom, woadwaxen)–bright, light green stems

Phellodendron amurense (Amur cork tree)–thick, ridged, corky bark

Pinus sylvestris (Scots pine)–foxy orange bark

Prunus maackii (Amur cherry)–bronze, exfoliating bark

Salix spp. (willow)–orange-red, golden late-winter stems

Poisonous Trees and Shrubs

Many common landscape plants have the potential to poison people who handle or eat them. *Rhus glabra* (smooth sumac), for example, causes occasional hives in some individuals, while *Daphne* species are potentially deadly if their fruit are eaten, even in small quantities. Apple and cherry seeds can produce cyanide, which can be deadly if ingested raw in large quantities.

The following list of poisonous plants is not exhaustive. Other plants could be poisonous if eaten in quantity, but they are not tasty enough to be appealing. The list is based on actual cases studies from Europe and North America.

Aesculus glabra (Ohio buckeye)–nuts and twigs

Andromeda polifolia (bog rosemary)

Artemisia spp. (sagebrush)

Daphne spp. (daphne)

Euonymus spp. (burning bush, spindle tree)

Hydrangea spp. (hydrangea)

Lonicera xylosteum (European dwarf honeysuckle, fly honeysuckle)

Mahonia spp. (Oregon grape)

Malus spp. (apple, crabapple)–seeds

Prunus spp. (cherry, plum, almond)–foliage and seeds
Rhus glabra (smooth sumac)
Sambucus racemosa (European red elder)

PLACEMENT: MAKING IT WORK

A PLANT'S PERSPECTIVE

As gardeners, we read books, browse through mail-order catalogues, and haunt nurseries and garden centers in search of the perfect plant for the perfect spot. In our mind's eye, we may picture a birch providing shade on a knoll or a juniper as a ground-cover below the dense canopy of a tree. But, although both scenarios "work" from a design perspective, they are an imperfect fit in terms of the physical needs of these plants. A birch requires even moisture and would forever struggle on the knoll without supplemental irrigation. Junipers do best in full sun.

The simplest way to categorize the environmental requirements of trees and shrubs is in terms of light, water, and soil. These differ among genera, from species to species, and even among cultivars of the same species. The more closely these needs are met, the healthier our plants. From a gardener's perspective, healthy plants look better and require less maintenance.

Light

Although there are exceptions, most trees require full sun. In their natural habitat, their crowns are situated at the top of the forest canopy where it's always "full sun." If placed in shade, most are unable to photosynthesize efficiently, and their form becomes loose, open, and irregular. In other words, they don't flourish. A few that are naturally adapted to the under-story are shade tolerant, but they are the exceptions.

Shrubs vary in their adaptability to sun and shade. Some, like honey-suckle, lilac, and roses, demand full sun. Others, like burning bush, hazelnut, and hydrangea, flourish in shade. Cedars and many dwarf spruce (which might have originated as witch's brooms within the canopy) do well in partial shade. Others might grow well in partial shade, but do not flower as profusely as they would in full sun.

But what is full sun? Partial shade? Full shade? Full sun is generally defined as a minimum of six hours of direct sunlight—not necessarily continuous. Anything less is partial shade. Full shade receives little or no direct sunlight.

If you garden in an older yard with mature trees and want to increase the available light, you have two options: tree removal and tree pruning.

Psychologically, tree removal is not easy for prairie people. Because trees take time and effort to grow and often have multi-generational emotional ties, the burden of guilt associated with their removal can be enormous.

Think, instead, in terms of tree health and function. If a tree is old, in declining or ill health, or poses a safety hazard, it might be beneficial to remove it. This might be especially true if it's in a grouping that is crowded or closely planted. Also think about function. Is the tree giving shade or screening an ugly shed? Is it providing wind protection or privacy? If it's removed, will nearby trees provide the same function? Will it be missed?

If you decide to remove a tree, the best time to do it is in late winter or early spring. You can see the branch structure clearly; branches weigh less without foliage, making the job easier and safer; and because it has not yet leafed out, the burden of guilt is somewhat reduced. This is also the best time to prune out major branches to allow greater light penetration.

Water

The trees and shrubs described in this book vary. There are wet-site species such as willow, which flourish in near boglike situations but can adapt to even moisture; those that demand even moisture, such as birch, Ohio buckeye, and hydrangea; those that are moderately drought tolerant, such as many *Prunus* species; and those that are extremely drought tolerant, like caragana, sea buckthorn, and Manitoba maple.

Moisture is a critical factor in sustaining the health of trees and shrubs. Lilacs, for example, are intolerant of flooding, while birches quickly fall prey to borers and die under drought conditions. Although many trees and shrubs will surprise you with their adaptability, the closer you can match their water demands, the healthier these plants will be.

Drought-tolerant Trees and Shrubs

Abies lasiocarpa (subalpine fir)
Acer ginnala (Amur or ginnala maple)
Acer negundo (Manitoba maple, box elder)
Amelanchier alnifolia (saskatoon berry)
Amorpha fruticosa (false indigo bush)
Arctostaphylos uva-ursi (bearberry)–once established
Aronia melanocarpa (chokeberry)
Artemisia spp. (sagebrush)
Berberis thunbergii (Japanese barberry)
Caragana arborescens (common caragana, Siberian pea shrub)
Celtis occidentalis (common hackberry)–once established
Cotoneaster spp. (cotoneaster)
Crataegus spp. (hawthorn)
Cytisus spp. (broom)
Diervilla lonicera (dwarf bush honeysuckle, diervilla)
Eleagnus angustifolia (Russian olive)
Eleagnus commutata (wolfwillow)
Fraxinus pennsylvanica var. *subintegerrima* (green ash)
Fraxinus mandshurica (Manchurian ash)
Genista spp. (broom, woadwaxen)
Halimodendron halodendron (Siberian salt tree)
Hippophae rhamnoides (common sea buckthorn)
Juniperus spp. (juniper)
Larix sibirica (Siberian larch)
Lonicera tatarica (Tartarian honeysuckle)

Malus baccata (Siberian crabapple)
and some cultivars

Ostrya virginiana (American hop
hornbeam)

Philadelphus lewisii (Lewis mockorange)

Physocarpus opulifolius (common
ninebark)

Picea pungens (Colorado spruce)–
once established

Pinus spp. (pine)

Prinsepia sinensis (cherry prinsepia)

Prunus spp. (cherry, plum, almond)

Pyrus ussuriensis (Ussurian pear,
Manchurian pear)–moderately,
once established

Quercus macrocarpa (bur oak)

Rhus glabra (smooth sumac)

Ribes alpinum (alpine currant)–
moderately

Sambucus racemosa (European
red elder)

Shepherdia spp. (buffaloberry)

Sorbaria sorbifolia (Ural false spirea)

Sorbus spp. (mountain ash, rowan)

Symphoricarpos albus (snowberry)

Syringa spp. (lilac)

Ulmus americana (American elm)

Viburnum lantana (wayfaring tree)

Viburnum lentago (nannyberry)

Viburnum trilobum (American
highbush cranberry)–moderately

Soil

Soil has many characteristics that,
together, influence plant growth.
The nature of the soil in your garden
should influence your choice of trees
and shrubs.

Prairie soils differ widely in
physical and chemical characteristics.
Ideally, most of us would prefer to
garden on rich loam, but we work
with what we have. Some soil
characteristics are easily improved.
Others seem immutable. (For more
on improving garden soils, see
Chapter Two, p. 18.)

The texture of our soils varies from
light sand to heavy clay. Soil texture
affects the availability of water and
nutrients. Plants that are drought
tolerant adapt more readily to sandy
soils; those that require rich, moist
conditions are easier to maintain on
heavier loam and clay-loam soils; and
those that require excellent drainage
likely need the addition of an under-
lying layer of gravel coupled with
raised beds or planting berms.

Prairie soils are typically fertile,
that is, they have sufficient nutrients
to maintain plant growth. The addition of organic matter improves the
availability of these nutrients. Because
prairie soils contain 5 percent, or less,
organic matter they may need to be
amended with peat moss, compost,
or well-rotted manure. Woodland
shrubs, such as hydrangeas, daphnes,
and some spireas, benefit from generous additions of these amendments,
which help the soil retain moisture.

Soluble salts are essential to
plant growth, as most nutrients are
absorbed as salts with soil water. But
high levels of soluble salts can be very
difficult for gardeners, because plants
vary in their tolerance for salts. Where
soluble salts are high, choose trees and
shrubs with a high salt tolerance such
as those listed on p. 16.

Salt-tolerant Trees and Shrubs

High Salt Tolerance
Amorpha fruticosa (false indigo bush)
Arctostaphylos uva-ursi (bearberry)
Artemisia spp. (sagebrush)
Berberis thunbergii (Japanese barberry)
Crataegus spp. (hawthorn)
Cytisus spp. (broom)
Eleagnus angustifolia (Russian olive)
Halimodendron halodendron (Siberian salt tree)
Hippophae rhamnoides (common sea buckthorn)
Rhus glabra (smooth sumac)
Salix pentandra (laurel leaf willow)
Shepherdia argentea (silverleaf buffaloberry)
Sorbaria sorbifolia (Ural false spirea)
Symphoricarpos albus (snowberry)
Syringa villosa (late lilac)
Ulmus spp. (American elm, Siberian elm)

Moderate Salt Tolerance
Acer negundo (Manitoba maple, box elder)
Caragana spp. (caragana)
Eleagnus commutata (wolfwillow)
Fraxinus pennsylvanica var. *subintegerrima* (green ash)
Juniperus spp. (juniper, some cultivars)
Lonicera tatarica (Tartarian honeysuckle)
Prunus virginiana (chokecherry)
Rosa rugosa (rugosa rose)
Ulmus davidiana var. *japonica* (Japanese elm)

Specimen Plantings: Going It Alone

"Specimen" trees and shrubs are those that stand out as individuals within our landscape. They do so because they possess an outstanding characteristic or combination of characteristics or because of their function—most often as a shade tree.

Generally, we plant them in the "negative space" of a lawn or against a solid fence or building where their beauty is accentuated and becomes a focal point that draws our eye and our attention. Although specimen trees and shrubs are often defined by their form, other attributes might include distinctive foliage, flowers, fruit, stem, or bark color. Trees and shrubs that combine all or several of these attributes, such as mountain ash, Amur cherry, and variegated red osier dogwoods, are welcome four-season assets for any garden. Evergreens are also excellent specimen trees with year-round value.

Depending on the size of the landscape, the number of specimen trees is generally limited to one per distinct area of a yard. Remember scale, and keep the size in proportion to the landscape as a whole.

Bordering on Togetherness

We often place trees and shrubs in informal groupings in tree and shrub borders or in mixed-layered borders with vines, bulbs, annuals, biennials, and perennials. These borders are "mixed" in terms of the types of plant material and "layered" in terms of height. Depending on the size of the landscape as a whole and the border itself, it might contain a few tall canopy trees, smaller trees, shrubs of varying heights, shorter herbaceous plants, and almost prostrate groundcovers.

From a design perspective, mixed-layered borders provide more interest and look more natural than a scatter-gun planting of individual trees and shrubs across a lawn. They allow for greater variations in height, as well as a more extended period of foliage, flowers, fruit, and bark and stem color. They also give the gardener a much greater choice of material because it is easier to meet the physical needs of plants given a specific soil type, exposure, or amount of water.

As well, tree and shrub borders and mixed-layered borders are easier to maintain than a host of individual plantings scattered about the lawn. Once planted and mulched, weeding is minimal and watering is reduced, and you only need to mow around one bed, nicely avoiding an afternoon spent literally "going in circles" around individual plants. Another advantage is that these designs reduce the incidence of mower and whipper-snipper damage to the base of trees and shrubs.

Exercising Restraint: Unity through Repetition

Restraint is an uncommon virtue among gardeners. Once we get started, it is all too tempting to create a "horticultural zoo" of as many different plants as we can squeeze into our landscape.

A more reasoned approach is to select a small number of trees and shrubs based on personal preference, their four-season landscape value, and their "fit" in terms of how well their light, water, and soil needs can be met. By repeating these theme plants individually or as groupings, you unify your landscape. And if, in the process, you leave space for the weird, the wonderful, the rare, and the unusual specimens we find so hard to resist, who's to find fault?

A Last Word

In the final scheme of things, we all have our own way of doing things—our own garden style. The best advice is to do what is comfortable for you and what makes you happy. In your garden, as in other facets of your life, to thine own self be true.

Plant Selection and Establishment

🍁

IS IT A TREE OR A SHRUB?

You would think this would be an easy question, but there is no clear dividing line between trees and shrubs. Often the same species will grow either in tree or shrub form, depending on environmental conditions or on pruning and training during its early years. *Funk and Wagnells Standard Dictionary of the English Language* describes a shrub as a "woody perennial plant of low stature, characterized by persistent stems and branches springing from the base," while *Native Trees of Canada* describes a tree as "a single stemmed woody plant of more than ten feet."

🍁

Native Trees and Shrubs

Native trees and shrubs such as green ash and highbush cranberry are used widely in prairie landscape plantings. There are many other native plant species that are less available or less widely adapted but still worthy of consideration for planting when they can be found. Finding plants for sale can be a challenge, but native plant nurseries are beginning to produce a wide variety of native woody plants.

Abies lasiocarpa (subalpine fir)
Acer negundo (Manitoba maple, box elder)
Amelanchier alnifolia (saskatoon berry)
Amorpha fruticosa (false indigo bush)
Andromeda polifolia (bog rosemary)
Arctostaphylos uva-ursi (bearberry)
Artemisia spp. (sagebrush)
Betula papyrifera (paper birch)

Celtis occidentalis (common hackberry)
Cornus alternifolia (pagoda dogwood)
Cornus sericea (red osier dogwood)
Corylus americana (American hazelnut)
Corylus cornuta (beaked hazelnut)
Crataegus succulenta (hawthorn)
Diervilla lonicera (dwarf bush honeysuckle, diervilla)

Eleagnus commutata (wolfwillow)
Fraxinus nigra (black ash)
Fraxinus pennsylvanica var. *subintegerrima* (green ash)
Juniperus horizontalis (creeping juniper)
Juniperus scopulorum (Rocky Mountain juniper)
Larix laricina (American larch, tamarack)
Lonicera involucrata (bracted honeysuckle)
Ostrya virginiana (American hop hornbeam)
Philadelphus lewisii (Lewis mockorange)
Picea glauca (white spruce)
Pinus flexilis (limber pine)
Populus sargentii (plains cottonwood)
Populus tremuloides (trembling aspen)
Potentilla fruticosa (potentilla, shrubby cinquefoil)

Prunus pensylvanica (pincherry)
Prunus virginiana (chokecherry)
Pseudotsuga menziesii var. *glauca* (Rocky Mountain Douglas fir)
Quercus macrocarpa (bur oak)
Rhus glabra (smooth sumac)
Rosa acicularis (prickly rose)
Rosa arkansana (prairie rose)
Rosa blanda (smooth rose)
Rosa woodsii (Wood's rose)
Shepherdia spp. (buffaloberry)
Sorbus americana, S. decora, S. scopulina (mountain ash, rowan)
Symphoricarpos albus (snowberry)
Thuja occidentalis (cedar, eastern white cedar)
Tilia americana (American basswood)
Viburnum lentago (nannyberry)
Viburnum trilobum (American highbush cranberry)

SITE PREPARATION

Before you go to the garden center for a load of plants to begin the exciting work of planting, take stock of what you need to do to prepare your site. "Rejuvenating" a poorly prepared site four years after planting is far less satisfying than doing it correctly at the start.

SOIL

The most important part of a tree or shrub is underground. The vigor of its roots depends on the availability of adequate water, air, and mineral nutrients for growth. Root health is affected by pH, salts, and the presence of toxic substances.

Soil provides mechanical support, water, and nutrients to plants. We think of soil as solid but, in fact, about 50 percent of most soil is pore spaces filled with water and air. The roots of plants grow in these spaces and take up water and dissolved nutrients from them. The solid portion of soil is made up of mineral particles of various sizes and of organic matter—the decaying remains of plants and microscopic organisms.

The mineral component of soil is formed from the breakdown of rock in the earth's crust. Soils have varying portions of sand, silt, and clay particles, and the relative portions of these various-sized particles determine soil texture. Soils high in sand are "light" in texture. They drain quickly and are easy to work, but tend to be droughty and infertile because they do not hold water and nutrients well. Light soils have a poorly developed structure, which makes them more prone to erosion. Soils with a high portion of clay particles are "heavy" in texture. They are difficult to work and are prone to compaction, but they hold water and nutrients well. Loam has nearly equal portions of sand, silt, and clay particles and is desirable for growing most plants.

The organic component of soil is composed mostly of decaying roots. This decomposition is accomplished by myriad insects, microscopic animals, fungi, and bacteria, which recycle nutrients and give soil its structure. The "humic" acids in organic matter provide glues and mucilage that stick soil particles together into aggregates and make them friable, or of "good tilth." They also hold nutrients in forms that are available to plants and contribute to the soil's water-holding capacity.

What Can I Do to Improve My Soil?

Problem: Heavy, compacted soil

To improve soil that is clay based and compacted, you must increase the large air spaces and improve the soil structure. To do this, add coarse sand (you'll need large quantities of it to have an appreciable effect) and organic matter. Avoid adding fine sand as it bonds to the clay particles and causes them to harden like concrete. Adding organic matter improves soil structure and makes it more friable. Because the organic matter breaks down over time, you need to add it regularly. Using organic mulches that eventually break down helps to accomplish this and prevents the soil from baking in the sun.

When adding amendments to any soil, be sure to incorporate them well. Layered soil textures impede both water percolation and root growth. Begin by tilling the soil, then add several inches of amendments, till again, and repeat the process as needed.

If your soil is very heavy and you want to grow plants that require excellent drainage, construct beds that are raised above the level of the existing soil to promote drainage. Special soil mixes can be added to these raised beds to accommodate plants with special needs.

Problem: Light, sandy soil

Light, sandy soils are easy to work, but dry out quickly. This is an advantage for many plants if sufficient water and nutrients can be added. However, if steps are not taken to improve the soil's water-holding capacity, plants will be vulnerable to damage during dry periods. To improve this type of soil, add organic matter to increase its water- and nutrient-holding capacity.

Problem: Alkalinity/high pH

Prairie soils are commonly formed from rocks that are high in lime and, as a result, are alkaline or basic. It is difficult and costly to change the pH of more than a small area of soil, but more-acidic, small planting beds can be created in well-drained areas by adding amendments such as peat moss, pine needles, and acid sand. Nonetheless, it is best to plant trees and shrubs that are tolerant of the existing pH.

Problem: Salinity, high salt concentration

It is difficult to remedy soils that are naturally high in salts. The only way to remove salts from the soil is to leach them out by improving drainage.

Overfertilization can cause salinity in poorly drained soils. Chemical fertilizers are salts, and the addition of excessive quantities of them will make the soil saline. On clay soils with poor drainage, this problem can be difficult to correct once it has been created.

The obvious recommendation for alleviating saline soil is to improve drainage and avoid overfertilization. But it is difficult to improve drainage if the soil is very heavy or if the water table is high. It is better to select a well-drained site for planting. For a list of trees and shrubs that are tolerant of saline conditions, see Chapter One, p. 16.

Problem: Low fertility

Adequate fertility levels are important for plant health and vigor. Soils that are low in fertility can be improved by

❦

Soil pH: Is Soil Acid or Alkaline?

The pH of soil is a logarithmic measure of its acidity or alkalinity on a scale of 0 to 14, with a neutral point of 7. Thus, a pH of 8 is 10 times more alkaline than a pH of 7, and a pH of 9 is 100 times more alkaline than one of 7.

Soil pH is largely determined by the "parent material," or rock, from which the soil originated, and it is extremely difficult to change. Most prairie soils are alkaline, or basic, with a pH of 7 or greater. Fortunately, most of the trees and shrubs described here are well adapted to these soils.

Among the few plants that prefer a more acidic soil are azaleas and rhododendrons. To temporarily acidify basic soils, dig deeply and add generous amounts of peat moss or use elemental sulfur or ammonium sulfate according to soil test recommendations. The change in pH will not be permanent and should be monitored for reapplication.

the addition of organic matter, such as compost or well-rotted manure. These amendments hold nutrients in forms that are available to plants over time. It is not possible to give good general recommendations for fertilizing trees and shrubs because soils vary as much as the needs of specific plants do. Nonetheless, trees and shrubs will benefit if they are fertilized with a high-phosphate (middle number) fertilizer at planting time. This should only be done once, as high phosphate levels in the soil can cause other nutrients to become unavailable. The safest way to add phosphate, which can cause plant burning and even the death of the plant, is in the form of bone meal or a water-soluble fertilizer. Follow the directions on the label.

After planting, trees and shrubs may benefit from periodic applications of fertilizer. However, more trees and shrubs are killed by too much fertilizer than by too little. A soil test is the best way to get an accurate indication of your plants' specific fertilizer needs. Sandy soils are more likely to require additions of fertilizer than loam or clay soils, which retain more nutrients. Be cautious about adding fertilizer to clay soils. Too much fertilizer can make the soil saline, which is difficult to correct. Avoid fertilizing in late summer, as this can induce growth that will not harden off for winter.

Adding organic matter will slowly release nutrients to the soil, which will contribute to the health of your trees and shrubs.

❦

How Much N, P, and K?

The major nutrients that are common to most fertilizers are nitrogen (N), phosphorus (P), and potassium (K). The numbers in the fertilizer analysis 15-30-15 indicate that the fertilizer is 15 percent nitrogen (N), 30 percent phosphate (P), and 15 percent potassium (K). In addition, many fertilizers contain micronutrients.

CHANGING THE GRADE

When preparing a site for planting, consider water drainage. Surface water should drain away from buildings, landscape features, and planting beds or areas. If there are already trees on your lot, you may have to change the grade level around them, but remember that good aeration is critical to the health of tree roots. Raising the grade level around trees, by adding soil over the roots, slows the infiltration of air into the soil. Its effect on a tree depends on the species and the amount and nature of the fill. A few centimeters of heavy clay could be deadly, whereas 10 to 15 cm (4 to 6 in.) of loose, gravelly soil might have little effect. For greater changes in grade, more elaborate preparations are necessary, such as dry wells and drain tiles to allow air movement.

PURCHASING AND PLANTING TREES AND SHRUBS

When you want to buy trees and shrubs, look for a nursery or garden center that has a knowledgeable staff and well-maintained and properly labeled plants. The information in this book should help you choose the right trees and shrubs for your needs. Look for plants that are healthy and are a good size in relation to their container.

PLANT HARDINESS

The best way to select trees and shrubs is by observing what grows well in your area.

The hardiest trees and shrubs are those from your own climatic area or from areas in Europe and Asia with similar cold, continental climates. On most open planting sites, the hardy "pioneer species"—poplars, green ash, Manitoba maple, and oak—are among the most likely to succeed. Where shelter is more established, the more favorable microclimate allows for the survival of less-hardy species and cultivars.

Using the most winter-hardy plants for the "bones" of your garden will contribute to your long-term satisfaction with your landscape. Trying more tender plants in favorable microclimates will make your garden a more exciting place.

The evaluation of plant hardiness is a complex process. Early plant-hardiness zone maps were based on minimum temperatures, but such factors as the loss of winter snow cover and the effects of winter chinooks were not taken into account. Although the new and much improved plant-hardiness zone map is based on seven climatic criteria, it still does not adequately reflect the effects of chinooks and significant microclimatic variations.

Even plants that are winter hardy will be injured if there is a frost during the summer when they are actively growing. As fall approaches, the tisues harden off, becoming ready for freezing temperatures. As part of this process, deciduous trees lose their leaves, and sugars and other chemicals accumulate in tissues to help the plant withstand freezing temperatures. In some instances, water is moved outside cells to protect them from damage from freezing.

Reduced day length triggers hardening off for winter in some plants. If placed close to street lights, these plants sometimes fail to harden off in time. Placing such plants in total shade for part of the day could extend their range by tricking them into hardening off sooner.

Variations in fertility levels can also affect the winter survival of woody plants. High levels of nitrogen in late summer encourage soft growth, which is vulnerable to winter injury. Adequate levels of nutrients such as potassium, however, are important for developing winter hardiness. The best strategy for growing plants in a cold climate is to maintain good fertility but not overfertilize or fertilize late in the summer.

Wind chill is felt by plants, just as it is by people. Some plants are more sensitive than others, but providing good shelter significantly improves your chance of successfully growing marginally hardy or tender cultivars. Plants that are marginal in flower-bud hardiness are much more likely to bloom if planted in sites that are protected from cold winter winds.

Freezing and thawing of the soil can cause root damage, due to soil heaving, but can be reduced by mulches and shading. Snow cover contributes to the moderation of soil temperature throughout the winter; generally, temperature fluctuations are a greater problem in heavier clay soils.

Rapid temperature changes, especially during the late winter, can damage trees. If daytime warming is followed by extreme cold, trees may develop frost cracks or a sunscald injury. Shading the trunks of vulnerable species such as mountain ash and Amur cherry may alleviate this problem.

In nature, some tree species range across several climatic zones. Manitoba maple, for example, is native from the Canadian prairies to Texas and Florida. Plants grown from seed collected from prairie stands can be expected to survive our winters, whereas plants grown from seed collected in Florida are unlikely to survive. It is not so much where a plant is grown that makes the difference as it is its genetics. The origin of a plant is called its provenance (documented source). Provenance is very important when you are buying nursery stock, both for grafted trees and for those grown from seed. A non-hardy rootstock can cause a grafted plant to fail.

Prairie nurseries have a vested interest in locating and growing plants that are winter hardy in their area. Researchers, gardeners, and nurseries have invested a great deal of effort over the past hundred years to identify and develop trees and shrubs that will be reliable in prairie gardens. This work is ongoing, but gardeners' sense of curiosity and their collective desire to push the limits also contribute to the development of new reliable cultivars for our gardens and to our knowledge of what will survive.

Trees and shrubs do not usually grow as isolated plants in open grassland. They are found in close association with other trees, shrubs, and plants where the microclimates and soil are favorable to their growing needs. Our landscape plantings will be most successful if we duplicate favorable conditions by establishing shelter, by mulching and amending the soil, and by giving careful thought to the location of more-tender plants.

PACKAGING

Until recently, spring was the only planting season for trees and shrubs. This allowed dormant bare-root plants a full season in which to become established. With the development of container-growing techniques, the planting season was extended. Healthy container-grown plants can be planted successfully at any time during spring, summer, and fall. Larger specimens are often sold balled and burlapped, and provided they have been dug at an appropriate time and properly handled, they too can be planted at

The Asian Connection

Over the millennia, plants have adapted to climates around the world through an accumulation of small genetic changes. We can expect that species and cultivars that are native to areas with similar climates to our own will be most successful when moved to the prairies.

In the early years of prairie settlement, many gardeners were disappointed when they tried to grow trees and shrubs from their former homelands in Europe. Woody plants native to the prairie region, however, are some of the most cold-hardy plants in the world, and plant breeders have used them to contribute hardiness to the more attractive garden varieties from Europe. The number of cold-hardy plants has also been greatly expanded by the introduction of plants from eastern Asia. Botanical explorers from Russia, Germany, France, and England brought seeds and specimens from these areas to the prairies in the eighteenth and nineteenth centuries. At the beginning of the twentieth century, a veritable flood of plant species became available from eastern Asia, in large part due to the collecting efforts of Ernest H. Wilson.

In the 1920s, plants of northeastern Asia became available for trial in prairie gardens. Professor Nils Hansen of the University of South Dakota traveled to Siberia and Manchuria, and others, notably Dr. Frank Skinner, from Manitoba, exchanged seeds with botanists in the area, particularly A. D. Woeikoff, Mr. Ptitsin, and others of Harbin, in the area then called Manchuria.

Many of the trees and shrubs listed in this book originated with seeds that came to us from eastern Asia: Amur maple (*Acer ginnala*), Japanese tree lilac (*Syringa reticulata*), Manchurian ash (*Fraxinus mandshurica*), and hedge cotoneaster (*Cotoneaster lucidus*). Others, such as the rugosa rose (*Rosa rugosa*), the early Korean lilac (*Syringa oblata* var. *dilitata*), and the Siberian crabapple (*Malus baccata*), have contributed their genetics to plant-breeding programs, which have resulted in hundreds of improved plants for the prairies.

any time during the growing season.

There are advantages to using bare-root plants, however. When large numbers of small trees are required for shelterbelts or hedgerows, bare-root plants are usually much cheaper. This method also allows you to buy cultivars not normally sold in garden centers from specialty growers through the mail.

PLANTING METHODS

Bare Root

With bare-root trees and shrubs, the key to success is keeping the roots moist from the time they are dug at the nursery until they are replanted. If they have moist packing material around their roots, leave the roots packed and keep them in a cool, shaded place until you are ready to plant, which should be as soon as possible. Dormant plants that have not yet leafed out may benefit from being plunged into warm water overnight before planting.

Dig a hole wide enough for the roots to be well spread out. It should be deep enough to allow the plant to be set at about the same level at which it was growing in the field at the nursery. Place the plant in the hole and pull soil in around its roots. Firmly tamp the soil, stepping on it to ensure that the roots are in firm contact with the soil. Once the soil has been firmed and the hole filled to about the original level, water the plant thoroughly to settle the soil around the roots. If the soil settles further, fill the hole to the proper level, and then apply mulch. Fertilizing with a high-phosphate transplant fertilizer encourages the quick re-establishment of roots. Follow label instructions and do not overfertilize.

Balled and Burlapped

The roots of balled and burlapped trees and shrubs are protected by the soil ball. The ball must be kept moist and intact. If you're not ready to plant when you get it home, place it in a shaded spot and cover the root ball with mulch to keep it cool and moist. The plant may be kept like this for weeks. Dig a hole that is 5 to 10 cm (2 to 4 in.) deeper than the depth of the ball and about 20 to 30 cm (8 to 12 in.) wider. Place the soil ball in the hole so that the tree stands straight and then pack soil about halfway up the ball. Untie the burlap and fold it back and down to ensure it is completely covered with soil; this prevents wicking of moisture out of the root ball into the air. Recheck that the plant is straight, and backfill to the top of the ball, making sure that the soil is tamped down firmly. When you're finished, there should be a well—about 5 cm (2 in.) deep—to hold water for the tree. Fill it with water and transplant-fertilizer solution diluted according to label instructions.

Container Grown

Container-grown plants can be held in their container until you are ready to plant, as long as the medium in the container is kept moist. Dig a hole about 5 cm (2 in.) deeper and about 20 cm (8 in.) wider than the root ball. Take the plant out of the container and examine the root ball. If the plant is root bound, and especially if there are roots spiraling around the outside of the root ball, take a knife and tease the roots out straight or cut through them in several places. This encourages the plant to root out into the soil. Fill the hole partway, check that the plant is straight, and finish filling with soil, leaving a 5-cm (2-in.) well around the tree for water. Water the plant until the water penetrates the root ball and percolates into the soil below.

Tree and Shrub Maintenance

❧

Even if you select trees and shrubs that have a minimum of serious insect and disease problems, any plant can become unhealthy as a result of environmental, nutritional, or other factors. Attention to these problems can significantly increase the plant's health and lifespan.

PRUNING

WHY PRUNE?

There are a number of reasons to prune trees and shrubs.

Transplanting bare-root or balled and burlapped trees or shrubs inevitably damages the roots. Broken or damaged roots should be cut back to healthy tissue so they can heal and regrow. To compensate for this reduced root system, the top growth is often reduced to minimize the stress on the newly transplanted tree or shrub. Use caution, however; leaves provide the energy to grow new roots, so severely reducing the top growth can slow the re-establishment of the roots and increase the stress on the plant.

Young trees and shrubs are often pruned to encourage a desired growth form. Judicious pruning helps to establish an attractive and desirable form, and it will improve the health and beauty of a plant over its lifetime.

Pruning to remove diseased and damaged wood helps control disease and allows the plant to heal. If done properly, it might significantly extend the life of a damaged tree or shrub.

Pruning encourages the growth of a strong and healthy tree, lessening the chance of wind and storm damage. Storm breakage can be dangerous to people and property, and low branches can cause injury.

Finally, pruning stimulates denser growth on trees and shrubs. Most trees and shrubs exhibit some degree of apical dominance. This occurs when buds behind the active growing point at the end of a stem are suppressed and do not grow. Pruning disrupts this dominance and stimulates growth from these side or lateral buds.

BASIC TECHNIQUES

Buy the right tools—the best you can afford. They will stay sharp much longer, make the job easier, and last longer. With proper care, good tools will often last a lifetime. You'll need secateurs or bypass pruners, loppers, a pruning saw, and a pruning knife. Hedge shears or pole pruners might also come in handy.

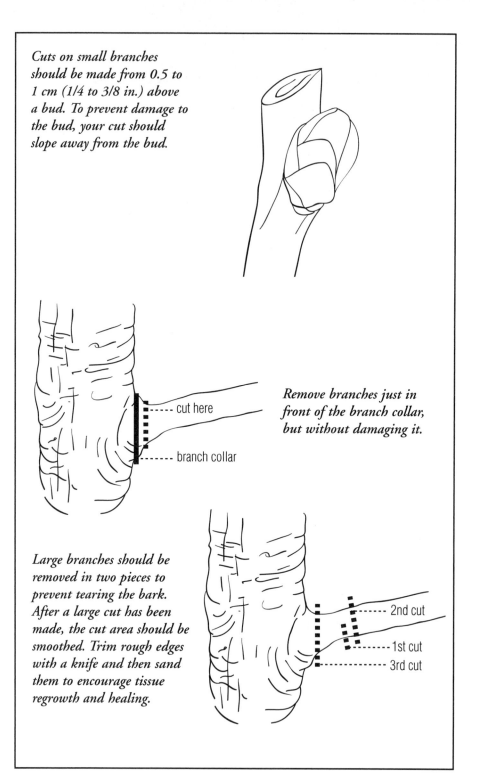

Cuts on small branches should be made from 0.5 to 1 cm (1/4 to 3/8 in.) above a bud. To prevent damage to the bud, your cut should slope away from the bud.

cut here

branch collar

Remove branches just in front of the branch collar, but without damaging it.

Large branches should be removed in two pieces to prevent tearing the bark. After a large cut has been made, the cut area should be smoothed. Trim rough edges with a knife and then sand them to encourage tissue regrowth and healing.

2nd cut

1st cut

3rd cut

DECIDUOUS SHRUBS

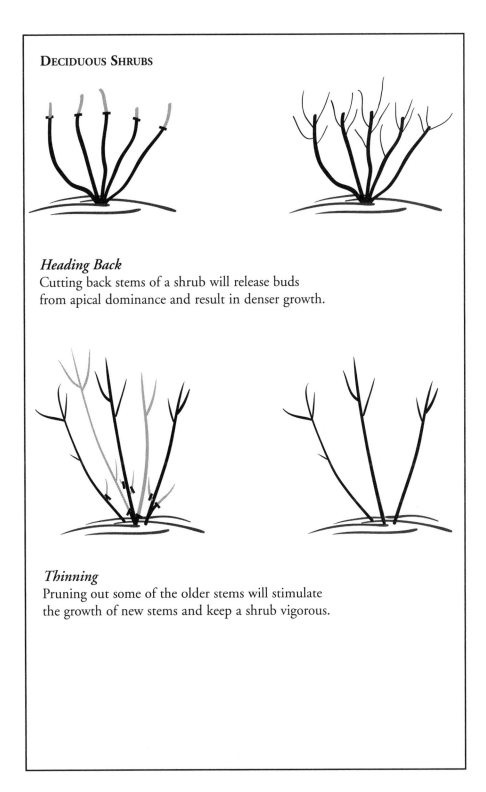

Heading Back
Cutting back stems of a shrub will release buds
from apical dominance and result in denser growth.

Thinning
Pruning out some of the older stems will stimulate
the growth of new stems and keep a shrub vigorous.

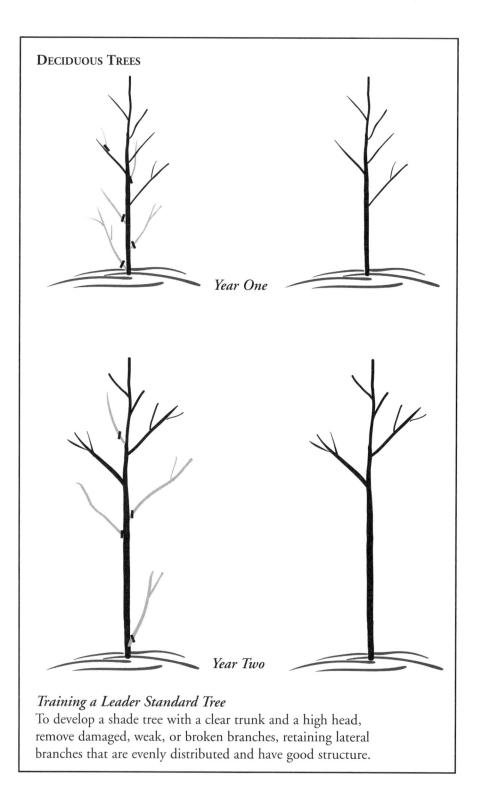

DECIDUOUS TREES

Year One

Year Two

Training a Leader Standard Tree
To develop a shade tree with a clear trunk and a high head,
remove damaged, weak, or broken branches, retaining lateral
branches that are evenly distributed and have good structure.

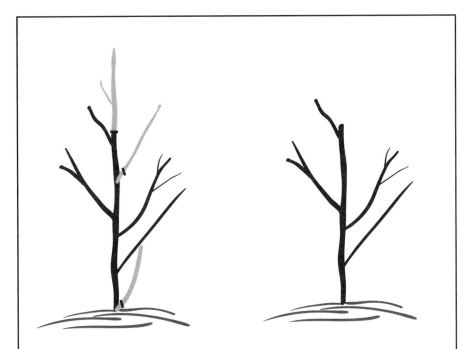

Training a Low-branching Standard Tree
This technique is often used for fruit trees or for low,
flowering trees in borders where a clear trunk is desired.
The leader is pruned out to encourage branch formation
and the development of a dense, low head. Branches are
removed from the lower portion of the trunk.

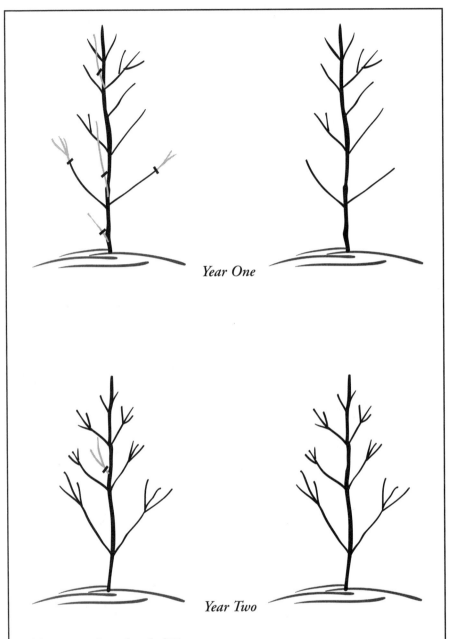

Year One

Year Two

Training a Low-headed Tree
To develop a tree that is branched close to the ground
for shelter or screening, remove broken, damaged, or
weak branches and encourage branches near the ground.

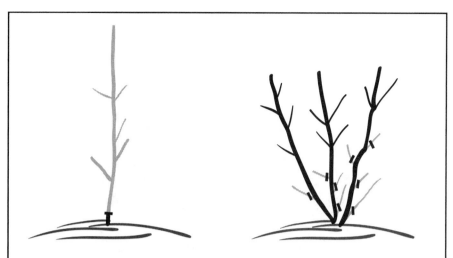

Training a Multi-stemmed Tree

At the end of the first year after planting, cut back the main stem to encourage the growth of several shoots from the base. At the end of the second year, select three or four strong, well-placed shoots and cut back the rest. In subsequent years, remove suckers that develop at the base and prune branches from the bottom of the stems.

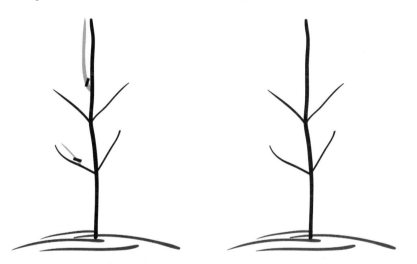

Removing Double Leaders

When trees with opposite buds lose their leader, they often develop competing leaders. If allowed to develop, the crotch between these forks becomes a weak point. To prevent this, remove the less-upright stem and train the other stem as a new leader.

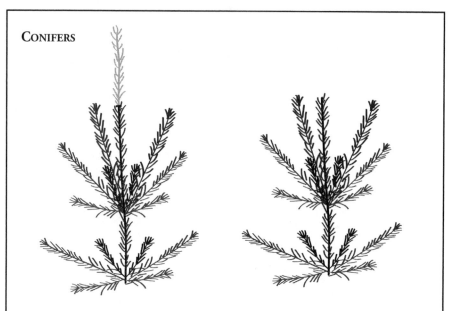

Heading Back New Growth

Pinching off new growth of conifers results in denser growth and controls the size of shrubby types like mugo pine. Do this pinching as the growth begins to become woody in late June, once the "candle" elongates vertically but before the new needles emerge horizontally. Leave at least 0.5 cm (0.25 in.) of growth.

Pruning Coniferous Shrubs

Prune back junipers and other evergreen shrubs to a main branch. For a natural look, never shear in a straight line. Other branches can be trained to fill gaps.

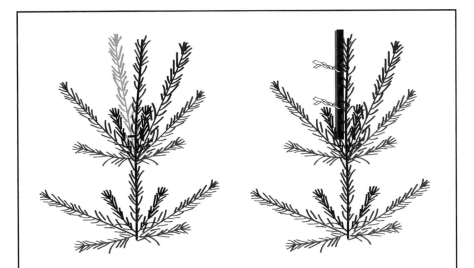

Training a New Leader for Coniferous Trees

If the top of a conifer is damaged, often two or more stems will grow up to form leaders. If you want a natural-shaped tree, remove the competing leader and, if necessary, tie the chosen leader to a stake within the tree to keep it straight.

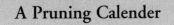

A Pruning Calender

EARLY SPRING: prune fruit trees and other deciduous trees, except birch and maple; prune summer-flowering shrubs that bloom on the current season's growth (*e.g.*, summer-blooming spirea, continuous-blooming roses, hydrangeas).

EARLY SUMMER: prune spring-blooming shrubs, such as lilac, immediately after they bloom to allow them to produce buds for the following season; prune birch and maple after the sap is up.

SUMMER: deadhead repeat-blooming shrubs; prune to correct storm damage, to remove sucker shoots on trees, or to remove diseased wood.

FALL TO EARLY SPRING: if a tree or shrub must be severely pruned, for the best results, prune while the plant is dormant.

Environmental Conditions

Protection from Extreme Cold

All gardeners want to try plants that are less than "iron-clad" hardy, but even the most winter-hardy species can be injured by unusual weather.

Ideally, plants grow vigorously through the summer and then harden off in advance of cold temperatures in early winter. If we provide plants with good growing conditions during the summer, they can build up the food reserves they need to survive over winter. As fall approaches, plants need to become less active and to go into a hardy state. We can encourage this by reducing water in late summer and by avoiding fertilizing or severe pruning after early summer.

Mulch such as post peelings, leaves, or straw helps to protect the roots from extreme winter temperature fluctuations. Apply winter mulches after growth has stopped and the soil has begun to freeze; if you apply it too early, the mulch might prevent the soil from freezing. Alternatively, mulches can be left in place as a permanent cover, reducing moisture loss and erosion. Winter mulches serve two purposes: they moderate soil temperature during the winter and prevent the premature warming of the roots in spring, discouraging early growth that can be frozen. This is especially important in areas where chinooks can stimulate plant growth in early spring.

Sunscald and frost cracks occur when bark is warmed by the sun during the day, followed by a rapid drop in temperature at night. Protect the bark by shading it from direct sunlight. You can do this by allowing branches to grow low on the trunk, particularly on the southwest side of susceptible trees, by covering the bark with ventilated plastic protectors, by screening it with burlap, or by painting it with a white latex paint to reflect the sun. Adjust protectors each year to avoid girdling the tree.

Drought Protection

Lack of moisture, both in the soil and in the air, is another significant limiting factor of our prairie climate. Lack of moisture can be dealt with by following these principles of xeriscape landscaping:

* Design for water conservation by placing plants with similar water needs together and by grading slopes to conserve water.
* Improve the soil's ability to hold water by adding organic matter.
* Reduce lawn areas that have high demands for water, fertilizer, and weed-control chemicals.
* Plant species vary greatly in their need for soil water, so select plants appropriate for the planting site.
* Install efficient irrigation systems, such as trickle irrigation.
* Mulch to conserve moisture.

Roots require air as well as water to grow. Keep the soil around newly planted trees moist to compensate for root loss, but allow it to begin to dry on top before watering it again. If water is applied too frequently and too heavily, the soil becomes waterlogged and will not provide a healthy environment for roots to become

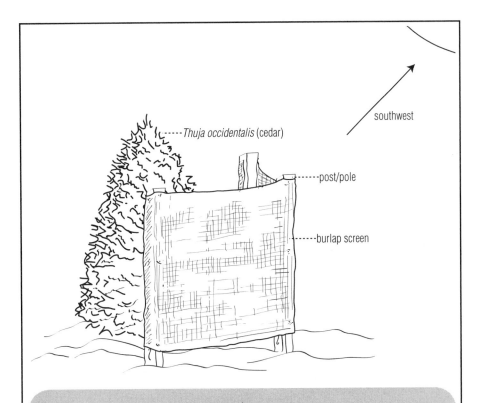

southwest

Thuja occidentalis (cedar)

post/pole

burlap screen

❦

Winter Browning of Evergreens

Needle browning in evergreens is not always cause for concern.
Evergreen needles are retained for only two to four years; the needles
naturally turn yellow and shed in the late summer or fall. If an unusually
large portion of the needles drop in a short time, it indicates drought.
Water the soil around the plant slowly and thoroughly until the water
percolates to a depth of 60 cm (24 in.).

During the winter, evergreens continue to lose moisture through
their needles. Because their roots are frozen, they may not be able to
take up water quickly enough to replace it, and this causes browning.
To alleviate browning, water evergreens well prior to freeze-up in the fall,
and place susceptible plants in sheltered locations, protected from wind
and from late-afternoon winter sun. Trunks can also be shaded from the
winter sun with burlap screens, but wrapping evergreens with burlap or
plastic is detrimental and not recommended.

Other causes of evergreen needle browning include herbicides, salt
spray, insects, and male dogs urinating on the lower branches.

established. On sandy soil, water thoroughly every three to four days; on more moisture-retentive loam soil, water approximately once a week. Reduce watering frequency if there is significant rainfall.

INJURY

MECHANICAL INJURY

The bark of a tree, like our skin, is its protective barrier, which enables it to survive in a hostile environment. Injury to the bark can result in serious harm to a tree or shrub.

Hail may cause small injuries that allow disease organisms to enter. Injuries that girdle the bark on a stem or trunk will cause the death of that stem.

Damage caused by the careless use of mowers and string trimmers is a common cause of death of young trees. Place protectors around the trunk and keep the surrounding tree well free of grass to reduce competition with the tree and to eliminate the need for cutting grass up to its base. Alternatively, place trees in a mixed-layered border.

Another preventable cause of injury to trees is girdling wires from labels or tree supports. As the tree grows, the wire cuts into it and eventually girdles the bark, which causes the death of the portion of the tree above the wire. Poorly tied support wire can also cause bark injuries by rubbing against the tree in the wind.

Mice, rabbits, porcupines, and deer can be devastating to trees. Mice chew the bark close to ground level, while rabbits feed higher up and porcupines climb into the tree to feed. Using screen or plastic wraps around the base in winter will deter mice, and fencing will keep rabbits or porcupines away. Deer cause damage by feeding on leaves, needles, and twigs or by rubbing their antlers on tree trunks. Fencing is effective in certain situations, but there are other options. Repellants either frighten animals away (*e.g.*, blood meal, human hair) or make the bark distasteful to them (*e.g.*, ground pepper or garlic). Blood meal is an effective deterrent, if deer have alternate food sources.

Branches are sometimes broken during severe weather. Pruning to develop a strong structure is the best preventative measure; prompt pruning back to sound wood using the guidelines in this chapter and avoiding stubs, helps the tree heal.

The most important part of the tree is underground. Trenching alongside a tree can cause serious damage to the roots and possibly death to the tree. If possible, trench beyond the tree's drip line. If this is not possible, damage to feeder roots can be alleviated by tunneling, rather than trenching, at least 0.5 m (1.5 ft.) below the surface within its drip line.

CHEMICAL INJURY

Trees and shrubs are susceptible to injury from herbicide drift, but sensitivity to particular chemicals varies among species. Ensure that non-target plants are not damaged when applying herbicides such as 2, 4-D, and glyphosate (Round-up). Before spraying, cover nearby plants and wrap exposed trunks with plastic.

Conifers such as *Pinus sylvestris* (Scots pine), page 125,
provide four-season shelter and privacy, as well as beauty.
SARA WILLIAMS

Juniperus communis 'Depressa Aurea' (common juniper), page 106,
and *Malus baccata* (Siberian crabapple), page 112, separate two areas
of the landscape, creating a garden room around a barbecue area.
SARA WILLIAMS

With careful pruning, a tree branch can frame other
attractive garden features below and beyond it.
SARA WILLIAMS

A low-maintenance, mixed layered border adds
structure and beauty to the winter prairie garden.
SARA WILLIAMS

Juniperus (juniper), page 102, provide a restful green
backdrop to bright perennials in a mixed border.
SARA WILLIAMS

Dwarf evergreen and deciduous shrubs guarantee year-round variety
in colour, texture, and height within a mixed border.
HUGH SKINNER

The brilliant fall color of *Ulmus davidiana* var. *japonica* 'Jacan' (Japanese elm), page 193, *Acer ginnala* (Amur maple, ginnala maple), page 62, and *Tilia mongolica* (Mongolian linden), page 194, is enhanced by the evergreen background of *Picea glauca* 'Densata' (Black Hills spruce), page 120

HUGH SKINNER

Variegated *Cornus* (dogwood), page 77, is a perfect partner for small evergreens and perennials in this beautifully textured foliage garden.

LIESBETH LEATHERBARROW

Columnar evergreens, such as
Thuja occidentalis 'Brandon' or
'Skybound' (cedar, eastern white cedar),
page 190, make beautiful and effective
screens for any size of garden.
LESLEY REYNOLDS

Abies balsamea (balsam fir), page 59
BAILEY NURSERIES

Abies lasiocarpa (alpine fir, subalpine fir,
Rocky Mountain fir), page 60
SARA WILLIAMS

Acer ginnala (Amur maple, ginnala
maple), page 62
SARA WILLIAMS

Acer negundo (Manitoba maple, box elder), page 63
Sara Williams

Acer saccharinum 'Silver Cloud'
(silver maple), page 64
Jeffries Nurseries Ltd.

Aesculus glabra (Ohio buckeye), page 65
Sara Williams

Amelanchier alnifolia (saskatoon berry), page 66
SARA WILLIAMS

Betula papyrifera (paper birch), page 70
BRIAN BALDWIN

45

Betula papyrifera (paper birch), page 70
Sara Williams

Berberis thunbergii 'Rose Glow'
(Japanese barberry), page 69
Sara Williams

Caragana arborescens 'Pendula' (weeping
caragana), page 74
Sara Williams

Cornus sericea (red osier dogwood),
page 79
Sara Williams

Cornus alba 'Argenteo-marginata' (syn. 'Elegantissima') (Tartarian dogwood), page 77
SARA WILLIAMS

Cotoneaster lucidus (hedge cotoneaster),
page 81
BRIAN BALDWIN

Crataegus x *mordenensis* 'Toba'
(Morden hawthorn), page 83
SARA WILLIAMS

Cytisus purpureus var. *procumbens* (purple broom), page 85
SARA WILLIAMS

Daphne burkwoodii 'Carol Mackie' (burkwood daphne), page 86
SARA WILLIAMS

Daphne cneorum (rose daphne), page 86
SARA WILLIAMS

Euonymus alatus
(winged burning bush), page 90
BAILEY NURSERIES

Eleagnus angustifolia (Russian olive), page 88
BRIAN BALDWIN

Euonymus maackii (Maack's spindle
tree), page 90

Euonymus nanus var. *turkestanicus*
(Turkestan burning bush), page 91

Forsythia ovata 'Northern Gold'
(Korean forsythia), page 91

Fraxinus pennsylvanica var. *subintegerrima*
(green ash), page 93

Genista tinctoria (dyer's greenwood), page 96
Sara Williams

Halimodendron halodendron (Siberian salt tree), page 97
Brian Baldwin

Hippophae rhamnoides (common sea buckthorn) page 97
Brian Baldwin

Hydrangea arborescens 'Annabelle'
(hydrangea, snowhill hydrangea), page 99
Sara Williams

Juglans spp. (walnut, butternut),
page 100
Liesbeth Leatherbarrow

Juniperus communis 'Depressa Aurea' (common juniper), page 106
Sara Williams

Juniperus horizontalis 'Mother Lode'
(creeping juniper), page 103
LIESBETH LEATHERBARROW

Juniperus sabina 'Arcadia' (Savin
juniper), page 104
SARA WILLIAMS

Juniperus scopulorum 'Medora' (Rocky
Mountain juniper), page 106
HUGH SKINNER

Larix decidua (European larch), page 107
HUGH SKINNER

Larix sibirica (Siberian larch), page 108
LIESBETH LEATHERBARROW

Lonicera tatarica 'Cameo' (Tartarian honeysuckle), page 109
SARA WILLIAMS

Malus baccata 'Thunderchild' (Siberian crabapple), page 114
LIESBETH LEATHERBARROW

Philadelphus lewisii (Lewis mockorange, mockorange), page 116
SARA WILLIAMS

Occasionally, people use soil sterilants on driveways or along fences. These chemicals can kill any tree whose roots reach into the area where they are applied, and if heavy rain causes runoff, the chemicals may cause injury at some distance from where they were applied. Don't use these chemicals anywhere near your valuable plants or those of your neighbors.

Motor oil, road salt, and excessive salts from overfertilization can also injure roots or stems. Air pollution can be harmful to both the leaves and the roots of plants. A sooty coating on leaves slows down processes like photosynthesis, and leaves can be damaged by acid rain. These types of injuries are most common near industrial areas.

INSECTS AND DISEASES

THE INTEGRATED PEST MANAGEMENT APPROACH

Beginning in the 1940s, people began to rely almost exclusively on chemicals to control insects and disease. Fortunately, over the years, we have come to realize the dangers these chemicals present to our environment.

Reliance on chemical controls can give rise to further problems. Pest organisms are part of a complex system in which most insects, fungi, and bacteria are beneficial. In this complex ecology, it is usually not reasonable to try to eliminate pests.

The integrated pest management (IPM) approach has two stages: first, it determines an acceptable level of injury; then, it looks at a variety of control strategies. The level of infection that requires the introduction of control measures might depend on the type of plant and where it is growing. For instance, the damage to plants that are viewed from close up will be visually more prominent than those that are viewed from a distance. The least environmentally harmful control strategies should be employed first.

IPM strategies are varied and consider the interaction of the plant in its environment. A key strategy pursued by plant breeders is the development of resistant cultivars. Excluding pest organisms can also be effective if the pests are not highly mobile and move slowly. A variation on this method is to eliminate one of the hosts if a pest organism needs more than one host to complete its life cycle (*e.g.*, juniper-saskatoon rust). However, sanitation is a more practical option with many pest species. Infected leaves are picked off and destroyed, while infected wood is pruned out and burned or disposed of in the garbage.

Diseases often hitch a ride to get to a susceptible host. This "vector," or carrier, is often an insect. An aphid, a bark beetle, or a bee can bring fungal spores or bacterial ooze to a potential infection site. Another common vector is the gardener, moving about in the garden, touching or pruning plants. Avoid handling plants when they are wet and disinfect pruning tools, especially when pruning diseased wood.

Effective, environmentally friendly control strategies include introducing predator insects (*e.g.*, ladybugs) and encouraging those that are already present; trapping insects using mechanical means, such as sticky strips or traps or pheromone traps; and removing weeds, deadwood, and debris to get rid of over-wintering eggs or pupae. In instances of severe infestations, dust plants with diatomaceous earth, use biological control agents such as *Bacillus thuringiensis,* or spray an insecticidal soap or a botanical insecticide such as rotenone.

CONTROLLING INSECT PESTS

The vast majority of insects are beneficial. The honeybee, for example, not only supplies us with honey but also pollinates plants. Insects such as ladybugs eat aphids and mites, dragonflies prey on mosquito larvae, and a variety of wasps are parasitic on various caterpillars, as are certain flies. Fireflies feed on snails, slugs, and the larvae of other insects. Chemical sprays often harm these beneficial insects more seriously than they do the pest insects. As a result, future infestations might be more severe and more difficult to control.

Aphids, which suck the juices from plant leaves, are common pest insects. If infestations are small and you're not squeamish, control them by squashing them with your finger. Larger infestations can provide good feeding grounds for ladybugs. Alternatively, the sharp crystals of diatomaceous earth can be applied to pierce the soft bodies of aphids, or their breathing passages can be sealed by insecticidal soap.

Spider mites are too small to be easily visible to the naked eye. If you suspect an infestation, place a sheet of white paper beneath the leaves and give the branch a sharp tap. If there is an infestation, some of the mites will drop onto the paper, where they will appear like specks of pepper. Spider mites prefer dry conditions and can often be discouraged by washing the plant with a strong spray of water. They are also prey for ladybugs and predatory mites. Severe infestations can be controlled by dusting with diatomaceous earth or by spraying with insecticidal soap.

Caterpillars are the larvae of moths or butterflies and cause damage by chewing the leaves of plants. You can often control light infestations by picking and squashing the offending insects. They are also food for wasps or birds, such as robins, and they may be parasitized by larvae of tachinid flies. Severe infestations of forest tent caterpillars or canker worms can completely defoliate trees or shrubs, and call for more drastic control methods. Female adult canker worms crawl up into the canopy of a tree to lay eggs. To prevent this, they can be trapped by putting sticky bands around the trunks. However, this method is only effective if most of the trees in the neighborhood are banded, because larvae are carried by the wind once they hatch. Caterpillars are controlled by *Bacillus thuringiensis*, which is available as a commercial spray product.

Scale insects infest a variety of ornamentals, such as pine and cedar. In small numbers, they can be rubbed off with a finger and destroyed. Control large infestations with ladybugs or chalcid wasps or with insecticidal soap or dormant oil sprays. Scale insects are protected by their covering scales and are difficult to control with chemicals.

Controlling Plant Diseases

Plant diseases can be effectively controlled by removing any one of the following factors:

* the presence of disease organisms
* a susceptible host
* environmental conditions that favor the disease organism.

Some diseases can be contained by excluding or eliminating disease organisms. Some viral diseases have been kept under control by restricting the sale and movement of plant material. This is one of the purposes of federal regulations that control the importation of plants. Where disease organisms are present, they can sometimes be controlled by pruning to remove infected wood and burning it to prevent reinfection. In some cases, removing or controlling insects that are vectors for the disease is effective. The progress of Dutch elm disease has been significantly slowed in some cities by removing dead wood that harbors elm bark beetles and preventing the movement of firewood.

Using resistant cultivars can be the most effective way to control such devastating diseases as fireblight. Flowering crabapple cultivars such as 'Thunderchild' have been developed with moderate to high resistance to fireblight. Although the most susceptible cultivars may be killed outright by the disease, those that are moderately resistant may only develop very

limited spur infections, and the most resistant will not show any symptoms of the disease. Unfortunately, the long and difficult search for elm species that are both fully hardy and resistant to Dutch elm disease has not yet been completely successful.

Sometimes, subtle differences in the environment can have a dramatic impact on disease infections. For instance, leaf spot diseases, like black spot on roses, need moisture on the leaves for a certain period of time for the fungal spores to germinate and infect the leaf. If a plant is growing in full sun and open to breezes, morning dew will dry much more quickly, reducing the chances of infection.

Bacterial diseases such as fireblight are caused by tiny, single-celled organisms that cause rots or wilts or form galls. There are no simple cures for bacterial diseases. Choose cultivars that are resistant and maintain good sanitation by pruning out and destroying diseased tissue. If it is necessary to remove an infected tree or shrub, don't replant a susceptible cultivar in the same location. Warm temperatures, high moisture levels, and an overabundance of nitrogen can favor bacteria. Normally, bacteria are spread by birds, animals, splashing rainwater, or pruning tools. They gain entry most easily through wounds. Keeping plants healthy and removing possible sources of infection are the most effective controls for bacterial diseases.

Fungal diseases such as black spot, shoestring root rot fungus, and Dutch elm disease produce leaf spots, mildews, rusts, root rots, and damping-off diseases. They are spread by insects or spores carried in the air. Control of vectors and removal of diseased tissue are effective control measures. Growing resistant cultivars removes the threat of certain diseases, such as black spot on roses. Pruning for better light and air circulation and removing damaged wood can reduce the incidence of disease.

Viral diseases and mycoplasma diseases, such as rose mosaic, are most often spread by insects such as aphids, mealy bugs, or whiteflies. The most effective control is the removal and destruction of infected plants, but control of aphids, leafhoppers, and other insect vectors can also reduce the spread of diseases.

PART II

TREES AND SHRUBS
FOR PRAIRIE GARDENS

Abies
ay-beez

Fir

Abies is derived from the Latin *abire* "to rise," which refers to the great height some species attain. Firs have a pronounced symmetrical growth habit, especially when young. Their needles are flattened, soft to the touch, and intensely aromatic.

How to Grow
Because their natural habitat is in areas of higher rainfall, most firs need consistent moisture to reach their full potential. Plant them in sheltered locations, protected from drying winds, with adequate mulch to ensure soil moisture. Firs should be transplanted either balled and burlapped or from containers.

Abies balsamea
ay-beez bal-sah-*mee*-ah
Balsam fir

Balsam fir is native to the boreal forest region across Canada, from the east coast to the Rocky Mountains. Adaptable to a variety of growing conditions, it is usually found on moist soils in association with aspen,

PLANT AT A GLANCE

TYPE: medium, coniferous, evergreen tree
HEIGHT/SPREAD: 10 to 15 m (33 to 50 ft.)/3 to 6 m (10 to 20 ft.)
LIGHT: full sun to partial shade
SOIL: moist, well drained; loam
DISTINGUISHING FEATURES: dark green needles; symmetrical habit
LANDSCAPE USE: specimen
PHOTO: page 43

birch, and spruce. It is cultivated for Christmas trees, and the sap is the source of "Canada balsam," which is used for mounting specimens on microscope slides and as an ingredient in fragrance.

When young, balsam fir forms a dense, symmetrical pyramid, with horizontal branches. It may look ragged as it ages because it tends to retain lower branches that have lost their needles. Other *Abies* species listed here are less inclined to this undesirable characteristic. 'Nana,' a dwarf form of *A. balsamea*, is an attractive, densely branched, globular shrub only 0.6 m (2 ft.) in height, with a 1.2-m (4-ft.) spread.

The bark of young balsam fir trees is smooth and silver gray, with prominent resin blisters, and forms rectangular plates with age. The needles are dark green, with two white stomatal lines on the underside. They are spirally arranged on the twigs, but are twisted at the base and often appear two-ranked, giving the branch with needles a flat look, especially on new growth. The violet cones are 5 to 10 cm (2 to 4 in.) long and are held upright on the branches, turning brown when ripe. The cone scales fall off when the seeds are ripe.

OTHER SPECIES AND HYBRIDS

- *Abies sibirica* (*ay*-beez sy-*beer*-i-kah), Siberian fir, is similar in appearance to balsam fir, but more tolerant of dry conditions. It is sometimes injured by late spring frosts and is seldom available in nurseries.

Abies lasiocarpa
ay-beez *las*-ee-oh-car-pah

Alpine fir, subalpine fir, Rocky Mountain fir

Alpine fir grows in the mountains of Alberta and British Columbia from 600 to 2,300 m (2,000 to 7,500 ft.) in the subalpine forest zone. *Lasiocarpa* is from the Greek *lasios*, "shaggy," and *carpos*, "fruit," referring to the rough cones.

Alpine fir is an ideal evergreen for a smaller landscape and is drought tolerant once established. It is narrow and pyramidal in habit, with a dense, elongated crown. The smooth, ash-gray bark breaks into gray-brown plates with age. The flattened needles are dark grayish green to bluish green, crowded on the stem, and directed forward. They have stomatal markings on both surfaces; on the lower surface, these appear as two white lines. The dark purple cones have scales

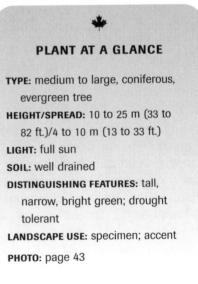

PLANT AT A GLANCE

TYPE: medium to large, coniferous, evergreen tree

HEIGHT/SPREAD: 10 to 25 m (33 to 82 ft.)/4 to 10 m (13 to 33 ft.)

LIGHT: full sun

SOIL: well drained

DISTINGUISHING FEATURES: tall, narrow, bright green; drought tolerant

LANDSCAPE USE: specimen; accent

PHOTO: page 43

sloping away from a central tip, and they shatter when ripe.

Acer

ay-sir

Maple

Acer is derived from the Latin word for "sharp" and refers to its generally hard wood, which the Romans used for spear handles. Maples grown on the prairies vary from the tough, ubiquitous, and often maligned native Manitoba maple to the coveted but generally unreliable sugar maple. They range from large trees to small shrubs and may have simple or compound leaves. Their only obvious commonalities are their flowers and seeds.

How to Grow

The cultural requirements of maples are diverse, but all will grow in full sun to partial shade. Most adaptable is *Acer negundo* (Manitoba maple), which grows well in a wide range of soil conditions, has a high tolerance for stress, and is extremely drought tolerant once established. *Acer ginnala* (Amur maple) is easily grown on any well-drained soil. Plant it in full sun for the best fall color. Once established, it is also extremely drought tolerant. *Acer saccharinum* (silver maple) prefers deep, moist, fertile soil and should be planted in a location sheltered from prevailing winds. Both Amur and silver maples may suffer from lime-induced chlorosis in high pH soils.

Spruce, Fir, Douglas Fir, or Pine?

True fir (*Abies*) can be distinguished from spruce (*Picea*) by their needles: spruce needles are four-sided, fir needles two-sided. A spruce needle will roll between your fingers, while a fir needle will not. Norway spruce is an exception. Its needles are four-sided, but are angled and will not roll.

Pine (*Pinus*) is easily distinguished from other conifers by its longer needles: 5 to 15 cm (2 to 6 in.) compared to 1.5 to 4 cm (0.5 to 1.5 in.) for the others. Pine needles are in clusters of two, three, or five, while the others have needles that are borne individually along the branch.

Fir cones stand erect on the branch and shatter when ripe. Those of spruce and Douglas fir (*Pseudotsuga*) hang from the branch and fall from the tree intact.

The winter buds of true fir are generally rounded and resinous; those of Douglas fir are pointed.

Acer ginnala
(syn. *A. tataricum* ssp. *ginnala*)

ay-ser gin-*nel*-la

Amur maple, ginnala maple

Native to the Amur River valley and other areas of northeastern Asia, *ginnala* is its common name within part of its native range. Ginnala maples hybridize naturally with the less-hardy Tartarian maples (*Acer tataricum*), which are native to southeastern Europe and western Asia. These hybrids vary in form and hardiness.

❀

PLANT AT A GLANCE

TYPE: large deciduous shrub or small tree

HEIGHT/SPREAD: 4 to 5 m (13 to 16 ft.)/3 to 4 m (10 to 13 ft.)

LIGHT: full sun

SOIL: well drained

DISTINGUISHING FEATURES: bright orange-red fall foliage; substitute for Japanese maple

LANDSCAPE USE: accent; grouping

PHOTO: page 43

Ginnala maples are particularly useful in a small landscape or as a grouping in a larger space and are easily pruned to suit their function. This maple is considered a large shrub when multi-stemmed, a small tree if pruned to a single stem. With its fall color and distinctly lobed leaves, ginnala maple is an ideal substitute for the non-hardy Japanese maples in oriental-style gardens or near a pond.

It has opposite leaves, which are a dark, glossy green, with two smaller lobes on either side of an elongated central lobe. They are coarsely toothed and accented by red veins and leaf stalks. Ruggedly hardy and extremely drought tolerant, they provide an awesome display of orange-red foliage in the fall. Coloration varies from plant to plant, so ginnala maples are best selected and purchased in the fall when those with the brightest colors are evident. Cultivars with superior red fall colour have been selected.

Small, greenish yellow flowers emerge with the leaves in dense, upright terminal clusters. The double samaras generally turn bright red in early fall, brown later, and usually persist throughout the winter, providing food for birds.

CULTIVARS

❀ 'Compactum' (syn. 'Bailey Compact'), at only 1.5 to 1.8 m (5 to 6 ft.) in height, is dense and compact, with lustrous, green leaves, which turn red-purple in fall.

❀ 'Flame' has red samaras, a fiery red fall color, and is 4.5 m (15 ft.) in height and spread. It is variable if seed grown.

❀ 'Seminowii' has smaller, more deeply cut leaves, with five lobes and red-purple fall color. It is 3 m (10 ft.) in height, with a spread of 5 m (16 ft.).

Leaving Home: Ways of Winging It

Like young adults, seeds need to get away from home where they can develop without competition from their parents and siblings for space, light, food, and water.

Birds not only disperse seeds over long distances, but scarify, or soften, the hard seed coats of certain species as the seed makes its way through their digestive tract. This avian aeroplan includes packaging the seed in a bit of nutritious bird droppings to get it off to a good start—at no extra charge.

In contrast, the one- or two-seeded fruit of maple, ash, and elm have thin, membrane-like wings, or "samaras," that spin like mini-helicopters on wind currents, enabling them to make their getaway.

Acer negundo

ay-ser ne-gun-doh

Manitoba maple, box elder

This tree is commonly called box elder because its leaves resemble those of elder (*Sambucus*) and because it was used to make boxes. *Negundo* is from its resemblance to another plant, *Vitex negundo*.

Found along rivers and streams of the prairie parklands, Manitoba maple has long been used in shelterbelts and as a shade and street tree. Without it, much of Saskatchewan's soil might have drifted to Manitoba. It flourishes in inhospitable sites where few other trees survive, and it is one of the best climbing/tree-house species available. Sometimes tapped for maple syrup, it needs 2 to 5 percent more sap than a sugar maple for an equivalent amount of syrup.

On the negative side, female trees self-seed to the point of being (almost) weedy. The wood is weak and prone to breakage in storms, and it often hosts box elder bugs and

PLANT AT A GLANCE

TYPE: large deciduous tree
HEIGHT/SPREAD: 12 to 15 m
(40 to 50 ft.)
LIGHT: full sun
SOIL: extremely adaptable, from sand to heavy clay
DISTINGUISHING FEATURES: ability to survive adverse conditions
LANDSCAPE USE: shade; specimen; shelterbelt
PHOTO: page 44

honeydew-secreting aphids. It is not a tree under which to park your car.

Manitoba maple has an upright, spreading, and somewhat open form and seems to fill the space available to it. The dark brown bark is furrowed. Burls are common and water sprouts, which require removal by pruning, sometimes develop at the base of the trunk.

It is the only prairie maple with pinnately compound leaves. They generally consist of three to five oval to oblong leaflets, light green above and gray-green below, which turn a clear yellow in the fall.

Male and female flowers are on separate trees, the male flowers in dense, red tassels, the female flowers in drooping, greenish yellow clusters. A double, yellow-green to ash-brown samara is produced by female trees.

CULTIVARS

* 'Baron' is a seedless male clone developed at Morden, Manitoba, with an upright, oval form, and a height and spread of 12 to 17 m (40 to 56 ft.).
* 'Variegatum' and 'Sensation' have not proved reliably hardy on the prairies.

Acer saccharinum

ay-ser sa-kah-*ree*-num

Silver maple

Saccharinum, "sugary," refers to the sap of the tree. The silver maple is native to much of eastern North America, but provenance is important: trees grown from seed collected in its most northerly and most western natural range will be the hardiest. Silver maples make excellent shade trees in sheltered locations that are protected from the prevailing winds. Deep, moist, fertile soil is ideal. They are prone to chlorosis on poorly drained soils.

Upright and oval in form, silver maples have a moderate to fast growth

---

❀

PLANT AT A GLANCE

TYPE: large deciduous tree

HEIGHT/SPREAD: 16 to 20 m (52 to 65 ft.)/5 to 7 m (16 to 23 ft.)

LIGHT: full sun to partial shade

SOIL: adaptable

DISTINGUISHING FEATURES: attractive light gray bark; dark green, lobed leaves with silver undersides, which turn clear yellow in fall

LANDSCAPE USE: accent; shade

PHOTO: page 44

---

rate, but the limbs are sometimes weak and may break in storms. The light gray bark is smooth and attractive when young, becoming rougher with age.

The leaves are opposite, simple, dark green above, silver below (hence, the common name), palmately lobed, and more deeply incised than the familiar sugar maple leaf on the Canadian penny. They turn a clear yellow in fall.

Separate male and female flowers are borne on the same tree. The densely clustered flowers are small, greenish yellow to red, and emerge before the leaves. The double samaras produced by the female flowers are often dispersed during early summer storms.

CULTIVARS

* 'Silver Cloud,' selected by Rick Durand, has an upright crown, a tendency to retain a central leader, reduced basal sprouting, and

golden yellow fall color. It is 18 to 20 m (60 to 65 ft.) in height, with a spread of 9 to 11 m (30 to 36 ft.). Hardy to zone 3 or 2, it is a seedless male clone.

OTHER SPECIES AND HYBRIDS

* *Acer pseudosieboldianum* (*ay*-ser *sue*-doe-see-*bol*-dee-a-num), Korean maple, is a small maple that, like the ginnala maple, could be substituted for the non-hardy Japanese maple in sheltered prairie locations. Native to northern China and Korea, where it attains a height of 5 m (16 ft.), expect a very dwarf version in well-protected locations on the prairies. The leaves are dark green, with reddish stalks, and turn a brilliant orange-red in the fall. Reddish cream flowers emerge before the leaves.

* *Acer rubrum* (*ay*-ser *rube*-rum), red maple, is sometimes grown in southeastern Manitoba. It is reliably hardy only to zone 3, although some specimens have survived in very protected locations in the colder regions. Its name refers to the brilliant orange-red fall color of the leaves, which otherwise are similar to those of the silver maple. The red maple needs full sun and even moisture to reach a height of 18 m (60 ft.) and a spread of 15 m (50 ft.). It adapts to a variety of soils, but in soils with a high pH it may develop lime-induced chlorosis. Although it has tremendous appeal as a shade and specimen tree, its value is limited by its questionable

hardiness throughout most of the prairies.

* *Acer saccharum* (*ay*-ser sah-*kare*-um), sugar maple, familiar on the Canadian penny, is also of questionable hardiness on the prairies, although it has survived in some locations. Used for sugaring in milder climates, its brilliant fall color and dense, oval to rounded form make it ideal as a small shade tree, reaching 10 m (33 ft.) in height, with a 6- to 7-m (20- to 23-ft.) spread. It requires an extremely sheltered location on well-drained, fertile, evenly moist soil, in full sun. 'Unity,' selected by Wilbert Ronald and Rick Durand, is hardy to zone 3.

Aesculus glabra
ess-*kul*-us glah-*brah*
Ohio buckeye

This is one of the best shade or specimen trees available to prairie gardeners. Native to the southeastern and central United States, Ohio buckeyes are nearly trouble free, fully hardy, and easy to grow, and they should be much more widely planted.

Aesculus is the classical Latin name for an oak with edible acorns. The Ohio buckeye, however, is not an oak and the nuts are poisonous, but even botanists go astray occasionally. It is

PLANT AT A GLANCE

TYPE: medium, flowering, deciduous tree

HEIGHT AND SPREAD: 6 to 12 m (20 to 40 ft.) or larger

LIGHT: full sun

SOIL: deep, fertile, well drained

DISTINGUISHING FEATURES: palmately compound leaves, which turn yellow-orange in fall; upright panicles of creamy white flowers

LANDSCAPE USE: specimen; shade

PHOTO: page 44

derived from the Greek *esca*, "food;" *glabra*, "smooth" or "hairless," refers to the shiny nut. The common name conjures up images of frontier America: Ohio is within its native range, while buckeye, another reference to the nut, reminds one of the eye of a deer.

A small to medium-sized tree, with a round to oval form, the bark is ashen gray and becomes rough and fissured with age. The leaves are opposite, palmately compound, and composed of five to seven oval to elliptical leaflets, with pointed tips. Dark green in summer, they turn a lovely yellow-orange in fall.

Large, attractive creamy white flowers are produced in upright panicles, 10 to 18 cm (4 to 7 in.) long in late June. These are followed by the buckeyes—shiny but poisonous nuts enclosed by a prickly husk.

HOW TO GROW

Ohio buckeyes do best in deep, fertile, well-drained soil, with even moisture, in full sun or partial shade. They are difficult to transplant if bare root; it is best to use container-grown stock.

Amelanchier alnifolia
ah-meh-*lang*-kee-er
al-ni-*fol*-lee-a

Saskatoon berry

Saskatoons are native from Alaska and the Yukon through to the north-central United States. Long used by Native peoples fresh and in pemmican, they were quickly adopted

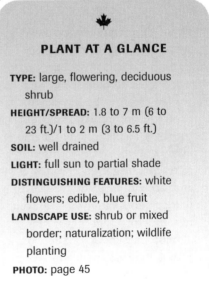

PLANT AT A GLANCE

TYPE: large, flowering, deciduous shrub

HEIGHT/SPREAD: 1.8 to 7 m (6 to 23 ft.)/1 to 2 m (3 to 6.5 ft.)

SOIL: well drained

LIGHT: full sun to partial shade

DISTINGUISHING FEATURES: white flowers; edible, blue fruit

LANDSCAPE USE: shrub or mixed border; naturalization; wildlife planting

PHOTO: page 45

by European settlers. Primarily grown for its fruit, the saskatoon is also an attractive ornamental. The genus name, *Amelanchier*, is from the French *amelanchus*, "honey," a reference to the sweet fruit.

One of the hardiest of our native shrubs, saskatoons can withstand winter temperatures as low as -50°C (-58°F). Although susceptible to various insects and diseases, they fruit successfully in most years.

Upright in form, the species can range from 1 to 7 m (3 to 23 ft.) in height, but most cultivars are considerably lower (1.5 to 5 m/5 to 16 ft.). They spread slowly and indefinitely by suckers. The common name is derived from a Cree word meaning "tree of much wood." *Alnifolia* means "with leaves resembling those of alder." The alternate leaves are oval to almost circular, simple, and singly toothed. Fall color varies from yellow through orange and purple.

The racemes of showy white flowers emerge in early spring and are generally self-pollinating. Edible, dark purple-blue berries follow within six to eight weeks. Most cultivars were selected from the wild for their superior fruit production.

How to Grow

Plant saskatoons in full sun to partial shade, in well-drained soil. They tolerate a wide range of soils and are drought tolerant once established. For greater fruit production, wind protection and even moisture are beneficial.

Cultivars

❀ 'Altaglow' (Brooks, Alberta, 1960) was selected for its ornamental rather than its fruiting qualities. It forms an erect, pyramidal shrub of 7 m (23 ft.) in height, with a spread of 2.5 m (8 ft.), and has brilliant deep purple, bright red, or orange to yellow fall foliage. The large, white fruit are sparsely produced.

❀ 'Honeywood' (A. J. Porter, Parkside, Saskatchewan, 1973) bears big clusters of large fruit on a bush with a height and spread of 2 to 3 m (6.5 to 10 ft.). It begins fruiting at an early age.

❀ 'Martin' is a 'Thiessen' seedling, with a height and spread of 2.5 m (8 ft.), selected by Dieter Martin of Langham, Saskatchewan. It has large fruit, with excellent flavor and uniform ripening.

❀ 'Northline' (Beaverlodge, Alberta 1960) is a very productive, freely suckering bush of 1.6 m (5.5 ft.) in both height and spread.

❀ 'Smoky,' also selected at Beaverlodge, has large, sweet berries in medium-sized clusters. At 4 m (13 ft.), in both height and spread, it is upright to spreading and suckers freely.

❀ 'Thiessen' was discovered in 1902 and introduced by George Krahn of Lakeshore Nurseries, Saskatoon. With a height of 5 m (16 ft.), and a spread of 2.5 m (8 ft.), it blooms early and produces large fruit.

On the Edge

❀ *Amorpha* is a genus that is represented by three species native to the prairie region. All have pinnately compound leaves, with many small leaflets, which give the shrubs a delicate texture, and spikes of tiny, purple flowers. They range in height from the 0.3-m (1-ft.) *Amorpha nana* (ah-mor-fah *nah*-nah), dwarf false indigo; to the 1-m (3-ft.) *A. canescens* (ah-*mor*-fah cah-*nes*-ens), leadplant; to the 2-m (6.5-ft.) and taller *A. fruticosa* (ah-*mor*-fah froo-ti-*koe*-sah), false indigo bush. All will adapt to dry, saline soil conditions that few other shrubs will tolerate.

❧ *Andromeda polifolia* (an-*drom*-i-dah paul-ee-*fow*-lee-a), bog rosemary, is a lovely evergreen groundcover shrub that grows in peat bogs of the northern hemisphere. It has narrow, evergreen needle-like leaves that resemble the herb from which it derives its common name. Because of its wide distribution, not all cultivars are hardy, including the commonly offered 'Blue Ice,' which has not survived in locations where locally native ones have. Bog rosemary prefers acid soil and is an interesting ground-cover for rhododendron enthusiasts.

❧ *Arctostaphylos uva-ursi* (ark-teh-*sta*-ful-us oo-va-*ur*-see), bearberry, is a dense and beautiful evergreen groundcover that is native throughout the prairie region. It is often found growing on limestone gravel in sun or partial shade. Its small, oval, dark green leaves are leathery and commonly turn to

bronze or burgundy in the fall. Small, urn-shaped flowers appear in spring and are followed by red berries in the fall. It can be used as a groundcover on banks or under trees.

❧ *Aronia melanocarpa* (ah-*row*-nee-a meh-len-oh-*kar*-pa), chokeberry, is a native plant that suckers vigorously to form thickets and is spectacular when used in large, mass plantings. The white flowers are borne in small clusters in late spring. The dark blue berries are similar to those of mountain ash. The dark, lustrous, green foliage turns a brilliant red in fall. 'Autumn Magic,' an outstanding selection from the University of British Columbia Botanical Garden, is noted for its brilliant red and purple fall color. Chokeberries grow in full sun or partial shade.

❧ *Artemesia* has two native shrub species that are occasionally grown in gardens. *Artemisia tridentata* (ar-teh-*mee*-see-ah try-den-*tah*-tah), big sagebrush, is valued in gardens in Europe for its unique foliage, which is covered with gray-white felt, and for its strong, pleasant sage odor. Each leaf has three teeth at the tip, hence, *tridentata.* It will reach 2 m (6.5 ft.) in height, tolerates infertile soils, and requires good drainage. *Artemisia cana* (ar-teh-*mee*-see-ah *cah*-nah), hoary sagebrush, is a smaller, gnarled shrub, growing to 1.2 m (4 ft.), with narrow, silver leaves. It naturally grows on sloping, well-drained, infertile clay soils.

Berberis thunbergii
ber-ber-is thun-ber-gee-ah

Japanese barberry

Berberis is from the Arabic *berberys*, the local name for the fruit. Barberry (barb-berry) takes its name from the needle-thin spines along the stems, which make it ideal for "traffic control" or as a barrier planting for gardeners with unkind hearts.

PLANT AT A GLANCE

TYPE: small to medium deciduous shrub

HEIGHT/SPREAD: 15 cm to 1.2 m (6 in. to 4 ft.)/30 cm to 1.8 m (12 in. to 6 ft.)

SOIL: well drained

LIGHT: full sun to partial shade

DISTINGUISHING FEATURES: yellow, pink, or red foliage, intensifying in color in fall

LANDSCAPE USE: barrier; rock garden; mixed or shrub border; hedge

PHOTO: page 46

Native to Japan, the species was introduced to Europe in 1864 and then to North America. But for almost half a century, barberry was illegal on the prairies because some species are alternate hosts of wheat stem rust, which devastated prairie wheat crops in the early twentieth century before the development of resistant wheat cultivars. In 2001, new federal legislation permitted the use of rust-resistant barberry cultivars.

Although some barberries are over 2 m (6.5 ft.) in height, many of the new cultivars are dwarf, compact shrubs, with dense foliage and an arching or rounded form. The small leaves are alternate and oval, and they range from yellow to red and purple to some that are mottled or variegated. Many turn reddish orange to purple in fall.

Small, yellow, cup-shaped flowers hang in clusters from the arching branches in early spring. They are followed by small, red berries, which persist throughout most of the winter.

HOW TO GROW

Plant barberries in full sun or partial shade in well-drained soil. Once established, they are very adaptable, quite drought tolerant, and easily pruned if they become too large. None of the following cultivars has been extensively trialed on the prairies. All are of unknown hardiness, so hedge your bets by placing them in a sheltered location.

CULTIVARS

* 'Golden Nugget' forms a low mound of 60 cm (24 in.), with a spread of 30 cm (12 in.) and has yellow foliage. It has done well in zone 2 through two winters with little snow cover.

* 'Rose Glow,' a Dutch introduction from 1957, is one of the largest (at 1 m/3 ft. in height, with an equal spread) and hardiest of the newly

introduced barberries, with outstanding rose red to pink variegated foliage.

* 'Royal Burgundy' ('Gentry') is a dwarf cultivar, with a height and spread of 50 to 60 cm (20 to 24 in.). It has burgundy-purple foliage, which turns very dark in autumn.

* 'Royal Cloak' is more upright and arching and, at 1 m (3 ft.), with an equal spread, is one of the largest of the new barberries. It has dark red-purple leaves.

* 'Ruby Carousel' ('Bailone') is low and mounded, with a height and spread of 1 m (3 ft.) and purple-red foliage.

Betula
bet-tuh-lah

Birch

Known for their peeling white bark, graceful form, and attractive foliage, birch have a long and honored place within the prairie landscape, but one that is in danger due to drought and the increasing presence of bronze birch borers.

Betula, the Latin name for this tree, was derived from *betu*, a Celtic name meaning "shine," which refers to the white bark. Birch have alternate, simple, oval to triangular leaves. Wind-pollinated male and female flowers are on the same tree. Male catkins are formed in late summer and elongate the following spring. Female flowers appear in early spring, before the leaves, and are less conspicuous. The seed is blown off the tree over winter.

Both native and introduced birch species have attractive bark, usually red brown to tawny in younger trees, maturing to white or brown once the stems reach 5 to 10 cm (2 to 4 in.) in diameter. Prominent horizontal markings, called lenticels, are openings that allow gas exchange between the tissue and the atmosphere. The mature white bark is useful in the landscape, for echoing nearby white flowers or variegated green and white foliage, or for contrasting with green, blue, gray, or purple conifers. Single-trunked, symmetrical birch trees reinforce a sense of formality, while those with multiple trunks lend a more informal ambience to the landscape.

HOW TO GROW
Birch are wet-site species, growing well on evenly moist, well-drained soils in full sun. They generally show dieback when planted on poorly drained, concrete-surrounded, or droughty urban soils.

Betula papyrifera
bet-tuh-lah pah-pi-*riff*-er-ah

Paper birch

Papyrifera is from the Greek *papyrus*, "paper," and the Latin *ferre*, "to bear," referring to the thin and easily peeled bark.

Native to much of Canada, including the boreal forests of the prairies, paper birch was once used extensively by Native peoples for canoes, baskets, snowshoes, and sleighs. The bark was utilized as a poultice to treat burns and skin injuries.

Paper birch is quite variable but, in general, it is a small to medium-sized tree, with long branches and an upright, oval form. Its shallow, spreading root system often intrudes onto the surface of lawns.

In nature, multi-stemmed trees are formed when animals browse the original stem. Trees in garden centers are either pruned by nursery professionals imitating deer or consist of several seedlings (sometimes with widely different characteristics) set in the same container. The bark of the paper birch is peeling, with horizontal lenticels; it turns white a little later than that of the European birch, generally when the trunk reaches 5 to 8 cm (2 to 3 in.) in diameter.

The dull, matte green leaves are doubly toothed and oval to triangular in shape, with a sharp tip. They turn a bright yellow in the fall. 'Chickadee' is a narrow, columnar form, with exceptionally white bark.

Betula pendula
bet-tuh-lah *pen*-dul-la
European or silver birch

The European birch is a medium-sized, upright, and oval tree, with a low canopy due to its weeping habit. *Pendula* is from a Latin word meaning "hanging, pendulous, or weeping." Its bark whitens sooner than that of the paper birch, and as it ages, the lower trunk develops a rough texture, with a black, diamond-shaped pattern. The leaves are smaller and glossier than those of the paper birch, with a flat base, but they have the same fine golden fall color.

CULTIVARS
* 'Fastigiata' is a small, narrow, columnar tree, shorter and much narrower than the species, with nearly vertical branches, becoming more oval with age.

- 'Gracilis' is a small tree, 4.5 to 6 m (15 to 20 ft.) in height, with a slightly smaller spread and finely cut leaves.
- 'Lacinata' is a large tree, 12 to 15 m (40 to 50 ft.) in height, with an 8-m (26-ft.) spread, weeping branches, white bark, and deeply incised, lacy leaves.
- 'Purple Rain'™ ('Monte') has a weeping habit and lustrous, dark purple leaves throughout the entire summer. It needs a well-sheltered location and does not appear to thrive in colder regions of the prairies. It reaches 12 m (40 ft.) in height, with a spread of 6 m (20 ft.).
- 'Youngii' (Young's weeping birch) is a dwarf birch, with very white bark and a weeping habit. It forms a low, mound-like, small tree, 5 m (16 ft.) in height, with a spread of 4 m (13 ft.). Left to its own devices, it would be an effective groundcover, but it is usually trained upward or budded or grafted onto a standard stem, giving it the appearance of a mushroom. Its leaves, less deeply incised than the species, turn yellow in fall.

OTHER SPECIES AND HYBRIDS
- *Betula fontinalis* (*bet*-tuh-lah fon-tin-*nah*-lis), the water birch, is a multi-stemmed, large shrub or small tree, up to 6 m (20 ft.) in height, with a spread of 3 m (10 ft.). It is less available than it should be. It has a special niche in the landscape adjacent to a pond or stream (*fontinalis* means

"growing near water"), yet it is adaptable to garden conditions. It appears resistant to borers and is being used to develop borer resistance in hybrids. On the grim side, bundles of its thin, shiny, bronze-red branches were once used to administer corporal punishment.

- *Betula glandulosa* (*bet*-tuh-lah glan-deh-*low*-sah), the shrubby or bog birch, is similar to the water birch, but smaller. An erect but somewhat spreading shrub (over 2 m/6.5 ft. in height and spread), it has shiny, green leaves, and dark gray to black, non-peeling bark, which has very conspicuous lenticels.

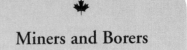

Miners and Borers

In the past few decades, bronze birch borers, birch leaf miners, and drought have all taken their toll on paper and weeping birches.

Small, gray areas on the surface of birch leaves in early June signal the presence of birch leaf miners, which are the larvae of black wasp-like sawflies. They hatch with a voracious appetite and immediately begin "mining" the interior of the leaves.

Female sawflies lay eggs in the upper-leaf surface in mid-May, and the small larvae hatch within a few weeks. Generally, there are two generations per season. The larvae of the second generation overwinter in the soil and emerge as adults the following spring.

Well-watered birches can tolerate several years of birch leaf miner infestations without harm. Insecticides also kill beneficial insects, thus their use is no longer recommended for birch leaf miners. Because the miners feed within the leaf, contact insecticides sprayed on the foliage are not effective. Within the last decade, natural predators in the form of parasitic wasps have migrated from eastern Canada and have been killing the larvae of birch leaf miners, significantly reducing both their numbers and their damage.

Bronze birch borers appear to be attracted to trees stressed by drought and by birch leaf miners, and they almost always spell doom for the tree. The best prevention is plenty of water; birches are, after all, wet-site species. Soak the soil within their drip lines to a depth of 60 cm (24 in.) every two weeks. There may also be a correlation between bark color and susceptibility to bronze birch borers: the darker the bark, perhaps the more resistant the tree.

If you are set on buying a birch, select one with dark bark, place it on well-drained soil, and water it very well.

On the Edge

❧ *Buxus microphylla* var. *koreana* (*buck*-sus mike-row-*fil*-lah koh-ree-*ah*-nah), Korean boxwood, is a dwarf, broadleaf, evergreen shrub that is largely untested on the prairies. It slowly forms a dense, compact, oval to mounded shrub of 50 cm (20 in.) in height, with a 1- to 1.2-m (3- to 4-ft.) spread. It is ideal for clipping into a dwarf, formal hedge. Exposed foliage turns bronze (or dies back!) in winter. It does well in full sun or partial shade in rich, well-drained soil. Because it is surface rooting, the shrub benefits from snow cover, a sheltered location, and a layer of organic mulch on the adjacent soil surface. 'Wintergreen' has smaller leaves than the species. Korean boxwood is thriving in the shade of trees in the Reader Rock Garden in Calgary.

Caragana
kare-rah-*gah*-nah

Caragana

Nowhere is the saying "familiarity breeds contempt" more appropriate than when applied to the caragana of our small-town hedges and farm shelterbelts. Introduced to western Canada in the 1880s, it's often regarded as a weedy, dust-catching, suckering, spiny, labor-intensive anachronism, requiring twice yearly trimming to look presentable. But like the Manitoba maple, caragana has served us well. It is fast growing, hardy, flourishes where nothing else survives, and extremely drought tolerant.

Caragana is from *karaghan*, its Mongolian or Tartar common name—it is native to Russia, Turkestan, Siberia, and northern China. Its flexible stems were once used there as rope and cordage in much the same way as willow was used.

All caragana have alternate, pinnately compound leaves, with the terminal leaflet usually reduced to a spine. Light to medium green, the young foliage is fresh and attractive in spring, but seems to become duller (and dustier) as the summer progresses. Yellow, pea-like flowers are produced in early summer. They are followed by long, narrow, yellow-green seed pods that mature to brown and make an audible "pop" as they open in late summer.

How to Grow

Caragana grows in almost any soil, in sun or shade, but it is intolerant of prolonged flooding. Occasional severe infestations of blister beetles or spider mites result in defoliation.

Caragana arborescens

kare-rah-*gah*-nah are-bore-*res*-sens

Common caragana, Siberian pea shrub

Arborescens means "tree-like" and this term differentiates it from shrubbier

❧

PLANT AT A GLANCE

TYPE: large, flowering, deciduous shrub

HEIGHT/SPREAD: 4 m (13 ft.)/ 3 m (10 ft.)

LIGHT: full sun or shade

SOIL: well drained

DISTINGUISHING FEATURES: one of the most drought- and shade-tolerant shrubs; yellow flowers in spring

LANDSCAPE USE: screening; accent; shrub border; groundcover; shelterbelt

PHOTO: page 46

species. Green stems form an erect, oval shrub, seemingly open but often impenetrable (as anyone who has tried to make their way through an old shelterbelt knows).

Cultivars

❧ 'Lorbergii' (fern-leafed caragana) has yellow flowers; its almost thread-like leaflets, which give the plant a look similar to an asparagus fern, are on long, graceful, sparsely branched shoots. It is generally grafted onto a 1.2-m (4-ft.) standard. Grafted plants may sucker from *C. arborescens* rootstock.

❧ 'Pendula' (weeping caragana) has foliage similar to the species but with heavy, pendulous branches, which become distorted, gnarled, and twisted. With a height and spread of 1 m (3 ft.), it is commonly grafted onto a 1.2-m (4-ft.) standard. It is considerably more

74

useful and attractive, though, on its own roots, either as a ground-cover on banks and slopes or as an accent plant in a mixed border or rock garden.

* 'Sutherland' (PFRA Sutherland Tree Nursery, Saskatchewan, 1944) is a tall, narrow, columnar shrub, 3 to 4 m (10 to 13 ft.) in height, with a spread of only 1 m (3 ft.). It is useful as a vertical accent, for screening, or to provide privacy between two adjoining properties.

* 'Tidy' (Morden, Manitoba) has finely cut foliage and an upright, rounded form, with a height and spread of 2 to 3 m (6.5 to 10 ft.). 'Tidy' refers not to its form, but to the fact that it is sterile and sets no seed.

* 'Walker' ('Lorbergii' x 'Pendula') (Morden) is a trailing, prostrate shrub, with asparagus fern-like foliage. On its own roots, it is extremely useful as a groundcover on slopes and other difficult sites. Unfortunately, most nurseries only offer it grafted onto a 1.2-m (4-ft.) standard, as an oddity.

OTHER SPECIES AND HYBRIDS

* *Caragana frutex* 'Globosa' (kare-rah-*gah*-nah frew-*tex*), globe cara-gana, was introduced by Frank Skinner of Dropmore, Manitoba, in the 1930s. *Frutex* means "shrub-like." As the common and cultivar names suggest, it is dense and globe-like, with a height and spread of 1 to 1.3 m (3 to 4 ft.). It suckers very little, has very tiny spines, and because it retains juvenile characteristics, neither flowers

nor fruits. It grows slowly into a compact, rounded shrub, which is ideal as a low, unpruned hedge or as a grouping. Its foliage is dark green, it is clothed to the base, and it appears much less susceptible to mite injury. No one could ask for a nicer caragana for a tough situa-tion, such as a planting bed in the middle of a sun-baked parking lot.

* *Caragana pygmaea* (kare-rah-*gah*-nah pig-*mee*-ah), pygmy caragana, forms an attractive mound, but with a stiffer and less-rounded appearance than that of globe caragana. Both names allude to its dwarf character—it reaches only 0.8 to 1 m (2.5 to 3 ft.) in height and spread. This non-suckering little shrub is native to northwest China and Siberia. It has fine-tex-tured, gray-green foliage, attractive flowers, and bears a profusion of spines. Place it in an open, sunny situation where it is less susceptible to spider mites and its form can be appreciated. Like the globe cara-gana, it is useful as a low barrier hedge or *en masse*.

* *Caragana rosea* (kare-rah-*gah*-nah row-*zay*-ah), rose-flowered cara-gana, is seldom offered by nurs-eries and remains largely untested on the prairies. Another dwarf caragana, it has a compact, mounding form, with a height and spread of approximately 1 m (3 ft.) and purple-red flowers.

On the Edge

* *Celtis occidentalis* (*kel*-tis ox-si-den-*tah*-lis), common hackberry, is

Why Fix N?

Gardeners with infertile soil, particularly sandy soil, can use nature to their advantage by planting trees and shrubs that fix N (nitrogen).

Since the early 1800s, scientists have observed that some plants, including those in the legume or pea family, clover and alfalfa, and certain trees and shrubs, are able to grow well in poor soils where other plants simply do not thrive.

Why? *Rhizobium* bacteria, which are found in the swollen nodules of the roots of these plants, are able to take nitrogen from the soil and "fix" it into a form that plants can use. The roots secrete compounds that attract *Rhizobia* living in the nearby soil. The bacteria enter the roots and stimulate a swelling; the swelling then develops into nodules in which the bacteria live and multiply. The bacteria absorb N_2 from the soil atmosphere and fix it into ammonium ions, which are absorbed by the plant's roots and transported to other parts of the plant. In a symbiotic relationship, the bacteria "fix" nitrogen for the plants and the plants provide sugars and carbohydrates to the bacteria through their roots. The plants also add nitrogen to the soil as they grow, die, and decompose.

Trees and shrubs that fix nitrogen are:
Amorpha spp. (false indigo bush)
Caragana spp. (caragana)
Cytisus spp. (broom)
Eleagnus spp. (Russian olive, wolfwillow)
Hippophae spp. (common sea buckthorn)
Shepherdia spp. (buffaloberry)

a tree that is native to eastern Canada and the United States; it appears in the prairie area of Canada in the Lake Manitoba delta, north of Portage la Prairie. It has a very beautiful form and is tolerant of a wide variety of soil conditions. Although rather slow growing and slow to leaf out in spring, it is a large tree, when mature, with a number of large, ascending branches. The leaves are oval and pointed, with an asymmetrical base. The bark on young twigs is a downy, light grayish brown, becoming gray with corky ridges as the tree ages. Small flowers appear singly in the axils of emerging leaves, followed by single-seeded, brown berries, which are attractive to birds. It is widely used as a boulevard tree in Regina. Trees grown from Lake Manitoba delta seed should be worthy of trial throughout the prairies.

Cornus
kor-nus

Dogwood

In general, our hardy dogwoods are shrubs of 1 to 3 m (3 to 10 ft.) in height, which are valued for their variegated foliage and bright winter twig color. The common name comes from a concoction once made from its bark to cure dogs of mange. *Cornus* is from the Latin *corneolus*, "of horn," implying that its wood is hard.

HOW TO GROW
Plant dogwoods in full sun to partial shade in well-drained soil. They do better with even moisture, but are moderately drought tolerant once established. Scale insects are an occasional problem. To promote new growth with bright stem color, each year, prune out one-third of the oldest and thickest stems in early spring before the leaves emerge. Remove them as close to ground level as possible, using long-handled loppers or a narrow pruning saw. Pagoda dogwoods are treated as a small tree and are not pruned in this manner. They do better when given shelter.

Cornus alba
kor-nus al-bah
Tartarian dogwood

Alba means "white," the usual color of the berries. The common name refers to Tartary, an older name for part of its natural range. An Asian species native to Siberia, northern China, and North Korea, Tartarian dogwood forms an upright shrub with an open appearance, which exposes bright red winter stems. The leaves, flowers, and fruit are very similar to those of our native red osier dogwood. Like the red osier dogwood, cultivars rather than the species grace our gardens.

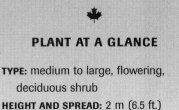

PLANT AT A GLANCE

TYPE: medium to large, flowering, deciduous shrub
HEIGHT AND SPREAD: 2 m (6.5 ft.)
LIGHT: full sun to shade
SOIL: moist; adaptable
DISTINGUISHING FEATURES: attractive variegated foliage; red winter stems
LANDSCAPE USE: shrub or mixed border; accent
PHOTOS: pages 42, 47

CULTIVARS
* 'Argenteo-marginata' (syn. 'Elegantissima'), silver leafed dogwood, has a height and spread of 1.5 to 2 m (5 to 6.5 ft.), variegated gray-green and creamy white foliage, and red winter stems. It does best in partial shade.
* 'Bailhalo' ('Ivory Halo') is an upright, compact selection of 'Argenteo-marginata.' The green leaves have white margins, and the stems are red in winter. Its rounded form is 1.5 m (5 ft.) in height and spread.

* 'Bud's Yellow' (Boughen's Nurseries, Saskatchewan) has outstanding yellow stem color and disease resistance. It has a rounded form, 2 m (6.5 ft.) tall and wide; its green foliage turns yellow in fall. It is exceptionally hardy but subject to sunscald, which blackens the bark.
* 'Gouchaltii' is more rounded than most, with a height and spread of 2 m (6.5 ft.). It has variegated green leaves with yellow margins, often with a pink tinge, and red winter stems. Unfortunately, it appears to be susceptible to aphids.
* 'Kesselringii' (purple twig dogwood) forms an upright, spreading plant of 1.8 m (6 ft.) in height, with a spread of 1.2 to 1.5 m (4 to 5 ft.). It has bronzy green foliage and deep purple stems, which turn almost purple-black in winter.
* 'Morden Amber,' a recent introduction from Morden Research Station, is hardy to zone 2. This medium-sized shrub is 2 to 2.5 m (6.5–8 ft.) in height with a spread of 1.2 to 1.8 m (4–6 ft.). It has white flowers and attractive yellow foliage that makes a striking contrast to its red bark throughout the growing season.
* 'Sibirica' (syn. 'Atrosanguinea'), Siberian coral dogwood, introduced in 1838, is an upright, spreading shrub, with a height and spread of 2 m (6.5 ft.). It has pale blue fruit, bright red stems, and soft green foliage, which turns scarlet in fall. In shade, it is susceptible to aphid infestation.

The Variation of Variegation

Gardeners have an enormous appreciation for variegated foliage—leaves that contain white, cream, pink, yellow, or purple in addition to the "normal" green.

Variegation can occur throughout a leaf, in the middle of it, or on its edge or margin. Different leaves on the same plant can show variation in their variegation.

Green plant cells contain other pigments besides the chlorophyll that makes them green. Yellow and orange come from carotenoids, while red and blue are derived from anthocyanins. These pigments can also bond with other compounds or elements, causing further variation of color. If the dominant green gene mutates out, these other pigments become evident.

Variegation occurs when a single cell either mutates spontaneously or is induced to mutate through the use of chemicals or irradiation. Viruses and growth hormones can also cause variegation in plants.

Some mutations are more stable than others. Stable mutations can be vegetatively propagated to produce additional plants, all exactly the same as the parent plant. These are called sports. Bud sports are mutations that occur on shoots, which are then vegetatively propagated, resulting in new cultivars.

❧ 'Silver Charm' (Boughen's Nurseries, Manitoba) is a dense, slow-growing, dwarf dogwood, approximately 1 m (3 ft.) in height and spread, with silver and green variegation.

Cornus alternifolia
kor-nus al-ter-ni-*fow*-lee-ah
Pagoda dogwood

This species is quite different from either Tartarian or red osier dogwoods. Although native to parts of the prairies, as the common name suggests, the layered habit of the

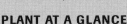

PLANT AT A GLANCE

TYPE: large, flowering, deciduous shrub or small tree
HEIGHT/SPREAD: 4 to 5 m (13 to 16 ft.)/2 to 3 m (6.5 to 10 ft.)
LIGHT: full to partial shade
SOIL: moist, well drained
DISTINGUISHING FEATURES: horizontal "pagoda" or layered branch pattern
LANDSCAPE USE: accent; tree/shrub or mixed border; oriental-style garden

branches lends it a pagoda-like or oriental appearance. Young stems are a deep purplish to reddish brown, becoming gray with age. Pagoda dogwoods form a distinctly vertical, large shrub or small tree. The oval leaves are often clustered at the ends of the branches, becoming scarlet to

red-purple in the fall. The leaves are alternate (thus, *alternifolia*) rather than opposite, like other dogwoods. The creamy white, somewhat fragrant flowers are in flat clusters and are followed by bluish-black berries, with attractive pinkish red stalks.

Cornus sericea
(syn. *C. stolonifera*)
kor-nus sir-*ree*-see-ah
Red osier dogwood

Sericea, "silky," refers to the hair on the plant's stems. Red obviously refers to the winter stem color, while *osier* refers to the long, flexible shoots of willows used in basketry and implies a similar use of dogwoods.

Native throughout the prairies, red osier dogwood is mound-like but widely spreading, often forming

PLANT AT A GLANCE

TYPE: large, flowering, deciduous shrub
HEIGHT/SPREAD: 2 to 3 m (6.5 to 10 ft.)/2 m (6.5 ft.) or greater, given time
LIGHT: full sun to shade
SOIL: adaptable
DISTINGUISHING FEATURES: bright red, golden, or olive green winter stem colour; some have variegated foliage
LANDSCAPE USE: naturalizing; mass planting; wildlife plantings; shrub borders
PHOTO: page 46

thickts. The stems of the species, once used for dyeing and tanning, are dull red when young and become gray when older.

The leaves are opposite and simple, display prominent veins, and are oval in shape, with a pointed tip. Green in summer, they turn red-purple in fall. White flowers in flat-topped clusters appear in May and June, followed by bluish white berries. Bitter but edible, the fruit was once used as famine food by Native peoples.

CULTIVARS

* 'Cardinal' has bright red winter bark. The dark green foliage turns red-purple in fall. It forms a large, rounded mound of 2.5 to 3 m (8 to 10 ft.) in both height and spread.
* 'Flaviramea' has an upright form, with a height and spread of 1.8 to 2.5 m (6 to 8 ft.). Its golden stems turn olive green in winter. It requires shelter in many regions of the prairies and is prone to sunscald or tip kill in the open.
* 'Isanti' is slow growing, dense, and compact, with a height and spread of 1.5 m (5 ft.). It has bright red stems and heavy fruit production. The foliage is dark green, turning red-purple in fall.
* 'White Gold,' with a height and spread of 2.5 m (8 ft.), has green and creamy white variegated foliage and bright gold winter stems.

On the Edge

* *Corylus americana* (*kor*-ril-us ah-meh-ri-*kah*-nah), American hazelnut, and *C. cornuta* (*kor*-ril-us core-*new*-tah), beaked hazelnut, are large shrubs with edible nuts, which were once commonly roasted or ground into flour. Both have alternate, simple, irregularly toothed leaves, with a pointed tip. Green during the summer, they turn yellow-green to yellow in the fall. The husk enclosing the nut resembles a helmet. The American hazelnut is a larger plant and produces larger nuts. It forms a rounded, multi-stemmed shrub, which can become open and leggy at the base, especially in shade. It suckers from the roots and eventually forms a substantial thicket. The nuts of the beaked hazelnut are covered in a long, green, beaked husk. Hazelnuts have few if any problems and grow well in full sun or partial shade, sheltered from wind, in moist but well-drained soil.

Cotoneaster
cuh-toe-nee-*ass*-ter
Cotoneaster

Cotoneaster is a genus of about fifty species of attractive and reliable shrubs, ranging from groundcovers to plants that are 3 m (10 ft.) in height. Most are native to northern Asia or northern Europe. The leaves are entire, meaning they are without teeth or lobes. The small, inconspicuous white or pale pink flowers are borne singly or in clusters in spring and are generally followed by red to black berries. The foliage of many species is a stunning orange-red in fall. The genus name is from the Latin *cotoneum,* "quince," and *aster,* "bearing an incomplete resemblance to"— perhaps referring to the fruit.

How to Grow

Cotoneasters prefer full sun and well-drained, fertile, moist soils, but will survive on dry sites. They tolerate pruning at any time of the year, but it will increase their susceptibility to fireblight and silver leaf disease. They can also be defoliated by "pear slug," the larvae of a sawfly. Plants that have been damaged by disease can be rejuvenated by pruning back to ground level; in any case, it is generally beneficial to rejuvenate hedges every fifteen to twenty years. Where space permits, cotoneasters can also be grown as an untrimmed, informal hedge, which will require less maintenance and be less susceptible to disease.

Cotoneaster lucidus

cuh-toe-nee-*ass*-ter loo-*sid*-dus

Hedge cotoneaster

Hedge cotoneaster, native to the Altai Mountains of Siberia, has been widely planted as a hedge because it is easy to transplant and thrives in any well-drained soil. It is often sold as Peking cotoneaster, but the true Peking cotoneaster is an inferior plant that is not winter hardy on the prairies.

Hedge cotoneaster stands out in the fall landscape with colors ranging

from yellow to red, but predominantly orange. During the summer, the small, oval leaves are a shiny, dark green—*lucidus* means "shining." It forms a dense, upright shrub, with slender, branched, upright stems. Bark on new growth is greenish, later becoming light to medium brown, with a thin, peeling surface. Tiny, inconspicuous, pinkish flowers, borne in clusters of two to five, are followed by small, black berries.

Other Species and Hybrids

🍁 *Cotoneaster integerrimus* (cuh-toe-nee-*ass*-ter in-teg-eh-*ree*-mus), European cotoneaster, is a spreading, mound-shaped shrub, 1 to 1.5 m (3 to 5 ft.) in height, with a 2-m (6.5-ft.) spread. It has gray-green leaves and attractive red fruit in fall. It is very tolerant of shade and grows well under trees.

🍁 *Cotoneaster horizontalis* 'Perpusillus' (cuh-toe-nee-*ass*-ter

Silver Leaf and Shear Responsibility

Silver leaf is a mycoplasma disease that affects cotoneasters and apples. The infected foliage appears more leaden than silver. The disease is initially limited to one or more branches. Browning of the leaf margins and midrib and a dark brown discoloration of the bark follow, and within a few years, the plant becomes less vigorous and dies.

Every time a cotoneaster hedge is pruned, thousands of wounds are created, allowing easy entry of the causal fungal organism (*Stereum purpureum*). In apple trees, the fungus enters through mower injury to trunks, hail injuries, and pruning cuts. Once inside, the fungus produces the toxin that gives the foliage that unique leaden sheen—and then kills it.

A cluster of shelf-like bracts may be present at the base of the dead branches. About 5 to 20 mm (0.2 to 0.8 in.) wide, the upper surface is grayish white, with a hairy or velvety texture, while the underside is a smooth purple.

There is no chemical cure. If silver leaf shows up, prune out the infected branches well below the point of infection. Disinfect your pruning tools after each cut. Then allow the cotoneaster to grow as a natural, untrimmed hedge.

hor-ri-zon-*tahl*-lis), ground cotoneaster, is a low-growing groundcover, 0.3 m (1 ft.) in height, with a 1.5 m (5 ft.) spread. Its small, round leaves are shiny and dark green. With an interesting herringbone branch structure, it is a valuable shrub for a protected location in a rock garden, for the edge of a border, or growing over a low retaining wall.

* *Cotoneaster racemiflorus* var. *soongoricus* (cuh-toe-nee-*ass*-ter rah-seem-i-*flor*-is soong-*gar*-i-cus), sungari rock spray cotoneaster, is a graceful arching shrub of 2 m (6.5 ft.) in height and spread, with grayish green leaves, which lend it a soft texture. The abundance of rose red fruit is attractive in fall.

Crataegus
krah-*tay*-gus

Hawthorn

The hawthorns are a substantial genus of large shrubs and small trees. The species are often difficult to separate and identify. Several species are native to the prairie region, and a number of exotic species are also worth growing. The Latin name is derived from the Greek *kratos*, "strength," and refers to the tough wood. The common name is derived from the Old English *haga*, "hedge," for which it was once used,

In past centuries, hawthorns were regarded with a sense of awe, respect, and fear. They were said to ward off both bad fairies and lightning. If oddly shaped, it was taboo to prune or move them. Their white flowers were considered a sign of purity and later their berries became a symbol of the blood of Christ.

Hawthorns provide outstanding beauty from summer to fall with their showy blooms and attractive fruit. Most hawthorns bear clusters of white flowers, which make a real statement in the spring. The alternate, simple leaves are double serrate and, in some species, lobed. They can be hairy or smooth and shiny. The smooth bark is gray to brown when young, breaking into strips with age. With a few exceptions, the branches are armed with sharp, woody thorns. These thorns protect nesting sites of small songbirds from predators.

There are a number of reasons why hawthorns are not more widely planted. If they've been growing in one location for more than three years, they do not transplant well. They are difficult to handle because of the thorns. If you like to wander around the yard in bare feet, be careful that all pruned and broken branches are removed, as the thorns can inflict painful wounds in bare feet and have been known to puncture tractor tires. Some species and cultivars are thornless and more user friendly.

How to Grow
Hawthorns are difficult to transplant. Buy small whips, container-grown plants, or balled and burlapped plants in early spring. They thrive in well-drained soils in sunny locations. Most hawthorns can be affected by cedar-apple rust, although we have never seen it on these species.

Crataegus x *mordenensis*
krah-*tay*-gus more-deh-*nen*-sis
Morden hawthorn

Morden hawthorns are hybrids of *Crataegus laevigata* 'Paul's Scarlet' and *C. succulenta*. They have no thorns and are very resistant to cedar-apple rust. They are susceptible to sunscald in colder parts of the prairies.

'Snowbird' has double, white flowers and is more winter hardy than 'Toba,' which has equally attractive double, pink flowers, inherited from its English parent, 'Paul's Scarlet' hawthorn. 'Toba' develops an interesting, somewhat twisting, bark and trunk form once it matures.

Other Species and Hybrids
❋ *Crataegus arnoldiana* (krah-*tay*-gus

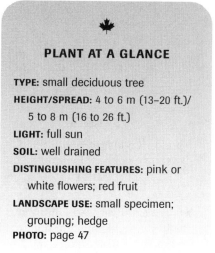

❋

PLANT AT A GLANCE

TYPE: small deciduous tree
HEIGHT/SPREAD: 4 to 6 m (13–20 ft.)/ 5 to 8 m (16 to 26 ft.)
LIGHT: full sun
SOIL: well drained
DISTINGUISHING FEATURES: pink or white flowers; red fruit
LANDSCAPE USE: small specimen; grouping; hedge
PHOTO: page 47

are-nol-dee-*ah*-nah), Arnold hawthorn, is an attractive round-headed, small tree, 5 m (16 ft.) in height, with a spread of 4 m (13 ft.). Clusters of white flowers in late spring are followed by quite large, red fruit, which ripen in late August. Branches are strongly angled, with gray bark and large spines.

* *Crataegus cerronis* (krah-*tay*-gus sir-*row*-nus), chocolate hawthorn, is an upright shrub, with shiny, dark green leaves, dark brown fruit, hence the common name, and large thorns. It makes a very attractive impenetrable hedge, 4 m (13 ft.) in height, with a spread of 2.5 m (8 ft.).

* *Crataegus chlorosarca* (krah-*tay*-gus klor-oh-*sar*-kah), Kamchatsk hawthorn, a native of northern China, is a shapely, round-headed, small tree of 5 m (16 ft.), and a spread of 2.5 m (8 ft.). It has dark purple bark, no thorns, and black fruit.

Cytisus
sy-*tis*-iss

Broom

Cytisus is a genus of small, deciduous shrubs in the pea family, mostly indigenous to Europe. The small leaves may be simple or trifoliate.

The typical pea-shaped, yellow flowers light up the landscape.

Henry VIII is said to have drunk an infusion distilled from broom flowers as protection against disease. Long-used medicinally, the fresh seed pods were believed to have intoxicating effects, while the seeds were often roasted as a coffee substitute. The common name suggests its past use as a household broom.

HOW TO GROW
Broom grows well on nutrient-poor soils, with good drainage, but is deep rooted and therefore difficult to transplant. Plant small, container-grown plants in spring, taking care not to overwater them. Prune to rejuvenate them and keep them healthy. Planting in full sun will help to avoid leaf blights, which can be damaging or even deadly.

Cytisus nigricans var. *elongatus*
sy-*tis*-iss *ny*-gri-kanz ee-long-*gah*-tis
Spike broom

Spike broom is a small, upright shrub, with trifoliate leaves. *Cytisus* was the Greek name for clover, to which the leaves of broom are similar. Numerous yellow flowers are produced on long racemes on new wood through July and August. Once dried, the flowers turn black, hence, *nigricans*. Because the flowers are produced on new growth, the plants can be pruned in early spring.

PLANT AT A GLANCE

TYPE: small, flowering, deciduous shrub

HEIGHT/SPREAD: 0.2 to 1 m (0.8 to 3 ft.)/0.5 to 1.5 m (1.5 to 5 ft.)

LIGHT: full sun

SOIL: well drained; infertile

DISTINGUISHING FEATURES: spiky form; bright yellow flowers

LANDSCAPE USE: front of border; rock garden

OTHER SPECIES AND HYBRIDS

❀ *Cytisus decumbens* (sy-*tis*-iss day-*kum*-benz), prostrate broom, is a low-growing, groundcover shrub, 10 to 15 cm (4 to 6 in.) in height, with a spread of up to 1 m (3 ft.). Its small, simple leaves are held close to the stem. In late spring, bright yellow flowers are borne singly or in clusters of two or three along the stem in great profusion.

❀ *Cytisus purpureus* var. *procumbens* (sy-*tis*-iss purr-purr-*ree*-us pro-*kum*-benz), purple broom, (photo on page 48) is a delicate, small shrub, 0.3 to 0.5 m (1 to 1.5 ft.) in height, with a spread of 0.5 to 1 m (1.5 to 3 ft.). The foliage is smooth, medium green, and trifoliate. The small, purple pea flowers are borne along the stems in early summer.

❀ ❀ ❀ ❀ ❀ ❀

Daphne
daff-nee

Daphne

Daphne is the Greek name for the bay tree or laurel, which this plant resembles. The mythological Daphne was a nymph, changed into a bay tree by the gods to save her from the presumably unwanted advances of Apollo.

Nymphs aside, never has a shrub been capable of such horticultural heartbreak. They die for no apparent reason. And yet we buy them, again and again, perhaps because some have flowers with a fragrance to die for. (Coincidentally, all are poisonous.) Dwarf shrubs, they range from evergreen to semi-evergreen to deciduous.

HOW TO GROW

Daphnes grow best in partial shade in sandy, well-drained soil, which has been well amended with organic matter and is kept evenly moist, but not waterlogged. Mulching the adjacent soil surface with a few inches of organic mulch ensures a cool root run. Place evergreen daphnes in the most protected part of your yard. If snow is lacking, cover them with loosely placed evergreen boughs.

Daphne burkwoodii 'Carol Mackie'

daff-nee burk-*wud*-ee-eye

Burkwood daphne

Burkwood daphne is a hybrid of *Daphne caucasica* and *D. cneorum*, introduced in 1931 by Albert and Arthur Burkwood, English nursery-men and hybridists. 'Carol Mackie' was discovered in 1962 by the real Carol Mackie as a sport in her New Jersey garden. It forms a low, round-ed, densely branched shrub, with variegated foliage.

🍁

PLANT AT A GLANCE

TYPE: small, flowering, semi-evergreen shrub

HEIGHT AND SPREAD: 0.6 m (2 ft.)

LIGHT: partial shade

SOIL: organic; well drained

DISTINGUISHING FEATURES: semi-evergreen, variegated foliage

LANDSCAPE USE: mixed border; shade garden

PHOTO: page 48

Semi-evergreen, it enters winter fully clothed. By spring, any foliage remaining on the plant appears toasted. But don't assume the worst. Within a few weeks, new growth appears. Although the species has blue-green foliage, 'Carol Mackie' is an attractive variegated, creamy white and green. The fragrant flowers are light pink to white, in 5-cm (2-in.) clusters in late summer. Even if it never flowers, it's worth growing as a foliage plant.

Daphne cneorum

daff-nee nee-*ore*-um

Rose daphne

🍁

PLANT AT A GLANCE

TYPE: low, evergreen, flowering shrub

HEIGHT/SPREAD: 0.3 m (1 ft.)/ 1 m (3 ft.)

LIGHT: partial shade

SOIL: organic; well drained

DISTINGUISHING FEATURES: fragrant, pink flowers in early spring; broad-leaf, evergreen foliage

LANDSCAPE USE: perennial or mixed border; shaded rock garden; near decks and patios for fragrance

PHOTO: page 49

The common name is undoubtedly a reference to the flower color. *Cneorum* is from the Greek *kneorum*, "shrub resembling an olive."

Native to central and southern Europe and into southwest Russia, rose daphne is usually described as most desirable but difficult to estab-lish and with a penchant for suddenly giving up the ghost and falling over dead. Yet, everyone notes they would try again—and again—to grow it.

Rose daphnes have long, trailing branches, which slowly spread to 30 to 60 cm (12 to 24 in.) as the stems root. The small, evergreen leaves are alter-nate, simple, narrow, and bright green. The small, deep pink, incredibly fragrant flowers are produced in terminal clusters.

OTHER SPECIES AND HYBRIDS

❦ *Daphne mezereum* (*daff*-nee meh-zer-*ee*-um), February daphne, is native from Europe and Asia Minor to Siberia and was cultivated in England prior to 1561. Russian and Tartar women once rubbed the berries on their cheeks, which became rosy thanks to its irritant compounds. Linnaeus wrote that six berries would kill a wolf, and the English herbalist Gerard claimed that a single berry would stop a drunk from drinking, such would be "the heat of his mouth." They form a small, erect, and well-branched shrub, about 0.6 m (2 ft.) in height and almost equal in spread, which has attractive olive green stems. They grow slowly and seldom sucker. The oval leaves are a rather dull, blue-green. Purple-rose flowers emerge in April, before the leaves, and arise directly from the stems in groups of two or three. They are followed by bright red berries, extremely attractive but very poisonous, which persist throughout much of the winter.

On the Edge

❦ *Diervilla lonicera* (der-*vill*-uh lon-*niss*-ur-uh), dwarf bush honeysuckle or diervilla, is a medium-sized, mounding shrub about 1.3 m (4 ft.) high and wide, which spreads by suckering. New growth is a metallic bronze green, maturing to

❦

Love and Loss

I kept company with a rose daphne for almost twenty years. I brought her home in a 15-cm (6-in.) pot and she gradually grew to a spread of 1.2 m (4 ft.). The fragrance was intoxicating, and I loved her dearly. One spring, I noticed some dieback. Over several years it grew worse and then she was gone. Out of respect, I waited a year, and then brought home another rose daphne. They come in gallon pots now and cost a whole lot more.

Sara Williams

a glossy green in summer and turning reddish in fall. Fall color is better when grown in full sun. The small, funnel-shaped, yellow flowers appear in mid-summer, in terminal clusters of one to five, and are attractive to birds. Adapted to many soils, they grow in sun or shade and under a range of moisture conditions. Once established, they are drought tolerant. They are ideal for mass plantings, naturalization, wildlife plantings, and on slopes.

Eleagnus
el-ee-*ag*-nus

Russian olive, wolfwillow

Eleagnus is from the Greek *eleia,* "oil," referring to the fruit, which resemble olives. Species of this genus are noted for their attractive silver foliage, fragrant but inconspicuous yellow flowers, and silver fruit. Because of their salt tolerance and ability to fix nitrogen, they can survive in inhospitable soils.

How to Grow

Salt and drought tolerant, *Eleagnus* are at home in well-drained, light soils in full sun.

Eleagnus angustifolia
el-ee-*ag*-nus an-gust-i-*foe*-lee-ah

Russian olive

Angustifolia, "narrow-leafed," describes the foliage. Native from Europe to western Asia, Russian olive is able to fix nitrogen, is drought tolerant, and has been widely used as a shelterbelt tree on the prairies. It is also quite salt tolerant. Because their branch structure is weak, Russian olive trees may break in storms. They have not been successful in some areas of zone 2.

The twigs of this oval to rounded tree are silvery white, while the older branches are almost black, providing a striking contrast with the silver foliage, stems, leaves, and fruit. The leaves are alternate, simple, long, and narrow, with smooth margins. Some are retained throughout most of the winter, providing color in the winter landscape. Generally thorny, Russian olives are not easily embraced or pruned. Inconspicuous but highly fragrant, yellow flowers, produced in June, are followed by small, fleshy, yellow-silver "olives."

PLANT AT A GLANCE

TYPE: medium deciduous tree
HEIGHT AND SPREAD: 4 to 7 m (13 to 23 ft.) or larger
LIGHT: full sun
SOIL: well drained
DISTINGUISHING FEATURES: narrow, silver leaves, retained into winter; dark trunk
LANDSCAPE USE: silver accent; specimen; shelterbelt
PHOTO: page 49

Other Species and Hybrids

* *Eleagnus commutata* (el-ee-*ag*-nus kom-mew-*tah*-tah), wolfwillow or silverberry, is familiar along fence lines, where the pleasant scent of its silver-yellow flowers still manages to catch us by surprise in June. A large shrub, with a height and spread of 2.5 m (8 ft.), wolfwillow has slender branches and an upright, loose form; it also suckers profusely and quickly to form large thickets. The small,

Wilt

Some strains of Russian olive seem susceptible to verticillium wilt (*Verticillium albo-atrum*), which is characterized by a branch or a portion of the tree suddenly wilting and dying within a few weeks or over several years. The fungus is soil borne, and infection is either through the roots or pruning wounds. It is more pronounced on heavier soils and less common on sandier soils. It has been suggested that watering and fertilizing with a soluble-nitrogen fertilizer enables the rapid formation of a thick layer of sapwood, which seals and isolates infected tissue.

silver, berry-like, oval fruit is dry and mealy, but nevertheless edible, and was once used as a famine food. Wolfwillow is exceptionally drought tolerant and flourishes in the toughest of exposed, dry sites in full sun. It finds a niche in rural landscapes for shelterbelts, naturalizing, and wildlife plantings. The cultivars are considerably more restrained and ornamental than the species. 'Coral Silver' has bright gray foliage and coral red fruit; 'Quicksilver' is a hybrid of *E. angustifolia* and *E. commutata*; and 'Zempin,' with larger, more attractive silver leaves, is taller than the species and less prone to suckering.

Euonymus
yew-*on*-im-us

Burning bush, spindle tree

The greatest attraction of many *Euonymus* species is their unusual and colorful fruit and the color of their fall foliage. Their unimpressive greenish flowers develop into colorful capsules, made up of three to five one-seeded cells. As they ripen, they open to reveal brightly colored, orange-pink seeds. The fall foliage of some species is a brilliant scarlet, adding to their autumn display. *Euonymus* vary from creeping groundcovers to small trees.

Euonymus means "of good name" and is thought to have been applied ironically, referring to the fact that burning bush was once used to poison animals. The leaves, bark, and fruit are also toxic to humans. The common name burning bush refers to its fall color.

HOW TO GROW
Euonymus are easily transplanted from containers or as balled and burlapped stock. They adapt to a variety of soils, as long as they are well drained. They are intolerant of flooding and should be mulched and watered during hot, dry weather. They tolerate pruning and adapt to sun or shade.

Euonymus alatus

yew-*on*-im-us ah-*lah*-tus

Winged burning bush

Winged burning bush is native to northeastern Asia. *Alatus,* "winged," like the common name, refers to the four corky wings on the stems.

The green-barked stems form an upright to vase-like shrub. On the prairies, winter dieback often limits it to a height of 1.5 m (5 ft.). The opposite leaves are medium green and oval and develop outstanding red fall color that's best in partial shade. The flowers are small, green, and inconspicuous, but the ripe fruit is an attractive red.

PLANT AT A GLANCE

TYPE: medium to large deciduous shrub

HEIGHT/SPREAD: 1.5 to 3 m (5 to 10 ft.)/1 m (3 ft.)

LIGHT: full sun to partial shade

SOIL: moist, well drained

DISTINGUISHING FEATURES: brilliant red fall color; attractive red fruit; corky, winged stems

LANDSCAPE USE: specimen; mass planting; screening

PHOTO: page 49

Euonymus maackii

yew-*on*-im-us *mack*-ee-eye

Maack's spindle tree

PLANT AT A GLANCE

TYPE: large deciduous shrub or small tree

HEIGHT AND SPREAD: 3 m (10 ft.)

LIGHT: full sun to partial shade

SOIL: moist, well-drained; loam

DISTINGUISHING FEATURES: vase shaped; red fall foliage; orange fruit

LANDSCAPE USE: screening; mass planting

PHOTO: page 50

Maack's spindle tree is native to northern China and to Korea and is named to honor Russian botanical explorer Richard Maack (1825–86). Its hard wood was once used to make spindles and skewers, as well as bows for violas and keys for pianos and organs.

It is a large, vase-shaped shrub of medium texture, with thin stems and mottled gray bark. The oval leaves are pointed at both ends. Small, yellow flowers develop into pink fruit, which open to reveal orange seeds. It is most effective planted in groups and most attractive in fall because of its red foliage.

Euonymus nanus var. turkestanicus

yew-*on*-im-us nah-*nus* tur-kes-*tahn*-i-kus

Turkestan burning bush

The species, *Euonymus nanus,* dwarf narrow-leafed burning bush, is a creeping groundcover, which roots where the stems touch the soil. Although not widely available, it makes an attractive semi-evergreen groundcover under trees. The more commonly available subspecies *Euonymus nanus* var. *turkestanicus,*

PLANT AT A GLANCE

TYPE: medium deciduous shrub
HEIGHT AND SPREAD: 1.5 m (5 ft.)
LIGHT: partial to quite dense shade
SOIL: moist; loamy
DISTINGUISHING FEATURES: narrow, bright red fall foliage; orange-red seed pods
LANDSCAPE USE: mass planting; groundcover
PHOTO: page 50

Turkestan burning bush, is more vigorous and upright than the species, forming an upright, globe-shaped shrub, with thin stems and green bark. The leaves are dark green, narrow, and linear. The inconspicuous, greenish flowers are followed by pink capsules, which open to reveal striking orange-red seeds.

OTHER SPECIES AND HYBRIDS

* *Euonymus obovata* (yew-*on*-im-us oh-bow-*vah*-tah), running strawberry bush, is a groundcover shrub, reaching 30 cm (12 in.) in height that quickly fills in, will tolerate shade, and has warty, scarlet fruit. The orange fall color often does not develop on the prairies.

Forsythia ovata

for-*sith*-ee-ah/for-*sy*-thee-ah oh-*vah*-tah

Korean forsythia

The genus *Forsythia* commemorates William Forsyth (1737–1804), a superintendent at the Royal Gardens in Kensington, England. *Forsythia* are native to eastern Europe and Asia.

PLANT AT A GLANCE

TYPE: medium to large, flowering, deciduous shrub
HEIGHT/SPREAD: 1.5 to 2.5 m (5 to 8 ft.)/1.5 to 2 m (5 to 6.5 ft.)
LIGHT: full sun to partial shade
SOIL: loose, loamy soil; adaptable
DISTINGUISHING FEATURES: bright yellow flowers in early spring
LANDSCAPE USE: shrub border
PHOTO: page 50

The four-lobed, yellow flowers in early spring are their outstanding ornamental feature. The flower buds of most forsythia species are killed by low temperatures common to prairie winters, so the only cultivars of interest to prairie gardeners are those with exceptional flower-bud hardiness.

The seed of *Forsythia ovata* was first collected in 1917 in the Diamond Mountains of Korea. It has smaller flowers than other species, but has been the source of hardiness for breeding forsythias that will bloom on the prairies. 'Northern Gold,' from Agriculture Canada in Ottawa, is the most flower bud–hardy cultivar. An upright shrub of up to 2 m (6.5 ft.) in height, and a spread of 1.2 m (4 ft.), it should flower most years on the prairies if planted in a reasonably sheltered spot.

Korean forsythias are upright to spreading shrubs. *Ovata,* "oval," describes the leaves, which are also opposite, dark green, smooth, and dull. The shrub's crowning glory is the yellow, bell-shaped flowers produced before the leaves emerge in spring. Flowering branches can be cut and forced for spring bouquets, along with pussy willows and plum blossoms. The thin, upright stems are yellowish, later becoming gray.

How to Grow

Forsythias have fibrous root systems, which transplant easily either bare root or from containers. They are heavy feeders and need adequate fertilizer and rich, well-drained soil. The best bloom is produced in full sun, although microclimates that are wind

protected and partially shaded may help protect flower buds from prairie winters. Prune immediately after bloom to encourage production of flower buds for the following year.

Fraxinus
fraks-in-us

Ash

Fraxinus is the name the Romans gave to the European ash species. It is derived from the Greek *phraxis,* "hedge," as ash was often used for this purpose. The common name is from the Norse *aska,* "man;" the Norse god Odin is said to have carved the first man from an ash branch.

Tall and long-lived, ash have opposite and pinnately compound leaves, composed of five to eleven leaflets. The bark is smooth when young, becoming rougher with age. The small, inconspicuous flowers emerge before the leaves. Ash are dioecious, with male and female flowers on separate trees. The female flowers are followed by clusters of dry, single-seeded samaras, the "helicopters" of childhood. Gardeners who object to these samaras landing on their lawns should purchase male trees.

How to Grow

Green ash tolerates wind and temperature extremes, thrives in a range of soils, and is exceptionally drought

Male and Female Plants

Fruiting and Commuting in the Botanical World

Flowers that have both female and male parts are said to be "perfect." If either part is missing, they are "imperfect." An imperfect flower is either male (with stamens) or female (with pistils).

If both the male and female flowers are on the same plant, it is monoecious. The word comes from the Greek *mono*, "one," and *oikos*, "house." It's like a couple living in the same house but in separate rooms, with a bit of wind- or insect-assisted commuting.

If male and female flowers are on separate plants, they are dioecious, from the Greek words *di*, "two," and *oikos*, "house." In this case, they are living in two "houses" or on separate plants. To ensure that dioecious plants produce fruit (if that's the objective), pollination must occur. To facilitate pollination, the male and female flowers on their separate plants must be within commuting distance, be it by wind or insect. If fruit and seed production are not desired, male clones can be selected.

tolerant. It does best in full sun. Unfortunately, it is prey to a number of insects, including lygus bugs, canker worms, and ash flower bud gall mites. None of these is life threatening, and the damage is mostly cosmetic. Manchurian ash is equally drought tolerant, while black ash does best under even-moisture conditions.

Fraxinus pennsylvanica var. *subintegerrima*

fraks-in-us pen-sil-*vah*-ni-kah sub-in-teg-eh-*ree*-mah

Green ash

Green ash is native to the prairies, as well as to much of central and eastern North America (*pennsylvanica* indicates that Pennsylvania is part of its native range). Like Manitoba maple, green ash seldom get the praise they deserve for the service they perform in the prairie landscape. They do have a relatively short foliage season and are susceptible to insect pests, but many

---

PLANT AT A GLANCE

TYPE: large deciduous tree
HEIGHT/SPREAD: 15 m (50 ft.)/8 to 10 m (26 to 33 ft.)
LIGHT: full sun
SOIL: well drained; adaptable
DISTINGUISHING FEATURES: golden fall color; tough and drought tolerant
LANDSCAPE USE: shade; specimen; street tree; shelterbelt
PHOTO: page 50

of the newer cultivars have been selected for their resistance to insects. Green ash are also fast growing and long-lived and have a deep taproot. This generally enables them to flourish where other trees flounder, in exposed and droughty sites.

Green ash is a medium to tall, upright tree, with a straight trunk and oval canopy. The grayish brown bark becomes furrowed with irregular ridges as the tree ages. The opposite and pinnately compound leaves consist of seven leaflets, each lustrous, dark green, oval in shape, tapering to a point, and toothed above the middle. *Subintegerrima* indicates that the twigs and leaf stalks are nearly hairless. Female flowers give rise to dry, winged, one-seeded samaras, which are borne in large clusters and are retained throughout much of the winter.

CULTIVARS

* 'Patmore' is a seedless male clone that reaches a height of 15 to 18 m (50 to 60 ft.), with a spread of 10 m (33 ft.). It was discovered by Richard Patmore of Brandon, Manitoba, as a seedling tree in Vegreville, Alberta. It is uniform and symmetrical in shape, with five to seven glossy, dark green leaflets. It leafs out earlier and holds its foliage later into fall than most green ash.
* Prairie Spire™ ('Rugby') is a seedless male selection with a narrow, pyramidal form, which becomes oval with age, a height of 15 m (50 ft.), and a spread of 7 m (23 ft.). It has golden fall color and is hardy to zone 3.

OTHER SPECIES AND HYBRIDS

* *Fraxinus americana* 'Northern Blaze' (*fraks*-in-us ah-meh-ri-*kah*-nah), white ash, is a Manitoba selection. It is 12 m (40 ft.) in height, with a 7 m (23 ft.) spread, and is upright and oval while young, becoming more open and rounded at maturity, while maintaining a central leader and even-branch distribution. The foliage first turns yellow and then a dark reddish purple to maroon in fall. It is highly resistant to ash plant bugs and ash flower bud gall mite. Budded onto green ash, it is hardy to zone 3, but still rare in prairie landscapes.

* *Fraxinus mandshurica* (*fraks*-in-us mand-*sure*-i-kah), Manchurian ash, as both the scientific and common names suggest, is native to Manchuria, as well as to other areas of China and Japan. Introduced to the prairies in the 1930s, several superior cultivars have since been selected. It forms a compact, oval, upright tree similar to green ash but slightly smaller—8 to 15 m (26 to 50 ft.), with a spread of 5 to 6 m (16 to 20 ft.). The large, green, compound leaves consist of nine to eleven sessile leaflets and turn a soft yellow in fall. The many long, narrow leaflets give the tree a lacy, delicate appearance. It is drought tolerant and resistant to insect infestations, and it deserves much greater use. 'Mancana' is a male (seedless) selection from Morden, Manitoba. It is 12 to 15 m (40 to 50 ft.)

in height, with a spread of 6 to 8 m (20 to 26 ft.), and has a dense, oval to round, compact canopy and outstanding yellow fall foliage.

* *Fraxinus nigra* (*fraks*-in-us ny-*grah*), black ash, is another native tree. It is similar to green ash but smaller, 10 m (33 ft.) in height, with a spread of 5 m (16 ft.), and more upright and oval to pyramidal in form. Its leaves consist of nine sessile leaflets, without leaf stalks or petioles. Found naturally in moist areas, it's not nearly as drought tolerant as green ash or Manchurian ash. 'Fallgold,' a Morden, Manitoba, introduction, is a male (seedless) cultivar with golden and persistent fall foliage. Only 10 to 12 m (33 to 40 ft.) in height, with a spread of 4 to 5 m (13 to 16 ft.), its columnar form and size make it an ideal boulevard, street, or shade tree.

* 'Northern Gem' and 'Northern Treasure' are hybrids of *Fraxinus nigra* x *F. mandshurica*, introduced from Morden, Manitoba. They are vigorous and harden off quickly in fall, when their foliage turns a pale orange-yellow. They produce low quantities of seed and appear resistant to flower bud gall mites. 'Northern Gem' is 10 m (33 ft.) in height, with a spread of 6 to 7 m (20 to 23 ft.), and is oval to round in form, with a wide crown, which makes it an ideal shade tree. 'Northern Treasure' is the same size, but has a more upright form,

making it suitable for street and boulevard plantings.

Genista
jen-*niss*-tah

Broom, woadwaxen

Genista is a genus of small shrubs in the pea family. Native to Europe and western Asia, the flowers are yellow and of typical pea-flower form. The very small leaves are simple or trifoliate and the stems are often green, performing the photosynthetic function of leaves. *Genista* was the ancient Latin name for this shrub.

Geoffry of Anjou (father of Henry II of England) was nicknamed Plantagenet (*Planta genista*) because he wore a sprig of broom in his hat, hence, the name of the English royal dynasty.

How to Grow
Genista grows well in infertile, well-drained soil in full sun. They are difficult to transplant and should be planted from containers in spring. Proper placement is critical at planting time; do not move these plants once they are established.

Genista lydia

jen-*niss*-tah *lid*-dee-ah

Lydia woadwaxen

Genista lydia is native to the Balkans and western Asia. The Lydia for which it is named is a city in western Turkey. Although most authorities list it as hardy to zone 6 or 7, it has bloomed faithfully in a well-drained, sunny, and protected spot in a zone 2 Manitoba garden for many years.

This interesting dwarf shrub develops into a mound of thin, green stems, with minute leaves. It is strikingly beautiful when in bloom in late June and early July. It needs a well-drained, sunny location.

PLANT AT A GLANCE

TYPE: dwarf, flowering, deciduous shrub

HEIGHT/SPREAD: 0.3 to 0.6 m (1 to 2 ft.)/1 m (3 ft.)

LIGHT: full sun

SOIL: well drained; infertile

DISTINGUISHING FEATURES: thin, green stems; striking yellow flowers

LANDSCAPE USE: rock garden; front of border

Genista tinctoria

jen-*niss*-tah tink-*tor*-ee-ah

Dyer's greenwood

PLANT AT A GLANCE

TYPE: dwarf, flowering, deciduous shrub

HEIGHT AND SPREAD: 0.6 to 1 m (2 to 3 ft.)

LIGHT: full sun

SOIL: well drained; infertile

DISTINGUISHING FEATURES: bright yellow flowers

LANDSCAPE USE: rock garden; mixed border

PHOTO: page 51

Plants used in dying cloth are often called *tinctoria*, from the Latin, "used in dying." The common name also refers to the plant's use as a dye; "greenwood" refers to its distinctly green branches. This plant dyes wool bright yellow; if the cloth is then dipped in blue dye from *Isatis tinctoria* (dyer's woad), it becomes the color known as Kendal green.

This upright shrub has slender, little-branched, green twigs and tiny, bright green leaves. Yellow flowers are produced in June and occasionally throughout the summer. The green stems photosynthesize.

Halimodendron halodendron

hal-im-oh-*den-*
dron hah-low-*den*-dron

Siberian salt tree

Halimodendron is a genus with only one species; it is in the pea family and related to caragana. The leaves and branches are covered with fine, gray down, which gives them a silvery appearance. The flowers are pale purplish pink. A very salt tolerant plant, it thrives where few other plants will grow.

Siberian salt tree is found across Siberia, from the Caucasus Mountains to the Altai Mountains. Its name is derived from three Greek words:

halimum, "maritime," *dendron,* "tree," and *halo,* "salt." It is a large shrub or small tree that tolerates the salty spray of a seacoast.

It is characterized by fine-textured, compound, silvery leaves, consisting of four leaflets. The central stalk of each compound leaf terminates in a spine and persists after the leaflets have fallen. Attractive pale lilac flowers in mid-summer are followed by inflated, dark brown pods.

How to Grow

Halimodendron halodendron will not tolerate wet soil. Growing on its own roots, it suckers freely and will form an open thicket of upright stems. It can be controlled by grafting it onto a caragana rootstock, or it can be top-grafted onto a caragana stem to produce a graceful small tree.

PLANT AT A GLANCE

TYPE: large, flowering, decidous, shrub
HEIGHT/SPREAD: 2 to 3 m (6.5 to 10 ft.)/2 m (6.5 ft.)
LIGHT: full sun
SOIL: well drained
DISTINGUISHING FEATURES: pale lilac flowers; very salt tolerant
LANDSCAPE USE: mass planting on dry or saline sites
PHOTO: page 51

Hippophae rhamnoides

hip-oh-fay ram-*noy*-deez

Common sea buckthorn

Sea buckthorn makes its most striking statement in the late fall and winter landscapes, with its bright orange fruit. High in vitamin C and saponins, the fruit has been promoted as a health food, but the berries are difficult to pick because they cling tightly to branches that are tipped by stout thorns. *Hippophae* is from the Greek *hippos*, "a horse," and *phao*, "to brighten," referring to its past use as a tonic for horses. *Rhamnoides* refers to its resemblance to the buckthorn genus *Rhamnus*.

Sea buckthorn is a large shrub, with upright, thorn-tipped stems, covered with silver or brownish scales. The alternate leaves are linear and gray-green and are covered with silvery scales, which are denser on the lower surface than the upper one. The flowers are inconspicuous, but give rise to highly showy orange berries on female trees, which persist throughout winter. Plants of both sexes must be grown in close proximity if berries are desired. An ideal ratio for fruit production is one male plant to six or seven female plants.

Two cultivars selected from the Agriculture and Agri-Food Canada (AAFC) Prairie Farm Rehabilitation Administration (PFRA) Shelterbelt

Water Conservation and Color

Pubescent, Tomentose, or Glaucous?

Gardeners consider silver foliage as another color in the palette of design, using it as an accent or contrast plant within their landscape. Plants, however, use this coloration as a means of water conservation, and plants with silver foliage, such as sea buckthorn, wolfwillow, sage, and Russian olive, are generally more drought tolerant than their cohorts with green foliage.

Like a mini-shelterbelt, small hairs on the leaf surface, called trichomes, together with silver or white scales, cool the leaf by reflecting light, provide shade for the leaf's surface, and deflect air currents that would desiccate or remove water from its tissue. These hairs also give the foliage a silver, white, or gray appearance. Plants coated with hair are called pubescent. If the hair is matted and flatter, they are called tomentose.

A fine, gray dust or waxy "bloom" is another way that plants conserve moisture. It gives them a silvery appearance, which is referred to as "glaucous."

Centre at Indian Head, Saskatchewan, are to be named in 2004. Currently known as selections 6582 and 6476, they were chosen from a seedling population of *Hippophae rhamnoides* ssp. *mongolica*, which was obtained from Russia in the mid-1990s. They are virtually thornless, with good yields of large, yellow-orange fruit, which are easily harvested by hand or by shaking. Their compact forms are easily trained to a single stem. The fruit of 6582 is slightly larger but not as sweet as that of 6476.

HOW TO GROW

Sea buckthorn grows best in full sun and well-drained soil, with wet sub-soil, such as that found on the sea-coast. It is sometimes difficult to establish on the prairies, but once established, it tolerates dry conditions, poor soil, salt spray from roads and vehicles, and saline soil. It is also nitrogen fixing.

Hydrangea
hy-*drain*-gee-ah

Hydrangea

Hydrangea is from the Greek *hudor*, "water," and *aggos*, "a jar," which refers to the cup-shaped seed capsule. Both species grown on the prairies have large flower heads, consisting of two types of flowers. Those in the center are fertile but inconspicuous.

Those in the outer ring are sterile and showy and serve to attract insects that are needed to pollinate the fertile inner flowers. They bloom on the current year's growth, so even if killed to snow or ground level each winter, they should still flower.

HOW TO GROW

Place hydrangeas in partial shade in well-drained but rich, fertile soil, which is well amended with organic matter. They require even moisture and protection from wind. In all but the most sheltered sites, they'll die back to snow or ground level, and the dead branches will need to be pruned out in spring. Because they bloom on the current season's wood, this is not a problem.

Hydrangea arborescens
hy-*drain*-gee-ah ar-bor-*ess*-enz

Hydrangea, snowhill hydrangea

Arborescens means "tree-like," but this is somewhat misleading as the plant rarely exceeds 1 m (3 ft.) in prairie gardens. Native to eastern North America, it is the plant of graveyards in Europe.

Snowhill hydrangea develops into a round mound, with numerous non-branched stems. The leaves are large, simple, and oval to elliptical, with a pointed tip and toothed margins. The long-lasting flowers, superb for dried or fresh arrangements, are produced in enormous, 10- to 15-cm (4- to 6-in.), rounded terminal heads in summer. The interior fertile flowers are a dull white. The outer sterile flowers open as an apple green color, mature to white, and then turn brown. 'Annabelle' was selected at the University of Illinois for its large, dark green leaves and its enormous, dense, long-lasting flower clusters, which bloom for three to four weeks. It is the best hydrangea selection for the prairies.

OTHER SPECIES AND HYBRIDS

* *Hydrangea paniculata* 'Grandiflora' (hy-*drain*-gee-ah pen-nick-yew-*lah*-tah), peegee hydrangea, takes its common name, peegee, from the initials of the species and the cultivar names. *Paniculata* means "with flowers in panicles." Native to Japan and to eastern and southern China, the species was introduced in 1861. Peegee hydrangea forms a tidy, upright to spreading shrub, with a height and spread of 1 m (3 ft.) and stout, reddish brown stems. The dark green leaves are smaller, usually opposite but sometimes whorled, and more attractive than those of the

snowhill hydrangea. Creamy white flowers are produced in dense, pyramidal panicles in late summer. They eventually fade to pink and then brown. Almost all of the florets are large and sterile, with panicles of up to 30 cm (12 in.) in length, and can be so heavy that the branches may bend.

Juglans
jug-luns

Walnut, butternut

Juglans (photo on page 100) is derived from the classical Latin *Jovis,* "of Jupiter," and *glans,* "acorn or nut." *Gual,* "wall" in Old Dutch, means strange or exotic, which was what the nuts of these non-native plants were to the early Europeans.

Walnuts are deciduous trees with very large, pinnately compound leaves. The trees are monoecious, with female flowers in clusters at the end of the current year's growth and male flowers borne in long catkins. The hard-shelled nuts are covered by thin or fleshy husks. Walnut roots produce compounds that inhibit the growth of other plants, so they should be used with caution in small gardens.

HOW TO GROW
Walnuts are difficult to transplant and should either be grown from seed or transplanted as young whips. They

prefer deep, rich, moist soil, but also grow well in drier soil of limestone origin.

Juglans cinerea

jug-luns sin-eh-*ree*-ah

Butternut

Butternut is native from New Brunswick to North Dakota and is worthy of trial in sheltered areas throughout most of the prairies. It is not always successful in zone 2 and grows best in protected microclimates. The butternut is a low-headed, open tree, with a trunk that usually splits into a number of large, ascending branches. *Cinerea* means gray or ash

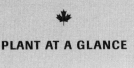

PLANT AT A GLANCE

TYPE: large deciduous tree
HEIGHT/SPREAD: 12 to 18 m (40 to 60 ft.)/10 to 12 m (33 to 40 ft.)
LIGHT: full sun
SOIL: rich; well drained, but tolerates some dryness
DISTINGUISHING FEATURES: large, pinnately compound leaves; edible nuts
LANDSCAPE USE: specimen; shade

colored, a reference to the bark, which has whitish ridges and dark gray to black furrows. The alternate, pinnately compound leaves are large and medium green. Each leaf is made up of eleven to nineteen leaflets, 25 to 50 cm (10 to 20 in.) long. The leaflets are pubescent; the rachis and petiole

have glands that exude sap. The edible, oblong nut is covered with a sticky husk, which is the source of an orange-yellow dye.

Juglans nigra

jug-luns ny-*grah*

Black walnut

PLANT AT A GLANCE

TYPE: large deciduous tree
HEIGHT/SPREAD: 15 to 22 m (50 to 75 ft.)/15 m (50 ft.)
LIGHT: full sun
SOIL: rich; well drained
DISTINGUISHING FEATURES: large, pinnately compound leaves, turning yellow in fall; edible nuts
LANDSCAPE USE: specimen; shade tree

A large shade tree, black walnut has an upright trunk, an open, high head, and dark brown to grayish black bark, broken into narrow ridges. *Nigra*, "black," could refer to the bark or the seeds. Its alternate leaves are pinnately compound, with fifteen to twenty-three leaflets, and are often missing the terminal leaflet. Leaflets emerge with fine hairs; they later become smooth and shiny on top. The male flowers are in long catkins. Female flowers give rise to large, edible, globe-shaped nuts, held singly or in twos, with smooth husks. Reliably hardy to zone 3, black walnut should be tried in the most favorable areas on the prairies.

Juniperus
jew-*nip*-per-rus

Juniper

Juniperus, the classical Latin name for the European species, form an extremely variable genus, from groundcovers a few centimeters in height to conical trees of 10 m (33 ft.). Mostly native to the northern hemisphere in Europe, Asia, and North America, their foliage colors include green, gray, blue, and yellow, as well as variegated forms. The bark, more noticeable in larger shrubs and trees, is thin and shredding.

Junipers are usually dioecious. The male flowers are inconspicuous, yellow cones. The female flowers develop into dark blue, berry-like cones, covered in a bloom; they ripen in their second or third year.

Sharp, needle-like leaves, often produced in whorls of three, are found on juvenile plants and don't invite touching. Generally, older plants have soft, scale-like foliage on older growth and needle-like leaves on newer growth. *Juniperus communis* (jew-*nip*-per-rus cuh-*mew*-nus), common juniper, and cultivars that originated as sports on newer growth, often retain their sharp, juvenile foliage for life.

How to Grow
Junipers do best in full sun in well-drained soils. In shady situations, most tend to be open and thin, although some creeping junipers have been used successfully as groundcovers under large canopy trees where there is sufficient indirect light. Most junipers are extremely drought tolerant once established. Some Rocky Mountain cultivars are open and require shearing to maintain a compact appearance, while others are quite dense. Spider mites, sometimes a problem on savin junipers during prolonged periods of hot, dry weather, are best washed off with regular, strong jets of cold water. Junipers are sometimes affected by saskatoon-juniper rust, but it is never lethal and seldom disfiguring. Simply prune off the galls.

Juniperus horizontalis
jew-*nip*-per-rus hor-ri-zon-*tahl*-lis

Creeping juniper

Horizontalis says it all—this prostrate plant is useful as a groundcover and in rock gardens. Creeping junipers form low mats of various colors. Rooting as they grow, the leading branches create attractive textured patterns as they slowly extend over the soil surface.

Less variable than other juniper species, creeping junipers are also exceptionally drought tolerant. There are numerous cultivars, ranging from green through silver to blue to golden variegated. Many turn purple in winter. The foliage is often plume-like. The berries, on female clones, are blue-black.

Cultivars
* 'Bar Harbor,' from coastal Maine, is somewhat salt tolerant. It has

soft, scale-like, bluish green foliage, which turns reddish purple in winter. It is 20 to 30 cm (8 to 12 in.) in height, spreading to 2 m (6.5 ft,), and its erect side branches lend it a deep-pile effect.

* 'Blue Chip,' from Denmark, forms a prostrate, dense, circular mound, 30 cm (12 in.) in height, with a spread of 2 to 3 m (6.5 to 10 ft.). It has bright blue foliage throughout the year.

* 'Blue Prince,' a powder blue color, is prostrate and is 15 cm (6 in.) in height, spreading to 2 m (6.5 ft.).

* 'Hughes' is low growing, with soft, scale-like foliage, which retains its silver blue-green color throughout winter. It has a radial or circular branching habit, is relatively fast growing, and attains a mature height of 30 to 40 cm (12 to 16 in.) and a spread of 3 m (10 ft.). It is vigorous and useful for massing in large areas.

* 'Mother Lode,' a very low sport of 'Wiltonii' that was supposedly induced by lightning, was introduced in 1982. It has unique golden variegated foliage and is only 10 to 15 cm (4 to 6 in.) in height, with a spread of 1 m (3 ft.).

* 'Prince of Wales,' selected on the Prince of Wales Ranch in High River, Alberta, in 1931, was released in 1967 by the Morden Research Station in Manitoba. This dense, ground-hugging plant—15 cm (6 in.) in height, spreading 2 to 3 m (6.5 to 10 ft.)—has bright green, soft, scale-like foliage, with a waxy blue bloom, which becomes purple in winter.

* 'Yukon Belle' has soft, bright silver-blue foliage, which turns purple in winter. Dense, ground hugging at only 30 cm (12 in.) in height, and very hardy, it has a spread of 2 m (6.5 ft.).

* var. 'Plumosa' ('Andorra'), introduced in 1916, is flat topped, with dense, short, erect branches. About 38 cm (15 in.) in height, it is considered one of the best of the low, mound-forming, spreading junipers. The branches radiate from the center, giving it a circular form of 2 to 3 m (6.5 to 10 ft.). Its sharp, juvenile needles are blue-green in summer, purple in winter.

* 'Wiltonii' ('Blue Rug') has dense, soft, scale-like foliage, which remains a glaucous blue all winter. Slow growing, it is only 15 to 20 cm (6 to 8 in.) in height and has a rather flat appearance, with long, trailing, prostrate branches,

which spread 2 to 3 m (6.5 to 10 ft.) and make it ideal for cascading over rocks and walls. It is a female selection, with small but intensely silver-blue berries.

Juniperus sabina
jew-*nip*-per-rus sah-*been*-ah
Savin juniper

Native to Europe, western Asia, and Siberia, savin junipers have been cultivated since ancient times and were in English gardens by 1548. Intermediate in height between the creeping and Rocky Mountain junipers, they have long been the mainstay of foundation plantings.

Although the species ranges from groundcovers to tree forms, our garden cultivars are generally symmetrical, arching, and distinctly vase shaped. Most have soft, scale-like leaves, usually green to blue-green, which release a strong, pungent oil of juniper aroma when bruised or crushed.

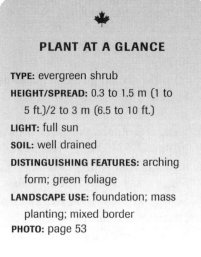

PLANT AT A GLANCE

TYPE: evergreen shrub

HEIGHT/SPREAD: 0.3 to 1.5 m (1 to 5 ft.)/2 to 3 m (6.5 to 10 ft.)

LIGHT: full sun

SOIL: well drained

DISTINGUISHING FEATURES: arching form; green foliage

LANDSCAPE USE: foundation; mass planting; mixed border

PHOTO: page 53

CULTIVARS

* 'Arcadia' is low and spreading— 0.6 m (2 ft.) in height, with a spread of 2.5 m (8 ft.)—and has graceful arching stems and a dense, layered form. The soft, scale-like, bright green foliage is retained throughout winter. Grown from seed from the Ural Mountains, it is an introduction from Morden, Manitoba.

* 'Blue Danube,' an Austrian introduction, is semi-upright, with soft, scale-like, blue-green to gray-blue foliage. Low (0.6 m/2 ft.) and spreading (2.5 m/8 ft.), the branches root as they grow. It may suffer from winter burn in exposed locations.

* 'Broadmoor' is a dwarf cultivar of 0.3 m (1 ft.), spreading to 2 m (6.5 ft.), with dense, bright green foliage. Hardy to zone 3, it should be placed in a protected location in colder regions.

* 'Buffalo,' at 0.3 m (1 ft.) in height, with a spread of 2 to 3 m (6.5 to 10 ft.), is a compact form of var. *tamariscifolia*. A female (berry-producing) selection, with bright green, mostly scale-like leaves, it retains good winter color and is ideal for covering a bank or wall. It was grown from seed imported from Russia in 1933.

* Calgary Carpet™ ('Monna') has soft, green foliage and a low, somewhat tufted, horizontal branching habit that is unique to savin junipers. It is 0.3 m (1 ft.) in height and spreads 2 to 3 m (6.5 to 10 ft.).

* 'Moor-Dense' ('Monard') is similar

to 'Broadmoor' but flatter, with dense, bright green foliage and tiered branching. It grows 25 cm (10 in.) in height and has a 1.5 m (5 ft.) spread.

❀ 'Skandia' is an extremely hardy, female (berry-producing) selection, with soft, scale-like, dark green leaves. At 20 to 45 cm (8 to 18 in.) in height, spreading to 2 m (6.5 ft.), it is relatively low and compact.

❀ var. *tamariscifolia* (ta-ma-ri-sa-*fo*-lee-ah) has been grown since 1789. It forms a round, mounded shrub, with stiff, arching branches and soft, scale-like, bright green foliage that reaches 45 cm (18 in.) in height and spreads 3 to 4 m (10 to 13 ft.).

Juniperus scopulorum
jew-*nip*-per-rus skop-yew-*lor*-um
Rocky Mountain juniper

Scopulorum, "of the cliffs" or "growing among rocks," aptly describes this juniper's dry, stony habitat in the Rocky Mountains from British Columbia and Alberta to New Mexico. Its wood, foliage, and fruit have long been valued by Native peoples for a wide range of uses, from snowshoe frames to medicinal remedies.

Rocky Mountain junipers form small, conical trees, generally with several main stems, which have thin, shredding, reddish brown bark. Slow growing, they are relatively long-lived. Their foliage is soft and scale-like and varies from light green to blue-green to silvery blue in color. They often

❀ PLANT AT A GLANCE

TYPE: small evergreen tree or shrub
HEIGHT/SPREAD: 4 to 10 m (13 to 33 ft.)/3 m (10 ft.)
LIGHT: full sun
SOIL: well drained; adaptable
DISTINGUISHING FEATURES: conical to pyramidal form; green, blue, or silver foliage
LANDSCAPE USE: shrub and mixed borders; accent; screening
PHOTOS: pages 41, 53

become too large to be used for foundation plantings.

CULTIVARS

❀ 'Blue Heaven' is a very hardy, bright silver-blue selection, with berries of the same color. It forms a small, fast-growing, conical tree, 3 to 6 m (10 to 20 ft.) in height, with a spread of 1.5 m (5 ft.). It generally requires shearing.

❀ 'Cologreen,' introduced in the 1930s, is a light forest green color, with a compact, pyramidal, almost cone-like form. It reaches 4 to 6 m (13 to 20 ft.) in height and has a spread of 1.5 to 2 m (5 to 6.5 ft.).

❀ 'Gray Ice' has silver gray-blue foliage, which remains very attractive throughout winter, and a symmetrical, pyramidal form, reaching 3 to 5 m (10 to 16 ft.) in height and about 1.5 m (5 ft.) in spread. Compact and dense, it does not require shearing.

* 'Medora' is a slow-growing, slender, nearly columnar selection, 3 m (10 ft.) in height, spreading to 1.5 m (5 ft.). A male clone (no berries), with blue foliage, it is resistant to saskatoon-juniper rust.
* 'Moonglow,' at 4 to 6 m (13 to 20 ft.) in height and spreading to about 1.5 m (5 ft.), is compact, conical, and dense, with intensely silver-blue foliage.
* 'Witchita Blue' has brilliant blue foliage and forms a small, open, pyramidal tree, 6 m (20 ft.) in height, spreading to 2 m (6.5 ft.). It requires annual shearing to keep it dense and compact.

OTHER SPECIES AND HYBRIDS

* *Juniperus communis* 'Depressa Aurea' (jew-*nip*-per-rus kom-*yew*-nis), common juniper, (photos on pages 39 and 52) is an exceptional plant in need of a marketing agent. Although much more attractive and better adapted to the prairies than the Chinese golden pfitzer juniper, it is seldom commercially available or seen in our prairie gardens. The leaves and young shoots emerge a bright golden yellow, maturing to blue-green by mid to late summer. The contrast of the new and mature foliage is stunning. It has a vase-shaped, spreading form, 1 m (3 ft.) in height, forming a circle of up to 3 m (10 ft.). In over a decade in a rural Saskatchewan yard, it has never shown any sign of winter dieback or spring browning. It is amazingly drought tolerant once established. Its only fault is its juvenility—all the leaves, in whorls of three, are needle-like and prickly. Unlike teenagers, it isn't a characteristic it will outgrow.

* *Juniperus communis* 'Effusa' (jew-*nip*-per-rus kom-*yew*-nis), common juniper, is a dwarf, spreading, bright green juniper, 23 to 30 cm (9 to 12 in.) in height, with an eventual spread of 1.2 to 1.8 m (4 to 6 ft.). Introduced from Holland in about 1944, it is extremely soft to the touch and drought tolerant and has shown no winter browning during the two (snowless) winters it has grown in zone 2. It is certainly worthy of more extensive trials.

* *Juniperus* x *media* 'Pfitzeriana Aurea' (jew-*nip*-per-rus meh-*dee*-ah), syn. *J. chinensis* 'Pfitzeriana Aurea' (jew-*nip*-per-rus chin-*en*-sis), Chinese golden pfitzer juniper, suffers from both over planting and winter burn. It should be replaced by *Juniperus communis* 'Depressa Aurea.'

* *Juniperus squamata* 'Blue Star' (jew-*nip*-per-rus skwah-*mah*-tah) forms a low, dense, dwarf "bun," 0.3 to .06 m (1 to 2 ft.) in height, spreading to 1 to 1.3 m (3 to 4 ft.), with steel blue foliage. *Squamata*, "scaly," describes the bark. Slow growing and ideal for a rock garden or mixed border, it benefits from a protected microclimate when grown in zone 2 gardens.

Larix
lair-icks

Larch

Found in boreal and alpine forest regions, larch are our only deciduous conifers. Their needles, borne singly on first-year shoots and in clusters on short spurs on older branches, turn golden in fall and are shed for winter. The cones often persist on the trees after the seeds are shed.

HOW TO GROW

Bare-root or balled and burlapped stock does not transplant successfully once the needles have expanded, so unless they are container grown, larch should only be planted in late fall or early spring. Place in full sun, and prune in mid-summer. All but the native *Larix laricina,* which is found in swamps in association with black spruce, grow on well-drained soils. *L. laricina* thrives in the garden under average moisture conditions, as long as competition from grass and weeds is minimized when the tree is small.

Larix decidua
lair-icks deh-*sid*-yew-ah

European larch

European larch is native to the mountains of central and northern Europe. *Decidua* indicates that, although this is a coniferous tree, it is deciduous

PLANT AT A GLANCE

TYPE: large deciduous tree
HEIGHT/SPREAD: 20 m (65 ft.)/ 8 m (26 ft.)
LIGHT: full sun
SOIL: well drained, moist
DISTINGUISHING FEATURES: spectacular golden yellow fall color; pyramidal form
LANDSCAPE USE: specimen; grouping or screening in large spaces
PHOTO: page 53

and loses its needles each fall. It is a large, pyramidal tree, with upswept branches, that become horizontal with age. The bark on new twigs is yellow, becoming gray, with deep, vertical fissures on older trunks. The soft, medium green needles turn golden yellow in fall and remain on the tree well into winter, especially if the tree is protected from wind. Fall color is spectacular, especially when groups are planted in large areas. The seeds are borne in cones, which are 2.5 to 4 cm (1 to 1.5 in.) long. *Larix decidua* 'Pendula' (weeping larch) develops into an attractive weeping tree, with a somewhat irregular form.

Larix laricina
lair-icks lair-ri-*see*-nah

American larch, tamarack

American larch, or tamarack, grows in swamps throughout the boreal forest regions of North America, from the Rocky Mountains eastward. Despite is well adapted to our prairie climate. It is fast growing and drought tolerant once established. Siberian larch is a large, pyramidal tree, which has upswept, young branches (later becoming horizontal), with upturned tips. The bark is yellowish on young twigs, aging first to reddish brown and later to dark grayish brown, with deep furrows. The needles are a soft, bright green, turning golden yellow and dropping in fall. Seeds are borne in small, leathery cones, with scales that turn in at the tips and open only slightly when ripe.

its wet native habitat, it adapts well when planted in normal garden conditions. Native peoples used this tree medicinally, to construct toboggans, snowshoes, and basketry, and for smoking hides. *Laricina* simply implies that our northern tamarack resembles (and, in fact, is) a larch.

American larch is narrowly pyramidal, with upswept, slender branches. The bark is smooth and gray when young and breaks into reddish brown, scaly plates with age. Needles are bright bluish green, turning golden yellow in fall. The small cones appear as tiny, wooden rosettes. They open and shed their seeds the first fall, but usually remain on the tree for another year.

Larix sibirica

lair-icks sy-*beer*-ri-kah

Siberian larch

Siberian larch, native from northeastern Russia through to western Siberia,

Lonicera

lon-*niss*-ur-uh

Honeysuckle

This genus consists of about 150 species of shrubs and vines that are native to the northern hemisphere. For the most part, they form vigorous plants, which require little attention and are well adapted to the prairies. Leaves are opposite and simple. The white, pink, or yellow flowers are borne in pairs in the leaf axils and are followed by yellow, orange, red, or blue fruit. One Siberian species, *Lonicera caerulea*, has edible fruit and may have potential as a commercial crop.

How to Grow

Honeysuckle grows in any well-drained soil in full sun or partial shade. Once established, it is remarkably drought tolerant and moderately salt tolerant. Select aphid-resistant cultivars.

Lonicera tatarica

lon-*niss*-ur-uh tah-*tare*-ri-kah

Tartarian honeysuckle

Tartarian honeysuckles are easy plants to grow—as long as the cultivar is aphid resistant. Tough and enduring, they provide two-season landscape value with their flowers and fruit.

They form large, upright shrubs, with hollow, arching stems, which are green when young and later turn brown. The blue-green, paired leaves are opposite, simple, and oval to oblong. The small, two-lipped, tubular flowers, borne in pairs, are freely produced in June and very showy, in white, pink, or rose. Golden orange to deep red berries, also grouped in pairs, follow.

PLANT AT A GLANCE

TYPE: large, flowering, deciduous shrub

HEIGHT/SPREAD: 2 to 3 m (6.5 to 10 ft.)/3 m (10 ft.)

LIGHT: full sun

SOIL: well drained; various

DISTINGUISHING FEATURES: white to pink flowers

LANDSCAPE USE: mixed or shrub border; wildlife planting; informal hedge; shelterbelt

PHOTO: page 54

Cultivars

* 'Arnold Red' has dark pink flowers, red fruit, and dark blue-green foliage; it grows to 3 m (10 ft.) in height, with a spread of 2.5 m (8 ft.).

* 'Cameo,' with white flowers and yellow fruit, and 'Flamingo,' with pink flowers and red fruit, are both from Boughen's Nurseries, Valley River, Manitoba. They reach 2.5 m (8 ft.) in height and spread 2 m (6.5 ft.).

* 'Honeyrose' has deep blue-green foliage, deep rosy red flowers, and red fruit; it grows 3 m (10 ft.) in

height and spreads 2.5 m (8 ft.).

* 'Sunstar' has white flowers and red fruit; it reaches a height of 2.5 m (8 ft.), with a spread of 1.2 m (4 ft.).

OTHER SPECIES AND HYBRIDS

* *Lonicera caerulea* var. *edulis* (lon-*niss*-ur-uh sir-*rule*-lee-ah eh-*dule*-liss), sweetberry honeysuckle, is native to Asia and was introduced to the prairies in 1937 via Skinner's Nursery in Manitoba. *Caerulea*, "sky blue," refers to the waxy bloom that gives color to the fruit; *edulis* means "edible"; the common name sweetberry also describes the berries. A rounded shrub of medium size, 3 m (10 ft.) in height, with a spread of 1.5 m (5 ft.), it is densely branched, with stiff, reddish brown, arching stems. The small, bright green leaves appear early in spring and turn yellow in fall. With pale yellow flowers, it is one of the earliest blooming shrubs, and it never fails to attract bees. The blue berries are edible and are used as preserves in parts of Russia and in Japan. Plants are very drought tolerant once established, nearly trouble free, immune to the honeysuckle aphid, and useful in a shrub or mixed border. Two cultivars selected for their superior fruit are 'George Bugnet' and 'Lac la Nonne,' both introduced by Bugnet of Legal, Alberta. New edible cultivars from Russia will be introduced in the near future.

❧

The Aphid and the Honeysuckle

Almost every prairie farmyard and many urban landscapes once hosted Tartarian honeysuckles. The introduction of the aphid *Hydaphis tataricae*, likely from Asia, changed all that. First reported in Quebec in 1981, it reached the prairies by 1983, and by 1990, most prairie honeysuckles were affected.

The tiny (2 mm/.08 in.), cream to pale green aphids over-winter on the honeysuckle, where they remain for their entire life cycle. Eggs hatch into female aphids, which can produce young without mating. The young aphids emerge just as the leaves begin to elongate, and feed on new growth throughout the summer.

They cause a distorted "witch's broom," which gives the flowers and new growth a purple, twist-ed, fasciated appearance and eventually kills the plant. Pruning out affected growth can some-what delay their demise, but the only real control is to plant resist-ant honeysuckle species and culti-vars, such as those listed under *Lonicera tatarica* and the accom-panying Other Species and Hybrids.

❀ *Lonicera spinosa* var. *albertii* (lon-*niss*-ur-uh spin-*now*-sah al-*ber*-tee-eye), Albert thorn honeysuckle, is a dwarf, mounded shrub native to Turkestan, with very narrow, glaucous leaves and fragrant, rose-colored flowers. Its branches and leaves have a pronounced linear texture, making it a rather unique plant for a mixed border or rock garden. It should be more available than it is.

❀ *Lonicera xylosteum* (lon-*niss*-ur-uh zy-low-*stee*-um), European dwarf or fly honeysuckle, is 1 to 2 m (3 to 6.5 ft.) in height, with a spread of 1.5 to 2 m (5 to 6.5 ft.). It has a round, mounded form, gray-green foliage, and spreading, arching branches, with shaggy, exfoliating bark. The dark wine-colored berries are poisonous. Native from Europe to western Siberia, this species is drought tolerant. The cultivars, which are seen more often than the species, are valuable as low hedges or for massing in full sun. 'Clavey's Dwarf,' a juvenile plant that seldom flowers, is used for hedging because of its dense, branching and mounded form; it has a height and spread of 1.5 m (5 ft.). 'Miniglobe' (*L.* x *xylosteoides* 'Miniglobe') (Morden, 1981) is also a juvenile plant that seldom produces flowers. Grown for its dark blue-green foliage and form, with a height and spread of 1 m (3 ft.), it is smaller than the species and used for low hedging.

❀ *Lonicera involucrata* (lon-*niss*-ur-uh in-vol-yew-*krah*-tah), bracted honeysuckle, is easily recognized in the open woods of our boreal forests by the conspicuous bracts that surround the flowers. A large, erect shrub, 1 to 3 m (3 to 10 ft.) in height, with a spread of 1 to 2 m (3 to 6.5 ft.), its leaves are simple, bright green, and oval, with a pointed tip. The tube-like, paired, yellow flowers emerge from the leaf axils and are followed by paired, shiny, purple-black fruit, which is relished by birds but possibly poisonous to humans.

On the Edge

❀ *Mahonia aquifolium* (mah-*hoe*-nee-ah ah-qui-*foe*-lee-um), Oregon grape, is more upright than *M. repens,* with shinier evergreen leaves and is likely to thrive only in the most favorable locations on the prairies.

❀ *Mahonia repens* (mah-*hoe*-nee-ah *rep*-penz), creeping Oregon grape, is native from British Columbia eastward to the Black Hills of South Dakota. Plants originating from the Black Hills should be winter hardy in sheltered locations across the prairies. Its attractive evergreen leaves are pinnately compound, with spiny teeth. Spikes of bright yellow flowers in June are followed by dark blue berries. Plant in well-drained soil in full or partial shade.

Malus baccata
mal-lus bah-*kah*-tah

Siberian crabapple

The fragrant and lovely flowers of this genus make it one of our most beloved harbingers of spring, while the fruit and fall color give it three-season ornamental value. It is a member of the rose family. *Malus*, Latin for "apple tree," was derived from the Greek word for melon. Apple seeds contain prussic acid, which reacts with enzymes in the digestive tract to form cyanide, but if swallowed whole, they are harmless.

Fireblight is the most common disease problem encountered on the prairies, but contemporary breeding programs have focused on fireblight resistance. All the cultivars listed here are moderately to highly resistant. Expect a lifespan of about twenty-five to thirty-five years.

There are about twenty-five species in the genus, all native to the northern hemisphere. Most are 5 to 7.5 m (15 to 25 ft.) in height at maturity, but can be quite variable in size and form. As their common name implies, Siberian crabapples are widely distributed in Siberia, as well as in Mongolia and China.

In general, most crabapples are upright to rounded, low headed, and spreading, with gray-brown bark and a deep and extensive root system. The leaves are alternate, simple, green, oval in shape, and finely toothed.

The flowers of *Malus baccata* are pink in bud, opening to single, pure white, fragrant flowers. Hybrids range from white to deep red-pink. The small fruit (*baccata* means berry-like), which are suspended from long, thin stalks, vary in color from yellow to red and are beloved by birds, which aid in their dispersal.

Extremely hardy and resistant to many diseases, Siberian crabapples have been used extensively in breeding ornamental crabapples for the prairies. They have been extensively crossed with *M. pumila* var.' Niedzwertzkyana,' a small tree, with purple-red flowers and dark red fruit, which is also native to Siberia. The resulting hybrids are known as rosybloom crabapples—noted for the reddish tint of their flowers, fruit, foliage, bark, and wood. These were originally hybridized in the 1920s and 1930s by Isabella Preston, in her work at the Central Experimental Farm in Ottawa.

PLANT AT A GLANCE

TYPE: flowering deciduous tree
HEIGHT/SPREAD: 5 to 10 m (15 to 30 ft.)/ 7 m (20 ft.)
LIGHT: full sun
SOIL: well drained, varied
DISTINGUISHING FEATURES: flowers; edible fruit
LANDSCAPE USE: specimen; grouping; mixed border; wildlife planting
PHOTOS: pages 39, 54

How to Grow

Plant crabapples in full sun and give them enough space to encourage air circulation. They adapt to a variety of soils, from sand to clay, but do best in those that are fertile and well drained, with even moisture. In lighter soils, mulching is beneficial. Prune in early spring before leaves emerge to remove water sprouts and suckers. Select cultivars that are resistant to fireblight.

Cultivars

* 'Kelsey' (Morden, Manitoba, 1969) honors Henry Kelsey, an early explorer of Manitoba. It has semi-double to double, purple-red flowers, with white centers. The foliage emerges red, changes to a copper green with red veins in summer, and becomes orange-yellow in fall. Small, purple fruit persist into winter. It has a height of 5 m (16 ft.) and a spread of 4 m (13 ft.).

* 'Morning Princess' (Lakeshore, Saskatoon) is a low, spreading, semi-weeping tree, 4.5 m (15 ft.) in height, spreading to 2.5 m (8 ft.), with an upright central leader. The new foliage is red, maturing to reddish green in summer and turning reddish orange in fall. Rose-pink, single flowers are followed by small, red fruit.

* 'Pink Spires' (Sutherland PFRA Tree Nursery, Saskatchewan), a rosybloom, is 6 m (20 ft.) in height, with a spread of 4 m (13 ft.). It has a narrow, upright, well-branched form. Its red-purple foliage turns greeny bronze in summer and copper in fall. The dark buds open to single, lavender-pink flowers, which are followed by small, purple-red, persistent fruit.

* 'Radiant' is a broad rosybloom, 8 m (26 ft.) in height, with a 6 m (20 ft.) spread and a compact, symmetrical form. The leaves are purple-red when young, changing to bronze by summer. Deep red buds open to single, dark pink flowers and are followed by bright red, persistent fruit. Place in a well-sheltered microclimate.

* 'Red Splendor' is an upright, spreading rosybloom, with a height and spread of 6 m (20 ft.) and an open, graceful form. The glossy, red-green foliage turns red-purple in fall. The large, light rose flowers mature to dark red fruit, which are retained throughout winter.

* 'Royal Beauty' is a small, weeping tree, with a height and spread of 3 m (10 ft.). It has slender, reddish purple stems and reddish purple foliage, which matures to dark green, with a purple underside. Deep red-purple to pink flowers are followed by small, dark fruit. It is a good selection for a smaller yard, in a well-sheltered location.

* 'Rudolph' (Frank Skinner, 1954) forms a small, symmetrical, upright, and rounded tree of 5 m (16 ft.), with a 4 m (13 ft.) spread. It is extremely hardy and disease resistant. Deep rose buds open to single, deep pink flowers, followed by ruby red fruit, which persist into winter.

* 'Selkirk' (Morden, Manitoba, 1962) is a rounded, vase-shaped rosybloom, 6 m (20 ft.) in height,

with an 8 m (26 ft.) spread. The glossy, red-green foliage later turns green bronze. Bright rose buds open to deep purple-pink flowers. It has exceptionally bright red fruit, which show up in the autumn landscape and persist throughout winter.

* 'Shaughnessy Cohen' (Morden, Manitoba, 1999) has cranberry red buds, which open to clusters of double, fuchsia-pink flowers, followed by small, reddish fruit. It is 6 m (20 ft.) in height, with a spread of 4 m (13 ft.).

* 'Spring Snow' (Porter, Inter-State Nurseries, Iowa, 1967) is a rounded tree, 8 m (26 ft.) in height, with a 6 m (20 ft.) spread and bright green, glossy foliage. The glistening, single, white flowers are fragrant and mostly sterile, so there is little or no fruit, a plus for those who hate mess.

* 'Thunderchild' (Percy Wright, 1978) has become one of the most

---

There's Bloom and There's Bloom

Bloom is the thin, waxy, or powder-like exterior coating that is found naturally on plums, apples, and other fruit. Easily rubbed off with a cloth or in your hands, it is nature's way of preventing desiccation, while adding yet another aesthetic layer to the color and beauty of the fruit.

---

popular rosyblooms on the prairies, and with good reason. It is a small, dense tree, 4 m (13 ft.) in height, with a 3 m (10 ft.) spread and a round to spreading form. It has dark purple-red foliage, single, pink-red flowers, purplish red fruit, and exceptional resistance to fireblight.

Microbiota decussata
mike-row-bee-*awe*-tah
deck-koos-*sah*-tah

Russian cypress, Siberian cypress

Microbiota is a genus containing only one species, which is native to Siberia. The genus name is from the Greek words *micros*, "small," and *biota*, "life." Russian cypress was first discovered in 1921 near Vladivostock, Russia, growing well above the treeline. It is a spreading, low, evergreen shrub, with a soft texture. The tips of new growth nod gracefully. *Decussata*, "with leaves in pairs," indicates that successive leaf pairs are at right angles. The needles are bright green and scale-like, similar to those of *Thuja* (cedar), turning to bronzy purple in fall. A single naked seed is surrounded by spreading cone scales, which open when ripe.

How to Grow

Russian cypress should be planted from balled and burlapped or container-grown plants. An alpine plant, it requires very well-drained soil. It does not tolerate heat and grows best in partial shade.

On the Edge

* *Ostrya virginiana* (oh-*stry*-ah vir-jin-ee-*an*-na), American hop hornbeam, grows on dry slopes in the forest understory, from Ontario into southeastern Manitoba. Grown successfully in the Patterson Gardens of the University of Saskatchewan, it is worthy of trial in sheltered locations throughout the prairies. *Ostrya* is derived from the Greek word *ostrys*, "shell," which describes the inflated, cream-colored floral bracts. The female catkins, with seeds enclosed in papery husks, resemble a hop and give the tree its common name. It is an attractive small, rounded, or pyramidal tree, with the trunk extending to near the top and with slender, horizontal branches. The simple, oval leaves are toothed and resemble elm leaves.

Paxistima canbyi
pah-*kiss*-ti-mah *kan*-bee-eye

Paxistima, cliff green

Paxistima is from the Greek words *pachys*, "thick," and *stigma*, which refers to the part of the flower that receives the pollen. The genus *Paxistima* includes only two species, both characterized by four-sided, square stems and both native to North America. Only *P. canbyi* is hardy on the prairies.

An evergreen shrub, paxistima

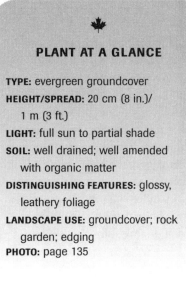

has horizontal branches, which form a dense mat and are spread by underground rhizomes. The roots are a bright unmistakable orange. The small, glossy, leathery leaves are narrow and opposite, with toothed margins.

How to Grow

Paxistima does best in well-drained but moist soil, which has been generously amended with organic matter. It tolerates full sun but grows best in partial shade and has no pest or disease problems. Snow cover and a sheltered site are recommended to protect it from late winter and early spring sunlight.

On the Edge

* *Phellodendron amurense* (fell-low-*den*-dron ay-mure-*en*-see), Amur cork tree, is native to the Amur region of northern China. A medium-sized tree, with a height and spread of 9 to 14 m (30 to 45 ft.), it develops several large, spreading branches. Its thick, corky bark becomes ridged and very beautiful with age. The opposite leaves are pinnately compound, much like ash, but give off a turpentine-like odor when crushed. The species is dioecious and the flowers are inconspicuous. Female trees produce small, black berries, with a tough skin. It is worthy of trial on protected sites on the prairies that have deep, rich, loamy soil.

Philadelphus
fil-ah-*del*-fus
Mockorange

Mockorange has numerous upright shoots, small, opposite leaves, and fragrant, white flowers in early summer. The genus is named for the ancient Egyptian king Ptolemy Philadelphus, who reigned from 285 to 247 BC. The flowers are similar to orange blossoms, hence, the common name.

How to Grow

Mockoranges transplant easily. They prefer moist, well-drained, fertile soil in full sun to partial shade, but will grow in less than ideal conditions. Prune immediately after flowering.

Philadelphus lewisii
fil-ah-*del*-fus lew-*wis*-ee-eye
Lewis mockorange, mock orange

Philadelphus lewisii is named after its discoverer, Meriwether Lewis of the 1804–06 Lewis and Clark expedition. It is native from southern Alberta and British Columbia to Montana, Washington, and Oregon; selections from plants native to southwestern Alberta make excellent garden plants for the prairies. It is an attractive upright shrub, with coarsely toothed leaves that are opposite and oval, with a pointed tip. The racemes of white

TYPE: medium, flowering, deciduous
shrub

HEIGHT/SPREAD: 1.5 to 2 m (5 to
6.5 ft.)/1.5 m (5 ft.)

LIGHT: full sun to partial shade

SOIL: well drained

DISTINUISHING FEATURES: fragrant,
white flowers

LANDSCAPE USE: back of border

PHOTO: page 54

flowers are sometimes lost to extreme winter cold in the more northern part of the area. Very showy in bloom but rather coarse the rest of the year, mockoranges are best suited to planting in large landscapes.

CULTIVARS

♦ 'Blizzard' was selected at Beaver-lodge, Alberta. It is very drought tolerant, has superior flower-bud hardiness, and is a profuse bloomer. It reaches 1.5 m (5 ft.) in height with a spread of 1 m (3 ft.).

♦ 'Waterton' is a tall shrub, 2.5 m (8 ft.) in height, spreading to 1.5 m (5 ft.). It has white flowers to its base in June and is an attractive plant for the back of the border.

OTHER SPECIES AND HYBRIDS

♦ 'Buckley's Quill' is double flowered, with quill-like petals, 1.8 m (6 ft.) in height, spreading to 1.2 m (4 ft.), and winter hardy

only in the most favorable locations on the prairies.

♦ 'Galahad' is a white, single-flowered cultivar of 1.2 m (4 ft.), spreading to 1.2 m (4 ft.), with attractive shiny foliage. It blooms to the branch tips in zone 3 and warmer areas.

♦ 'Minnesota Snowflake' is a double-flowered form, 1.5 m (5 ft.) in height and spread, that is winter hardy to zone 3.

♦ *Philadelphus coronarius* 'Aureus' (fil-ah-*del*-fus core-row-*nare*-ree-us), golden mockorange, can be found in protected locations in prairie gardens. It is a rather coarse shrub, with golden foliage and white flowers.

♦ ♦ ♦ ♦ ♦ ♦

Physocarpus opulifolius
fy-soh-*kar*-pus
op-yew-li-*foe*-lee-us

Common ninebark

Physocarpus is from the Greek words *physa*, "bladder," and *karpos*, "fruit," which refers to its bright orange, inflated seed pods so evident in late summer and autumn. A member of the rose family, the genus consists of ten species that are native to North America and Asia. The genus is characterized by vigorous plants, with upright, arching stems and exfoliating bark. Only one, *P. opulifolius,* is found in prairie gardens.

Common ninebark forms a medium to large shrub, with arching branches. The common name, ninebark, describes the many layers of shredding bark. The thin, brown bark peels in narrow strips, providing interest throughout winter. The fibrous roots are deep, but not widely spreading. The distinctly three-lobed leaves are alternate, simple, and coarsely toothed. Leaves of the species are green, while those of the cultivars can be golden yellow or a rich deep purple. Creamy white to pinkish flowers are produced in terminal clusters in early spring. These are followed by very attractive inflated seed pods, which mature to salmon red and are useful in dried floral arrangements

HOW TO GROW

Ninebark will grow in almost any soil in full sun or partial shade. It is disease and insect free and remarkably drought tolerant once established.

CULTIVARS

* 'Dart's Gold,' 1.5 m (5 ft.) in height, with a 1 m (3 ft.) spread, is a smaller, more compact selection of 'Luteus.' It has white flowers and golden foliage that is retained longer into summer before turning yellow green. It is easily sheared into a low hedge.

* 'Monlo' (Diabolo®) has dark purple leaves, pinkish white flowers, and salmon-colored seed pods. It is very adaptable, but at 3 m (10 ft.), with a spread of 2 m (6.5 ft.), it is taller than catalogues generally indicate. The foliage turns an almost iridescent red-purple in fall when grown in full sun.

* 'Luteus,' often called golden ninebark, has greenish yellow foliage, which is more intense if grown in full sun. It is 2.5 m (8 ft.) in height, with a spread of 1.2 m (4 ft.).

* 'Nugget' is a compact, dwarf golden ninebark, with a height and spread of 1.2 m (4 ft.). It has white flowers and dense, deep golden yellow foliage, which matures to lime green by mid-summer and turns yellow in fall.

Picea

pie-*see*-ah

Spruce

Picea is the ancient name for spruce and is derived from the word *pix*, "pitch," the resin used for caulking.

Spruce are the most common evergreen conifers of the boreal forest. In their natural forms, all species grow to be very large trees, most exceeding 25 m (82 ft.) in height when mature. They provide exceptional shelter from winter winds, cover and food for wildlife, and year-round beauty in the landscape, and are the most important forest trees for lumber and paper.

Because they often outgrow their setting, they should be used with caution in the urban landscape. A large number of dwarf forms have been selected, however, which are better suited to urban gardens. Propagated from cuttings or by grafting, they are expensive in comparison to seed-grown forms, but worth the price. Like art, these trees appreciate in value with age.

How to Grow

Plant balled and burlapped or container-grown plants. They are generally adapted to well-drained, moist soils. They tolerate some shade, but become thin and open in heavy shade. Prune in early to mid-summer, as the soft, new growth becomes woody.

This stimulates new bud formation and results in denser growth the following year.

Picea abies

pie-*see*-ah *ay*-beez

Norway spruce

Norway spruce is the common spruce of central and northern Europe. A large number of distinct forms and cutivars have been selected from the varied populations over its wide range.

This large, broadly pyramidal tree generally has horizontal branches, which are sometimes bowed downward, with upturned tips. Secondary branches often hang, giving the tree a weeping appearance. The bark is reddish brown and develops into thin

PLANT AT A GLANCE

TYPE: large, coniferous, evergreen tree, numerous dwarf and shrub forms

HEIGHT/SPREAD: 30 m (100 ft.)/ 15 m (50 ft.)

LIGHT: full sun to partial shade

SOIL: moist, well drained

DISTINGUISHING FEATURES: bright green needles; drooping branches; quite drought tolerant if kept well watered during establishment years

LANDSCAPE USE: shelter; in large open areas, such as parks, golf courses

PHOTO: page 136

scales with age. The needles are dark green and sharply pointed. Although four sided, the needles will not roll easily between your fingers like those of other spruces. The seeds are borne in relatively large, hanging, cylindrical cones, 10 to 15 cm (4 to 6 in.) long. They are green to purple when young, maturing to light brown. They ripen in fall, and the seeds are released the following spring.

CULTIVARS

❧ 'Nidiformis,' nest spruce, is a dense, flat-topped, globular shrub, only 1 m (3 ft.) in height, with a 1.5 m (5 ft.) spread.

❧ 'Ohlendorfii' is shrubby and flat topped when young, but becomes a dense, pyramidal, upright shrub or small tree, 2.5 m (8 ft.) in height, with a 1.5 m (5 ft.) spread.

❧ 'Pendula' is a variable group. The most common clone is a creeping form, which can be trained to grow upright.

Picea glauca

pie-*see*-ah *glock*-kah

White spruce

White spruce is typical of the boreal forest region across Canada, growing in mixed stands in association with trembling aspen, paper birch, and balsam fir. It is one of the most important trees in Canada's forests for lumber and pulp.

Pyramidal in shape, with near-horizontal branches, white spruce has thin, grayish brown, scaly bark. *Glauca*, "glaucous," refers to a dull, grayish green or blue covered with a

❧

PLANT AT A GLANCE

TYPE: large, coniferous, evergreen tree

HEIGHT/SPREAD: 30 m (100 ft.)/ 15 m (50 ft.)

LIGHT: full sun to partial shade

SOIL: moist, well drained

DISTINGUISHING FEATURES: bluish green needles; pyramidal form

LANDSCAPE USE: shelter; in large, open spaces

PHOTO: page 42

powdery bloom and describes the needles, which are a dull, dark green to bluish green and pointed but not sharp. The cylindrical cones are 3 to 6 cm (1.25 to 2.5 in.) long, green when immature, and light brown later.

The best specimens grow in moist, well-drained soils.

CULTIVARS

❧ 'Conica,' dwarf Alberta spruce, seldom performs well on the prairies. A false cypress growing in Steinbach, Manitoba, emerged from winter in perfect condition, while the dwarf Alberta spruce beside it was completely brown above the snowline. The key to growing this spruce successfully is to shield it from winter sun by placing it on the north side of a fence or building. Dwarf Alberta spruce grow to 2.5 m (8 ft.) with a spread of 1.5 m (5 ft.).

❧ 'Densata,' Black Hills spruce, reaches 13 m (42 ft.) with a spread of 5 m (16 ft.), has denser growth, and is better adapted to dry conditions than the species.

Picea pungens
pie-*see*-ah *pun*-genz
Colorado spruce

Colorado spruce grows in the Rocky Mountains from Colorado and Wyoming to Utah and New Mexico at elevations of from 2,000 to 3,300 m (6,500 to 10,000 ft.). The common name tells us that Colorado is part of its native range; *pungens*, "sharp-pointed," refers to the needles, which are stiff and sharp and can cause skin irritation when handled. They vary from bright green to silvery blue, but most are bluish green. Selected blue forms are a favorite ornamental. The blue color comes from a waxy bloom on the needles.

❋
PLANT AT A GLANCE

TYPE: large, coniferous, evergreen tree
HEIGHT/SPREAD: 30 m (100 ft.)/ 15 m (50 ft.)
LIGHT: full sun
SOIL: moist, well drained
DISTINGUISHING FEATURES: bluish green to silvery blue needles; the most drought tolerant of the spruce
LANDSCAPE USE: shelter; specimen in large areas; dwarf forms are more suitable for urban yards
PHOTO: page 136

Pyramidal in form, with stiff, horizontal branches, Colorado spruce has grayish brown bark that becomes deeply furrowed with age. The 6- to 10-cm (2.5- to 4-in.) cones hang from the branches. Green when young, they ripen to straw colored to light brown, with thin, wavy scales.

CULTIVARS
❋ 'Bakeri' is a deep blue, compact, conical tree form reaching 3.6 m (12 ft.) with a spread of 1.8 m (6 ft.).
❋ 'Fat Albert' is semi-dwarf, very dense, and broadly pyramidal. It grows to 4.6 m (15 ft.) tall and wide.
❋ 'Glauca Globosa' is a silvery blue, irregular, dwarf globe, only 1.2 m (4 ft.) in height, with a 1.8-m (6-ft.) spread.
❋ 'Glauca Pendula' may spread as a groundcover or grow at an angle. The main stem can be staked upward to form a graceful speci-men. The height and spread are variable depending on how the tree is trained.
❋ 'Hoopsii' is a large, silver-blue, densely pyramidal selection. It needs pruning and staking when young to develop a dense, upright shape.
❋ 'Iseli Fastigiate' is steely blue and very narrow, with ascending branches. It grows to 3.6 m (12 ft.) in height with a spread of 1.5 m (5 ft.).
❋ 'Montgomery' forms a silver-blue, dwarf, broad pyramid 3.6 m (12 ft.) tall and wide.

❧ *Picea omorika* (pie-*see*-ah ah-*more*-ri-kah), Serbian spruce, has not been widely tried in prairie Canada, but occasional specimens can be found of the species and of *P. omorika* 'Nana,' a dwarf, pyramidal form. It is a beautiful spruce, sometimes very narrow and conical in form, 1.5 m (5 ft.) tall and wide, and deserves wider testing. The foliage is dark green on the upper surface, with two white bands on the lower surface.

Pinus
pie-nus
Pine

Pinus is the classical Latin name for this genus, which is distributed worldwide, mostly in the northern hemisphere. Many pines, both native and introduced, ranging from dwarf "buns" to towering trees, do well on the prairies. Generally, they are tougher than spruce or fir, with a taproot that enables them to "tap" water from the subsoil during drought.

Depending on the species, the needles are in bundles of two, three, or five, and they may remain on the tree for two to five years (or longer), then turn yellow, and fall in the autumn. Needles on the "inside" of the tree, closest to the trunk, are the oldest, and these brown and fall first.

As pines become older, they often (but not always) lose their lower branches, exposing their attractive furrowed bark. Deer love the younger needles (especially those with softer needles, such as Swiss stone pine) and may denude branches within browsing level.

HOW TO GROW

Plant most pines in full sun in well-drained, loamy soil. Once established, they're moderately drought tolerant. Sapsuckers find some of the larger pines attractive. Scale insects can be a problem in mugo and Scots pines

Pinus cembra
pie-nus *sem*-brah
Swiss stone pine

Cembra is the Italian common name of this lovely tree, native to the Carpathian and Alps Mountains, as well as parts of Asia. The Swiss stone pine is long-lived but very slow growing—a tree you plant for your grandchildren. Narrow, columnar, dense, and clothed to ground level (if not browsed by deer), it is one of the loveliest pines available. The bark is gray-green and smooth. The long, soft needles are dark green, with bluish white, stomatal lines on their undersides. In bundles of five, they're resistant to sunscald and retained for up to five years, giving the tree a very dense appearance. Although it has a painfully slow growth rate from a gardener's point of view, the Swiss stone pine is one of the best pines for a small landscape. Certainly, it will not outgrow its location—not in your lifetime or in mine.

The erect cones are greenish violet when young, mature to purple-brown, and fall without opening in their third year. They are prickle free, with edible seeds (pine nuts), which are very attractive to blue jays and other birds. 'Columnaris' is a narrow and columnar cultivar.

Pinus flexilis

pie-nus *fleks*-i-lis

Limber pine

Limber pine is an alpine/subalpine species, often found in exposed areas of the foothills of the Rockies. It was discovered by Edwin Jones, an American army doctor who accompanied an 1820 expedition to the Rocky Mountains. Both *flexilis* and the common name, limber pine, refer to the supple, young branches.

Dense and pyramidal when young, it becomes rather broad and flat topped with age (like many of us), developing a large and uneven crown.

It can be single or multiple trunked; in both cases, the trunk and the branches appear thick in proportion to their length. The bark is a soft gray-green, which becomes darker with age.

The needles, in bundles of five, are blue-green to gray-green, stiff and slightly curved, with lines of stomata. They persist for five or six years and give the tree its very dense appearance. The cylindrical and resinous cones are erect when young, but become pendulous once they mature and hang at right angles to the stem. The seeds are edible and can be eaten raw or roasted or ground into flour.

Although slow growing, limber pines can live for over a hundred years. Dwarf and columnar cultivars are sometimes available, but none have been widely tested on the prairies.

Pinus mugo

pie-nus *mew*-go

Mugo pine

Mugo is this pine's old Tyrolese name from the Austrian Alps. Native to the mountains of southern and eastern Europe, from Spain to the Balkans, mugo pines are an extremely varied species, ranging from prostrate mounds to small, pyramidal trees over 7 m (23 ft.) high. The brownish gray bark is covered with bumpy stumps, from which older needle bundles have fallen. The green needles, in bundles of two, are rigid and slightly curved, and they are retained for five years or more. Their tips may become yellow-green in winter. The cones are small and round.

Species and older varieties, such as var. *mughus* and var. *pumilo*, are

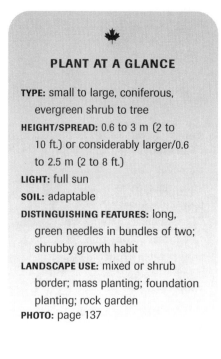

PLANT AT A GLANCE

TYPE: small to large, coniferous, evergreen shrub to tree

HEIGHT/SPREAD: 0.6 to 3 m (2 to 10 ft.) or considerably larger/0.6 to 2.5 m (2 to 8 ft.)

LIGHT: full sun

SOIL: adaptable

DISTINGUISHING FEATURES: long, green needles in bundles of two; shrubby growth habit

LANDSCAPE USE: mixed or shrub border; mass planting; foundation planting; rock garden

PHOTO: page 137

generally seed grown and often from different strains of seed. What is available is a dog's breakfast, complicated by the fact that many of these may have been pruned to look cute and dense, but eventually they will grow up to fulfill their genetic potential. When purchasing a seed-grown plant, if you want a short, dense plant, look for the one with the shortest needles and the shortest distance between whorls of branches. Vegetatively propagated cultivars will be uniform and identical to the parent plants from which they were derived.

For a denser, more compact appearance, mugo pines should be pruned each spring, once the "candles" have fully elongated but before the needles have begun to emerge laterally. At least 0.5 cm (0.25 in.) of candle should be left.

CULTIVARS

* var. *mughus* (*mew*-gus) is a low-growing form from the eastern Alps and Balkans, usually less than 2 to 4 m (6.5 to 13 ft.) tall and twice that width, but variable, depending on the seed source.

* var. *pumilio* (pooh-*mill*-ee-oh), also from the mountains of eastern and central Europe, is generally prostrate and 3 m (10 ft.) wide, but variable if raised by seed.

* var. *uncinata* (un-see-an-*nah*-tah), syn. *P. mugo* var. *rostrata*, mountain mugo pine, is usually taller—5 to 8 m (16 to 26 ft.) in height, with a 2 to 3 m (6.5 to 10 ft.) spread—and has a single trunk. Native to the Alps and Pyrenees, it is considered by many to be a tree form of

mugo pine. The very dense and rigid needles are in bundles of two.

* 'Mops' is compact, with a height and spread of 1 m (3 ft.) and a neat, mounded form.
* 'Slowmound' is low and dense, at 1.2 m (4 ft.) in height, with a spread of 2 m (6.5 ft.), and has rich, green foliage.

Pinus sylvestris

pie-nus sil-*ves*-tris

Scots pine

"Scots" is somewhat misleading as this species is widely distributed, with a native range from Scandinavia through Spain and Siberia. *Sylvestris* is from the Latin word *silva*, which means "of the forest." The wood was once widely used for the masts of sailing ships because its resin slowed decay.

Scots pine are fast growing and long-lived. Although generally almost symmetrical and pyramid-like when young, they become more open and flat topped as they mature, with all the character of a "Group of Seven" painting. Their bark is foxy orange to reddish brown, later becoming rough and fissured. They have a deep and wide-spreading root system, especially when grown on sandy soil.

The needles, in bundles of two, are sharply pointed, blue-green, stiff, and slightly twisted, often becoming yellow-green by late winter. The cones point backward toward the trunk in clusters of two or three. Retained for two years before falling, the cones have no prickles on their scales, but are rock hard and exceedingly tough

PLANT AT A GLANCE

TYPE: large, coniferous, evergreen tree

HEIGHT/SPREAD: 15 to 30 m (50 to 100 ft.)/6 to 8 m (20 to 26 ft.)

LIGHT: full sun

SOIL: well drained; adaptable

DISTINGUISHING FEATURES: foxy orange bark; irregular "Group of Seven" form

LANDSCAPE USE: specimen or character tree; grouping, shelterbelt; wildlife planting

PHOTOS: pages 39, 138

on lawn-mower blades. They are a good reason to apply mulch below these trees!

'Fastigiata,' introduced in 1856, is a narrow, columnar cultivar, 6 m (20 ft.) in height, with a spread of 1.2 m (4 ft.). It has vertical branches, which are held close to the main trunk, and bright blue needles. It is excellent as an accent plant or in a shrub or mixed border. Place it in a well-sheltered location as it is not as reliable on the prairies as the species.

OTHER SPECIES AND HYBRIDS

* *Pinus aristata* (*pie*-nus air-ris-*tah*-tah), bristlecone pine, is native to the southwestern United States, where it is one of the slowest-growing and longest-lived trees and may eventually reached 12 m (40 ft.) in height. On the prairies, it is considered a somewhat

marginal, short-lived, dwarf, accent shrub for a protected rock garden or other well-sheltered location. The blue-green needles, in bundles of five, have white, resinous flakes (often mistaken for scale insects) and persist for up to fifteen years, giving the branch a bottlebrush appearance. The cones are cylindrical, with bristle-like prickles on the scales, hence, its common name.

❧ *Pinus banksiana* (*pie*-nus bank-see-*an*-nah), jack pine, is the most widely distributed pine across Canada. Other than extreme hardiness and the ability to survive adversity, it has little to recommend itself as an urban ornamental conifer, with the possible exception of epitomizing a Charlie Brown Christmas tree. They have an open, irregular form; a height of 20 m (65 ft.) and a spread of 7 m (23 ft.); dark brown, furrowed, irregular bark; and short, dull green needles in bundles of two. Poorly adapted to lime soils, they are better left growing at the lake.

❧ *Pinus contorta* var. *latifolia* (*pie*-nus con-*tor*-tah la-ti-*foe*-lee-ah), lodgepole pine, is native to the Cypress Hills region of Saskatchewan and Alberta. As the common name suggests, its long straight trunks were once used by Native peoples to build lodges. It has a narrow form with a height of 18 m (60 ft.) and a width of 6 m (20 ft.). The twisted needles are in bundles

of two. Lodgepole pine does well on light soils and is drought tolerant once established.

❧ *Pinus ponderosa* var. *scopulorum* (*pie*-nus pon-deh-*row*-sah scop-yew-*lor*-um), ponderosa pine, is native to the Black Hills of South Dakota, eastern Wyoming, and the eastern foothills of the Rocky Mountains. At 20 m (65 ft.) in height, with a spread of 6 m (20 ft.), it is smaller and hardier than the species *(P. ponderosa)* and better adapted to the prairies. Broadly pyramidal in form, its bark is dark gray, nearly black, and its sharp needles are in bundles of three. Obtain trees from seed collected from its northernmost range.

❧ *Pinus pumila* (*pie*-nus pooh-*mil*-lah), Japanese stone pine or dwarf Siberian pine, needs further hardiness testing on the prairies. It is similar and closely related to Swiss stone pine, with needles in bundles of five. Smaller in all its parts and very slow growing, it has a prostrate form, with short, upsweeping branches, making it ideal for a rockery or mixed border. It reaches a height of 45 to 60 cm (18 to 24 in.), with a 90- to 120-cm (36- to 48-in.) spread, but is variable if not grafted.

❧ *Pinus strobus* (*pie*-nus *strow*-bus), white pine, is probably the softest and most sensuous pine available to prairie gardeners, but be aware of provenance. Plants grown from

Pine Needle Scale: Weighing the Damage

If you notice waxy, oval, white specks about 3-mm (.13-in.) long (called "scales") on the needles of your pine or spruce, the chances are good that immature insects lurk beneath. What you're looking at is a cozy nursery with a ready food supply—the needles—beneath a protective covering.

About mid-June, the newly hatched nymphs or crawlers, armed with a voracious appetite, begin to leave the safety of the scale, seeking their fortune in the wider world. At this stage they are very tiny, oval, and red, but like any infant, they have the ability to sit still and suck—conifer needles. If infestations are severe, their damage is more apparent than they are— yellow to gray needles, often stunted and reduced in size.

By August, the young scale insects have matured to adults. After mating, as is the fate of many insects, the males die. The females secrete a waxy white scale, lay thirty to fifty eggs beneath it, and also die, their own bodies adding to the protective covering of their young. The eggs overwinter under the scale, hatching the following spring. There is only one generation per year. Scale insects also attack cedar; those on cedars are a bronzy brown.

Although the symptoms of their infestations are very visible, scale insects seldom do much damage. Natural predators include ladybird beetles and tiny parasitic wasps. High temperatures or heavy rain also reduce populations during the crawler stage, as will a strong stream of cold water from a garden hose.

seed originating in the most northern and western portion of its natural range are more likely to be hardy on the prairies than those from farther east or south. A white pine that came as a seedling from a ditch west of Thunder Bay has grown and prospered in a garden near Saskatoon, whereas two earlier attempts with white pines of unknown seed origin failed.

White pines are graceful, pyramidal trees, 15 m (50 ft.) in height, with a spread of 7 m (23 ft.). Their thin, gray bark becomes brown and furrowed with age. The long, soft, pliable, blue-green needles are in bundles of five and are generally retained for two years. Needles fall to leave smooth, clean-looking branches. The attractive lilac purple, curved cones are long and cylindrical. Fast growing, especially when young, white pines live for well over one hundred years. Place them where they are sheltered from wind and where they can be touched, so their softness can be appreciated. They prefer fertile, moist, well-drained

Needle Browning: Fall Fall-Out Is Fine

Most evergreen leaves, scale-like or needle-like, have a lifespan of two to four years, then turn yellow, then brown, and fall. These are the oldest leaves on the plant, closest to the trunk, and generally hidden by younger foliage on the outer portion of branches. Generally, the "fall" occurs gradually through the course of autumn, so we seldom notice it.

Occasionally, due to heat or drought stress, needles seem to fall overnight, and we notice a pile of brown needles at the base of the tree or shrub. While it's natural for these to fall, to do so within a few days should sound an alarm bell: water the soil below the plant slowly and thoroughly so the water percolates to a depth of 60 cm (24 in.). Other causes of needle drop may be:

* Frost: If a hard frost occurs just as the soft new spring growth of spruce or pine is elongating, it may freeze, droop, and turn brown. Only the new growth will be effected. Wait until next year.
* Herbicides: If evergreens come into contact with 2, 4-D, new growth may appear twisted and distorted. The tree itself usually recovers, so be patient. Soil sterilants and pre-emergent herbicides can also cause damage from which plants may or may not recover.
* Drought: Trees that are drought stressed usually show yellowing and browning from the top down and the outside inward—the last parts to receive water through the plant's plumbing system. Water deeply and thoroughly.
* Winter: Damage can be caused by low temperatures or drying (desiccation of tissue) or both, and shows up as brown foliage in the spring. Water deeply in late fall. Only apply fertilizer in the spring. Summer or fall applications may delay hardening off. Select hardy cultivars. Place burlap screens 1 to 2 m (3 to 6.5 ft.) in height about 30 cm (12 inches) away from cedars on their west and south sides. These will shade the plants from reflected light and reduce wind desiccation. Do not wrap evergreens with burlap or plastic or other materials as this increases temperatures leading to further drying out and may cause them to break dormancy prematurely in the spring.
* The big male dog next door: Junipers and cedars are particularly vulnerable to urine damage from dogs marking out their territory. Try repellents that can be tied or sprayed on the foliage.
* Salt: Evergreens planted near roadways that are salted during the

winter are subject to damage when the salty slush is sprayed onto their foliage. The salt acts as a desiccant and the needles brown and fall. Plant evergreens beyond the reach of salt splash or place a temporary screen between the road and the evergreens. Saline soils can also cause browning, generally leaving the foliage with a reddish purple tinge. Do not plant evergreens on saline soil. Junipers are more salt tolerant than many other evergreens, but even they are not happy campers in this situation.

* Insects: Severe infestations of insects that feed on needles cause browning. Before applying an insecticide, see who's home. Use a magnifying glass or hand lens to ensure that the cause is an insect. Get positive identification and control measures from a local extension expert. Often a strong spray of cold water from a garden hose reduces the insect population considerably.

soil in full sun or partial shade. Neither white pine blister rust nor weevils has been a problem on the prairies, where these pines are relatively uncommon.

Populus
pop-yew-lus
Poplar

Populus is the classical Latin name that arose from the ancient Roman practice of using these trees in public squares frequented by the *populus*, "people." Poplars are valuable shelter trees in parks, greenbelts, farm shelterbelts, and very large suburban lots. However, most of them are too large, and their root systems are too aggressive, for urban landscapes.

Pioneer Poplars

Poplars are a large group of fast-growing trees. Our native poplars are "pioneer" species. They grow in the transition zone between forest and grassland, where they "invade" grasslands by sending up sucker shoots from established roots, thus shading the grass and providing conditions that are favorable for other forest species. In the wild, clones of aspen are among the largest living organisms, with single clones covering many acres.

Although this suckering ability is important to the natural regeneration of forests, it can be troubling in the landscape. Some of the cottonwoods and hybrids, however, have much-reduced

129

suckering tendencies. Poplars are more prone to sucker when their extensive root systems are disturbed through cultivation. Mulched poplars generally sucker a lot less. The extent of suckering is also dependent on species and variety.

The male and female flowers are on separate trees, and female trees produce large amounts of fluffy seeds, which can be objectionable in the landscape. Most poplars offered in nurseries are male clones, so fluff is not a problem.

How to Grow

Poplars are easy to transplant bare root in the spring or from containers throughout the growing season. Small, bare-root trees are used for shelterbelt plantings. Poplars grow most vigorously in moist, well-drained, fertile soils, but are very adaptable and tolerate dry soil, saline conditions, and a wide pH range. Poplar species and cultivars vary widely in their susceptibility to diseases, and it is important to plant those that thrive in your area.

Populus alba

pop-yew-lus *al*-bah

White poplar, silver-leafed poplar

The silver-leafed poplar is a large, round-headed tree. The bark is whitish to grayish green, with large,

dark blotches, and breaks into dark gray ridges as it becomes older. The leaves are dark green on top, with dense, white, hairy undersides—*alba* means "white"—and are distinctly lobed, with three or five lobes. Although the foliage is very attractive, this tree should be avoided, except in open spaces where their suckering habit and aggressive roots will not create problems. The cultivar 'Nivea' has prominently lobed leaves that resemble those of maple, with white undersides and white young twigs, and it is

---

🍁

PLANT AT A GLANCE

TYPE: large deciduous tree
HEIGHT AND SPREAD: 12 to 20 m (40 to 65 ft.)
LIGHT: full sun
SOIL: moist, deep loam, but adaptable
DISTINGUISHING FEATURES: dark green leaves, with white undersides
LANDSCAPE USE: screening or shelter in large areas; shade

---

sometimes incorrectly referred to as "silver maple." Maple leaves are opposite on the stem; poplar leaves are alternately arranged. This poplar has a bad habit of suckering, especially as the main stems mature and die out.

Populus hybrids

Poplar hybrids

Hybrids of eastern cottonwood and plains cottonwood are frequently planted as shelter trees and occasionally as street trees. These hybrids are very fast-growing trees and provide quick shelter for farmyards and in large, open spaces. Their form varies from upright to spreading and round headed. The bark on young twigs is either green or yellowish, becoming light grayish green to light gray with age. The leaves are shiny and medium green.

CULTIVARS

* *Populus* x *jackii* 'Northwest' (*pop*-yew-lus *jack*-ee-eye) is a large, open-headed tree, up to 15 m (50 ft.) tall and 12 m (40 ft.) wide, with large, horizontal branches. It is resistant to rust but quite susceptible to canker.
* 'Assiniboine' is broadly pyramidal form, similar to 'Northwest,' but more disease resistant. It grows to 15 m (50 ft.) tall and 4 m (13 ft.) wide.
* 'Katepwa,' selected at the AAFC-PFRA Shelterbelt Centre at Indian

Head, Saskatchewan, in 1986, is extremely hardy, vigorous, and fast growing. It has a semi-upright crown and a height of 18 m (60 ft.) at twenty-three years of age. It has a spread of 5 to 6 m (16 to 20 ft.). Resistant to poplar gall mite and common poplar diseases, it is a male (fluffless) clone, which is well adapted to shelterbelt, riverbank, and forestry-woodlot plantings.
* 'Prairie Sky' is a narrow, upright form, 15 m (50 ft.) tall and spreading to only 2 m (6.5 ft.). It is highly disease resistant.

Populus tremula 'Erecta'
pop-yew-lus *trem*-yew-lah
Swedish columnar aspen

Swedish columnar aspen was discovered in the wild in Sweden in the 1920s. A highly ornamental, columnar form (thus, the cultivar name 'Erecta') of the European aspen, it has proven to be well adapted to our prairie climate. 'Erecta' was once thought difficult to propagate, but improved methods have been developed and it is now widely available.

The gray-green bark has a white bloom, and the branches are narrowly upright. Its alternate leaves are dark green and round, with an undulating margin. Flattened petioles allow the leaves to tremble in even the slightest breeze. Swedish columnar aspen is a male clone, so has no "fluff."

OTHER SPECIES AND HYBRIDS

❦ *Populus* x *canescens* 'Tower' (*pop*-yew-lus kah-*nes*-entz) is a hybrid between *P. tremula* 'Erecta' and *P. alba*. It is 15 m (50 ft.) in height, with a 1.5 m (5 ft.) spread, and is very upright in form, though not as dense as the Swedish columnar aspen. Its leaves are silvery green on the underside, with numerous fine hairs.

❦ *Populus deltoides* (*pop*-yew-lus del-*toy*-deez), eastern cottonwood, and *P. sargentii* (sar-*gen*-tee-eye), plains cottonwood, are large, round-headed trees, with few, but large, branches. The bark is yellowish on young twigs, but later turns light gray and breaks into deep, vertical ridges. The leaves are shiny, triangular in shape, and have flattened petioles, which allow the leaves to flutter in the slightest breeze. Cottonwoods are handsome trees, but are best left growing in the wild. They are too open to be effective as a shelter tree; female trees produce objectionable fluff, and their wood is weak and subject to breakage. Their hybrid

progeny (see *Poplar* hybrids) are superior trees in the landscape.

❦ *Populus grandidentata* (*pop*-yew-lus gran-di-den-*tah*-tah), bigtooth aspen, is similar to trembling aspen, but its larger leaves are more distinctly toothed. It is not as drought tolerant as trembling aspen. The cultivar 'Sabre' is a seedless selection, which has a balanced and open branch structure.

❦ *Populus tremuloides* (*pop*-yew-lus trem-yew-*loy*-deez), trembling aspen, is the most common tree of the parkland and boreal forest regions. They generally have upright trunks, with round, open, oval heads. If you value an aspen bluff in the landscape, you should protect it. They do not tolerate soil compaction over their roots, so restrict activity beneath them and protect understory shrubs.

Potentilla fruticosa
poh-ten-*till*-uh
froo-ti-*koe*-sah

Potentilla, shrubby cinquefoil

The genus name is from the Latin word *potens*, "powerful," which refers to the value once placed on its medicinal properties. The genus *Potentilla* is composed of about five hundred species of annuals, perennials, herbs, and shrubs, most of them found in the temperate, boreal, and arctic regions. Potentilla is a member of the rose family; the flowers have five petals and small, compound leaves. After an initial flush, it blooms over a long period.

Most garden shrub cultivars are now listed under *Potentilla fruticosa*. Native to the prairies, it is also circumpolar. *Fruticosa* is from the Latin *frutex*, meaning "shrubby." This small shrub has a fibrous root system and rough, peeling, dark brown bark, once used as tinder. The alternate leaves are pinnately compound, with three to seven leaflets, although they generally have five, as the common name cinquefoil, from the French *cinq*, "five," and *foil*, "leaf," suggests. The small leaflets are gray-green, narrow, and covered with fine hairs.

Circumpolar in the northern hemisphere, the species itself is highly variable and seldom commercially available. It usually has yellow or occasionally white flowers, but those of the cultivars range from white through yellow to orange and pink. They bloom intermittently in small, dense clusters throughout the summer.

HOW TO GROW

Older cultivars, with single, white or yellow flowers, seem able to handle a tougher situation in open areas in poor soil with little moisture. These cultivars do well in full sun, while those with pink or orange flowers fare better with even moisture in partial shade, where their flowers are less likely to fade.

All potentillas adapt to a variety of soils, as long as they are well drained. Keep potentillas evenly moist until they're well established, at which point many of the older, yellow-flowered cultivars are quite drought tolerant.

Most potentillas, once mature, require annual thinning of the old wood, or rejuvenation, every four to five years, through hard pruning to ground level. Spider mites can be a problem, but are seldom serious. Hose the plants down with cold water during hot weather.

CULTIVARS

❧ 'Abbotswood' is a dwarf cultivar, 0.6 to 1 m (2 to 3 ft.) in height, with a dense, spreading form to 1 m (3 ft.), dark blue-green foliage, and a profusion of large, pure white flowers, with prominent yellow stamens all summer.

133

- 'Coronation Triumph' (John Walker, University of Manitoba) honors the coronation of Queen Elizabeth. Upright, dense, and mounded, with a height of 1 to 1.2 m (3 to 4 ft.) and a 1-m (3-ft.) spread, it has soft gray-green foliage and a profusion of large, bright yellow flowers over a long period.
- 'Goldfinger' (Holland, 1970), forms a dense and compact but upright plant with a height and spread of 1 m (3 ft.). It has dark green foliage and blooms profusely with large and showy, golden yellow flowers over a long period of time.
- 'Katherine Dykes' is an old reliable cultivar, 1 m (3 ft.) in height, with a 1.2 m (4 ft.) spread. It has large, soft yellow flowers, silver gray-green foliage, and spreading, arching stems.
- Mango Tango® ('Uman') (Louis Lenz, University of Manitoba) forms a tidy, compact plant, 0.6 to 0.8 m (2 to 2.5 ft.) in height, with a 0.8- to 1-m (2.5- to 3-ft.) spread. It has dark green foliage and bicolored, red-orange, and deep yellow flowers.
- 'McKay's White,' a sport of 'Katherine Dykes,' is low and mounding, with a height and spread of 0.8 m (2.5 ft.), soft gray-green foliage, creamy white flowers, and no seed heads.
- 'Orange Whisper' (Louis Lenz, University of Manitoba) is mounded and compact, with a height and spread of 1 m (3 ft.), soft apricot peachy yellow flowers, and light green foliage.
- 'Pink Beauty' (Louis Lenz, University of Manitoba, 1995) has a low, mounded form, with a height and spread of 1 m (3 ft.), bright dark green foliage, and free-flowering, semi-double to double, deep pink flowers.
- 'Primrose Beauty' has a profusion of soft yellow, cup-shaped flowers on a dwarf, dense plant of 1 m (3 ft.), in both height and spread, with silver-gray foliage.
- 'Snowbird' (Louis Lenz, University of Manitoba) is a vigorous, upright, compact cultivar of 0.8 m (2.5 ft.), with a spread of 0.5 to 0.8 m (1.5 to 2.5 ft.). It has glossy, dark green foliage and a profusion of semi-double to double, white flowers.
- 'Yellow Gem' (University of British Columbia) is a spreading potentilla, only 0.5 m (1.5 ft.) in height, with a spread of 1 m (3 ft.), bright yellow, ruffled flowers, and gray-green foliage.

Prinsepia sinensis
prin-*sep*-ee-ah sin-*nen*-sis

Cherry prinsepia

Prinsepia, a small genus of shrubs closely related to *Prunus*, is native to northern and western China. The genus name commemorates James Prinsep (1799–1840), a secretary of the Asiatic Society of Bengal.

Microbiota decussata (Russian cypress, Siberian cypress), page 114
SARA WILLIAMS

Paxistima canbyi (paxistima, cliff green), page 115
SARA WILLIAMS

Physocarpus opulifolius Diabolo®
(common ninebark), page 118

Picea abies 'Ohlendorfii' (Norway spruce),
page 120

Picea pungens 'Glauca Pendula'
(Colorado spruce), page 121

Picea pungens 'Iseli Fastigiate'
(Colorado spruce), page 121

Pinus cembra (Swiss stone pine), page 122
BRIAN BALDWIN

Pinus flexilis (limber pine), page 123
SARA WILLIAMS

Pinus mugo 'Slowmound' (mugo pine), page 124
SARA WILLIAMS

Pinus sylvestris (Scots pine), page 125
BRIAN BALDWIN

Pinus sylvestris bark (Scots pine) page 125
SARA WILLIAMS

Populus 'Tower' (poplar hybrid),
page 132
JEFFRIES NURSERIES LTD.

Populus tremula 'Erecta' (Swedish
columnar aspen), page 131
BARBARA KAM

Potentilla fruticosa 'Pink Beauty'
(potentilla, shrubby cinquefoil), page 134
JEFFRIES NURSERIES LTD.

Potentilla fruticosa 'Yellow Gem'
(potentilla, shrubby cinquefoil), page 134
SARA WILLIAMS

Prinsepia sinensis (cherry prinsepia), page 134
BRIAN BALDWIN

Prunus x *cistena* (purple-leafed
sandcherry, cistena cherry), page 152
LIESBETH LEATHERBARROW

Prunus maackii (Amur cherry),
page 152
SARA WILLIAMS

Prunus pensylvanica (pincherry),
page 154
JOHN DAVIDSON

Prunus tomentosa (Nanking cherry)
page 155
LESLEY REYNOLDS

Prunus triloba var. *multiplex*
(double-flowering plum, double-
flowering almond), page 156
BRIAN BALDWIN

Prunus virginiana 'Schubert'
(chokecherry), page 158
BRIAN BALDWIN

Pyrus ussuriensis (Ussurian pear,
Manchurian pear), page 158
SARA WILLIAMS

Quercus macrocarpa (bur oak),
page 160
LIESBETH LEATHERBARROW

Ribes alpinum (alpine currant), page 162
BRIAN BALDWIN

Rosa Explorer Series 'George Vancouver'
(hardy shrub rose), page 166
HUGH SKINNER

Rosa Explorer Series 'William Baffin'
(hardy shrub rose) page 166
LESLEY REYNOLDS

Rosa 'Hazeldean' (hardy shrub rose),
page 169
SARA WILLIAMS

Rosa Parkland Series 'Morden Blush'
(hardy shrub rose), page 167
LESLEY REYNOLDS

Rosa Parkland Series 'Prairie Joy'
(hardy shrub rose), page 167
HUGH SKINNER

Rosa Parkland Series 'Winnipeg Parks'
(hardy shrub rose), page 168
LESLEY REYNOLDS

Salix exigua (coyote willow), page 172
SARA WILLIAMS

Sambucus racemosa 'Dropmore Fernleaf' (European red elder), page 174
SARA WILLIAMS

Sorbaria sorbifolia 'Aurora'
(Ural false spirea), page 175
SARA WILLIAMS

Sorbus decora (showy mountain ash), page 177
SARA WILLIAMS

Sorbus aucuparia (European mountain ash, rowan), page 177
SARA WILLIAMS

Spiraea x *bumalda* 'Goldflame' (dwarf bumalda spirea), page 179
SARA WILLIAMS

Syringa meyeri 'Palibin' (dwarf Korean lilac, Meyer lilac, littleleaf lilac), page 183
SARA WILLIAMS

Syringa reticulata (Japanese tree lilac),
page 184
SARA WILLIAMS

Syringa x *prestoniae* 'Miss Canada'
(late lilac), page 185
SARA WILLIAMS

Syringa vulgaris 'Charles Joly' (common
lilac), page 186
AGRICULTURE AND AGRI-FOOD CANADA,
MORDEN RESEARCH STATION

Syringa x *hyacinthaflora* 'Maiden's Blush'
(early flowering lilac, American hybrid
lilac, hyacinth flowering lilac), page 187
AGRICULTURE AND AGRI-FOOD CANADA,
MORDEN RESEARCH STATION

Syringa x *hyacinthaflora* 'Sister Justina' (early flowering lilac, American hybrid lilac, hyacinth flowering lilac), page 187
Sara Williams

Thuja occidentalis 'Smaragd' (cedar, eastern white cedar), page 190
Brian Baldwin

Thuja occidentalis 'Little Giant' (cedar, eastern white cedar), page 190

Tilia cordata (linden, basswood),
page 192

Viburnum lantana (wayfaring tree),
page 194

Viburnum lantana (wayfaring tree), page 194
SARA WILLIAMS

Viburnum lentago (nannyberry),
page 195
LIESBETH LEATHERBARROW

Viburnum trilobum (American highbush
cranberry), page 196
SARA WILLIAMS

Prinsepia has a typical "haystack" form, with stiff, arching branches. The bark is yellowish, becoming gray and exfoliating in strips on older stems. The lance-like, bright green leaves are alternate on new growth and clustered on older stems. It has sharp spines at the base of each leaf, which make it ideal for barrier plantings.

Prinsepia is among the first shrubs to leaf out in spring. The round, yellow flowers are borne in clusters of one to four on the previous year's wood. They're followed by very sour, red, juicy fruit, about 1.5 cm (0.5 in.) in diameter, which are used for making jelly in their native range, which, as *sinensis* suggests, is China.

How to Grow

Prinsepia is very drought tolerant and should be planted on well-drained soil. It is tough once established and

adapts well to full sun or partial shade, competition from other plants, and pruning.

Prunus

proo-nus

Cherry, plum, almond

Flowering plums, cherries, and almonds are among the showiest of prairie shrubs and small trees. Some are prized for their early spring blooms, others for their attractive purple foliage, and many for their smooth and glossy bark. *Prunus* is the classical Latin name for a plum tree.

Their leaves are opposite, entire, and, usually, oblong to lance-like. Prairie-hardy species are deciduous. The white or pink flowers open early in the spring and have five petals, except for double-flowered forms. The flowers are borne singly (almonds and plums), in clusters or corymbs (cherries), or in racemes (chokecherries and mayday trees). The fruit of all *Prunus* are single-seeded drupes (stone fruit).

The leaves and seeds of cherries and plums contain prussic acid, which reacts with digestive enzymes to release cyanide, a poison that can be deadly if eaten in large enough quantities.

How to Grow

Flowering plums and cherries grow best in sunny sites in well-drained soil of average fertility, which is high in organic matter. Some, such as chokecherries, pincherries, sandcherries, and Russian almond, are among the most drought tolerant of all plants. *Prunus* species can be transplanted bare root, balled and burlapped, or container grown in the spring. Plants should be pruned after blooming in the spring. Keeping trees vigorous through proper care—watering, fertilizing, and pruning—minimizes the impact of several serious diseases and insects.

Prunus x *cistena*

proo-nus sis-*tee*-nah

Purple-leafed sandcherry, cistena cherry

One of the most attractive purple-leafed shrubs, purple-leafed sandcherry has an upright form and dark purple to black bark. The leaves emerge red and darken to deep purple. Smooth and shiny, they are

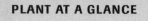

PLANT AT A GLANCE

TYPE: small to medium, flowering, deciduous shrub
HEIGHT AND SPREAD: 1.5 to 3 m (5 to 10 ft.) in milder climates
LIGHT: full sun
SOIL: well drained
DISTINGUISHING FEATURES: attractive purple foliage
LANDSCAPE USE: accent; mixed border
PHOTO: page 140

oval in shape, with a sharp point and toothed margin. The light pink to white flowers are attractive in combination with the purple leaves. The fruit are dark purple but rarely appear.

Purple-leafed sandcherry dies back to snow level on the prairies, but with spring pruning of deadwood, it quickly grows back to good form.

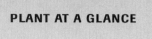

PLANT AT A GLANCE

TYPE: small, flowering, deciduous tree
HEIGHT/SPREAD: 8 to 12 m (26 to 40 ft.)/5 to 8 m (16 to 26 ft.)
LIGHT: full sun
SOIL: well drained
DISTINGUISHING FEATURES: white flowers; bronze, exfoliating bark
LANDSCAPE USE: small specimen
PHOTO: page 152

Prunus maackii

proo-nus *mack*-ee-eye

Amur cherry

Amur cherry is native to northern China, Korea, and Siberia, in the region of the Amur River, and was introduced to Britain from St. Petersburg in 1910. The species was named in honor of Richard Maack (1825–86), a Russian naturalist.

It is an upright, oval tree, which becomes more rounded with age. The trunk generally branches low into several large, upright branches, with extremely attractive smooth golden to bronze, exfoliating bark. The oval leaves are medium green and about half as wide as they are long. Racemes of creamy white flowers are produced in abundance after the tree has leafed out in spring. The small, black cherries are too astringent to eat, but are attractive to birds. They contain a dark purple dye, which will stain furniture below them.

The trunk of the Amur cherry is susceptible to sunscald and frost cracking during rapid drops in winter temperatures, and to shoestring fungus (affecting the root system and causing above-ground dieback accompanied by clusters of mushrooms at the base of the tree), so it should not be pruned, except to remove dead branches. These problems often combine to limit its lifespan to fifteen years. Despite this drawback, Amur cherry grows quickly and can be quite worthwhile in the landscape.

Prunus nigra

proo-nus ny-*grah*
Canada plum

Canada plum, a small, low-headed tree, with upright branches, is native into the southeastern corner of Manitoba and is hardy if grown from northern seed source. The smooth, shiny, reddish brown to grayish brown bark breaks into vertical strips and becomes dark gray to near black with age, hence the name *nigra*, and the branches are usually armed with thorns. The dull, medium green leaves are elliptical, with a sharp point.

Showy flowers are produced in clusters of three or four on lateral spurs. Although bloom time varies among seed-grown plants, they are among the earliest of spring flowers and are very attractive. The petals open white and often fade to pink. The fruit are red to yellowish red, about 3 cm (1.25 in.) long, with thick skin and sour, edible flesh.

CULTIVARS

* 'Muckle' plum (*Prunus* x *nigrella* 'Muckle'), a hybrid between Canada plum and Russian almond, is a spectacular pink-blooming, small tree.
* 'Princess Kay' is a white, double-flowered cultivar found in the wild in northern Minnesota. It was introduced by the University of Minnesota Landscape Arboretum.

OTHER SPECIES AND HYBRIDS

* *Prunus padus* (*proo*-nus *pah*-dus), mayday tree or European bird cherry, is a small, flowering, deciduous tree, 6 to 12 m (20 to 40 ft.) in height, with a spread of 5 to 12 m (16 to 40 ft.). It grows best in full sun in well-drained soil. *Padus* is the Greek name for a wild cherry. The common name,

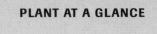

PLANT AT A GLANCE

TYPE: small, flowering, deciduous tree
HEIGHT AND SPREAD: 3 to 5 m (10 to 16 ft.)
LIGHT: full sun to partial shade
SOIL: well drained
DISTINGUISHING FEATURES: white flowers in spring
LANDSCAPE USE: small specimen tree in border

Chokecherries, Maydays, and Black Knot

Black knot is caused by the fungus *Dibotryon morbosum*. The rough, black galls that form on the branches have a striking resemblance to cow pies wrapped carefully around a branch. Once they encircle a branch, it dies. Although other *Prunus* species can be infected, it is most common on chokecherry and mayday trees. Cultivars vary in their susceptibility to black knot. The most effective control is to prune out infected branches, but it is difficult to keep black knot under control where it is rampant in nearby wild chokecherry stands.

mayday, comes from the pagan Roman holiday that celebrated the onset of spring and coincides in Europe with the flowering of *Prunus padus*. Among the earliest trees to leaf out in the spring, the mayday tree is a fast-growing and rather open-headed tree when young; later, it becomes denser and more rounded. The trunk divides into a number of large, upright branches. The bark is dull silvery gray, and the dark green leaves are oval and quite rough. Many cultivars have purple foliage. The showy white or pink flowers are produced in racemes, from 8 to 15 cm (3 to 6 in.) long, followed by small, black berries similar to those of the chokecherry, but its seeds are ridged while those of choke-cherry are smooth. Unfortunately, it has serious problems, chiefly its susceptibility to black knot disease, which limit its usefulness.

♣ 'Colorata' is a pink-flowered cultivar introduced from Sweden. The leaves emerge bronze purple and then turn purplish green above and dark purple underneath. It is marginally hardy in colder parts of the prairies.

♣ 'Dropmore' is a cultivar selected for its large, white flowers.

Prunus pensylvanica

proo-nus pen-sil-*vah*-ni-kah

Pincherry

Pensylvanica refers to part of its natural range, and pincherry refers to the fruit, which have elongated stems and are said to look like pins in a pincushion.

Pincherry develops into a low, round-headed tree, with a central trunk. The bark is a shiny, reddish brown, with prominent horizontal lenticel markings. The shiny, green leaves are narrowly oval, with a long pointed tip, and turn brilliant orange in fall. The leaf edges have numerous small, uneven teeth. The flowers, which are produced in clusters of five to seven, give rise to small, red, intensely sour but edible cherries.

CULTIVARS

♣ 'Jumping Pound' is a small, weeping form with excellent ornamental

Prunus tenella

proo-nus teh-*nel*-ah

Russian almond

Russian almond is striking during its short blooming period. An upright, suckering shrub, with branched, gray stems, it develops a globular to spreading form. The shiny, dark green leaves are oblong, with toothed edges, and turn scarlet or yellow in fall. *Tenella* means "dainty" or "delicate" and may refer to the delicate twigs or numerous pink flowers that are produced on old wood before the leaves emerge.

PLANT AT A GLANCE

TYPE: low, flowering, deciduous shrub
HEIGHT/SPREAD: 1 m (3 ft.)/suckers to fill space available
LIGHT: full sun to partial shade
SOIL: well drained
DISTINGUISHING FEATURES: pink flowers in spring
LANDSCAPE USE: mass planting in borders where its suckering habit is not objectionable

---

Prunus tomentosa

proo-nus toe-men-*toe*-sah

Nanking cherry

Nanking cherry is native to northern and western China. Its pale pink early spring bloom is very pretty, and it makes an attractive hedge in well-drained soil.

PLANT AT A GLANCE

TYPE: small, flowering, deciduous tree
HEIGHT AND SPREAD: 3 to 5 m (10 to 16 ft.)
LIGHT: full sun
SOIL: well drained
DISTINGUISHING FEATURES: white flowers in early spring; orange fall foliage
LANDSCAPE USE: small specimen; feature in border
PHOTO: page 140

and fruiting qualities, 2.5 to 3 m (8 to 10 ft.) in height and spread. It was found in the Jumping Pound district in the Alberta foothills in 1936, is well suited to smaller gardens and should be more widely available that it is.

🍁 'Lee #4,' introduced by Mr. Lee of Camp Creek, Alberta, in the early 1990s, produces large fruit on long racemes, generally on the outside of a compact bush, with a height and spread of 1.5 to 1.8 m (5 to 6 ft.), for easier picking.

🍁 'Mary Liss' was selected from the wild by John Liss of Sangudo, Alberta, in 1937. It produces large, mild fruit, with thin, tender skin and a pleasant flavor suitable for processing. The tree is non-suckering and upright and has a single, sturdy trunk and a height and spread of 2.5 to 3 m (8 to 10 ft.).

It develops from numerous upright stems, which spread with age. The stems have brown bark that exfoliates in strips. The dull, dark green leaves are oblong and distinctly hairy on both surfaces—*tomentosa* means "densely woolly." Yellow-orange autumn foliage color is only produced where plants are grown in dry conditions and mature early. The white flowers, opening from pink buds, arise singly or in pairs on the previous year's growth and are very showy for a short period in early spring, followed in summer by sweet, edible, round cherries held on short stalks. Normally bright red, there are forms with white or dark red fruit.

Prunus triloba var. *multiplex*

proo-nus try-*low*-bah *mul*-tee-pleks

Double-flowering plum, double-flowering almond

The double-flowering plum is a large, spreading shrub. *Triloba*, "three-lobed," describes the leaves, which are medium green, pubescent, three lobed at the tip, and doubly toothed. *Multiplex*, "much-folded," refers to the double, pale pink flowers, which are produced in clusters along the stems just as the leaves emerge. It is striking in bloom, but flower buds may be lost to extreme winter cold. The double-flowering form from Chinese gardens was described by western scientists before the single-flowered wild form. Hardier, single-flowered forms have been used to develop double-flowered cultivars that have better flower-bud hardiness, but they aren't widely distributed.

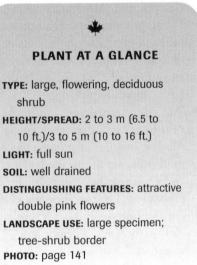

Prunus virginiana

proo-nus vir-gin-nee-*an*-nah

Chokecherry

Virginiana, "of Virginia," may refer to where it was first described. Widely distributed across North America, it was introduced to England in 1724. The purple-leafed forms are derived from a plant found in the wild and introduced as 'Schubert' chokecherry by the Oscar H. Will Co. nursery of Bismarck, North Dakota.

Chokecherry grows naturally as a large, upright, suckering shrub, but it is often trained as a small, round-headed tree. The bark is a smooth, grayish brown, later becoming dark gray. The species has shiny, dark green foliage, but most commercially available cultivars are purple-leafed forms. Their leaves emerge green and turn dark purple by early summer, except for those on new mid-summer growth. The flowers, which bloom after the leaves emerge, are creamy white and tightly packed in racemes that are 8 to 15 cm (3 to 6 in.) long. The small, dark purple cherries are astringent but edible.

Many cultivars are strongly suckering. This can be controlled by budding them onto non-suckering rootstocks, such as *Prunus padus*.

Chokecherries are susceptible to black knot disease, which should be controlled by pruning.

CULTIVARS

* 'Bailey's Select Schubert' choke-cherry is an oval to rounded form with vigorous growth, 6 m (20 ft.) in height, with a spread of 4 m (14 ft.).
* 'Boughen's Yellow,' introduced by W. J. Boughen of Valley River, Manitoba, has attractive yellow fruit, with little astringency and good ornamental value. It is 3.6 m (12 ft.) in height, with a 3-m (10-ft.) spread.
* 'Garrington,' introduced by Len Pearson of Bowden, Alberta, consistently produces high yields of large, tart, black fruit of good processing quality. It has a height and spread of 3 to 4 m (10 to 13 ft.).
* 'Lee Red,' introduced by Lloyd Lee of Barrhead, Alberta, has large, tasty, red fruit (good for wine), along with attractive rose to burgundy foliage. It is 3 to 3.6 m (10 to 12 ft.) in height, with a 3-m (10-ft.) spread.
* 'Midnight Schubert' chokecherry is a non-suckering selection from Lakeshore Tree Farms in Saskatoon. It has a broad head and

---

PLANT AT A GLANCE

TYPE: large, flowering, deciduous shrub or small tree

HEIGHT AND SPREAD: 3 to 8 m (10 to 26 ft.)

LIGHT: full sun to partial shade

SOIL: well drained

DISTINGUISHING FEATURES: dark purple foliage; white flowers

LANDSCAPE USE: small specimen tree; screening; shelter

PHOTO: page 141

very dark purple foliage, reaching 8 to 10 m (26 to 33 ft.) in height with a spread of 6 to 8 m (20 to 26 ft.).

* 'Mini Schubert' chokecherry is a very dense, small tree or shrub. It could be attractive as a top-grafted tree.

* 'Pickup's Pride' was obtained from a native bluff on the farm of John and Myrna Pickup at Broadview, Saskatchewan, and introduced by AAFC-PFRA Shelterbelt Centre in Indian Head, Saskatchewan. It was selected for its high yields of large fruit, which have superior processing quality. Plants are 4 to 5 m (13 to 16 ft.) high and wide.

* 'Robert,' also introduced by Lloyd Lee and of similar size to 'Lee Red,' has large racemes of grape-sized fruit, with foliage similar to the 'Schubert' chokecherry.

* 'Schubert' chokecherry is a small (4.5 m/15 ft. height and spread), upright, oval tree. The new leaves emerge green and turn purple as they mature. White flowers are produced in racemes after the leaves come out.

On the Edge

* *Pseudotsuga menziesii* var. *glauca* (soo-doh-soo-*gah men*-zee-eye *glaw*-kah), Rocky Mountain Douglas fir, is native to the western edge of the prairie region, with its easternmost native stand within the city of Calgary, Alberta. Trees from selected seed sources are worthy of trial on well-drained, wind-protected sites, with adequate moisture.

It is a large, pyramidal conifer, with ascending upper branches and drooping lower branches. The bark is smooth, with numerous resin blisters on young trees and with deep, brown, vertical fissures developing with age. The drooping cones are distinctive, with prominent three-pronged bracts extending beyond each cone scale.

Pyrus ussuriensis
pie-rus oo-sir-ree-*en*-sis

Ussurian pear, Manchurian pear

Twenty species of pear are native to the temperate regions of Europe and Asia and are all a member of the rose family. The flowers, each with five petals, bloom before the leaves emerge. Although the nectar in pear blossoms has a relatively low sugar content, because they flower so early, when little other food is available, they still attract bees, ensuring that pollination will occur. The flowers, along with their form and fall coloration, lend them three-season ornamental value.

Pyrus is the classical Latin name for this tree; *ussuriensis* denotes the Ussuri River, which forms the border between Russia and China and then joins the Amur River (of Amur maple fame). Native to northern China, Korea, eastern Siberia, and northern Japan, Ussurian pear comes with both a hardy pedigree and conspicuous thorns. It was introduced to western Canada by Frank Skinner, who obtained seed from the Arnold Arboretum of Harvard University.

Although variable in form and with fruit better left to the birds, it can make a fine ornamental tree. Upright and oval to rounded, Ussurian pears are generally dense and low headed, with stiff, upright branches. The oval leaves are alternate and simple, with finely toothed margins and a pointed tip. A lustrous, dark green throughout summer, the leaves turn yellow to reddish purple in fall. The bark is yellow, and the thorns (which are really modified twigs) are long, stout, and plentiful. This is not a tree to be pruned with impunity!

Fragrant, white flowers appear in early spring, but pear trees require patience. Slow to mature, they generally don't flower until they are eight to ten years old, but it is well worth the

wait for their lovely bloom. The fruit of the species are small, greenish yellow, gritty, astringent, and inedible—although they are much loved by bears, squirrels, and birds, which eat them once the fruit has fallen. It is a messy tree, not to be planted near walkways.

How to Grow

Ussurian pears perform better when sheltered by wind and when planted in fertile, well-drained soil in full sun. Mulching is beneficial. They are moderately drought tolerant once established, but give them even moisture when young. Even with less than ideal conditions, they'll still survive. Suckers and water sprouts may need to be pruned out occasionally. Wear eye protection and be aware of thorns.

Cultivars

♦ 'McDermid' is a seed-propagated cultivar released in 1990 by USDA, Bismarck, South Dakota. It is useful for shelterbelts and wildlife. The fruit is 2.5 to 4 cm (1 to 1.5 in.) in diameter.

♦ 'Mountain Frost' ('Bailfrost') is a vigorous, upright pear of 6 m (20 ft.), with a spread of 5 m (16 ft). It has glossy, green foliage, lightly fragrant, white flowers, and few fruit.

♦ 'Prairie Gem' ('MorDak') is oval when young, becoming more rounded later; it reaches 6 m (20 ft.) in height and spread. It has bright green foliage, which turns golden yellow in fall, white flowers, and few fruit.

♦ 'Ure' (Morden, Manitoba) has an

upright growth habit, reaching 5 m (16 ft.) in height, with a 4-m (13-ft.) spread. It has large, showy flowers and 5-cm (2-in.), greenish yellow fruit in mid-September, which can be used fresh or for canning.

Quercus macrocarpa
kwer-kus mah-krow-*car*-pah

Bur oak

Quercus, the Latin name for oak, means "tree above all others." Oaks have been a symbol of strength and durability since ancient times. This large genus has more than five hundred species, both evergreen and deciduous, which are native from the tropics to the temperate zones almost worldwide. Large and long-lived, they are grown for timber and for their ornamental value. The bark of some species is used for dyes, tannins, and cork. Acorns are sometimes used as hog feed.

Native to eastern North America, including Manitoba, bur oaks are handsome, high-headed trees, with straight trunks and a deep taproot, which allows underplantings to thrive without competition. The almost-black bark develops corky ridges and becomes deeply furrowed with age.

The alternate leaves are simple, oblong, and deeply lobed. A glossy, leathery, green, they turn yellow through golden brown and sometimes red-purple in fall. Male flowers are drooping catkins, appearing with the leaves in spring. In Greek, *makros* means "large," and *karpos,* "fruit;" the words describe the edible acorns. They are enclosed by a fringed cup and develop from the female flowers.

How to Grow

Bur oaks are amazingly adaptable, thriving in the heavy clay soil around Winnipeg (which boasts one of the largest urban oak forests in North America) and in the sandy soil south of Saskatoon. They grow in full sun or partial shade and are extremely drought tolerant once established. If you grow them from seed, transplant them early—remember, they have a taproot. Several types of tiny cynipid wasps cause the formation of galls on the twigs. These galls remain long after the insects have left, but their damage is mainly cosmetic.

PLANT AT A GLANCE

TYPE: large deciduous tree
HEIGHT/SPREAD: 10 to 15 m (33 to 50 ft.)/8 to 10 m (26 to 33 ft.)
LIGHT: full sun to partial shade
SOIL: adaptable
DISTINGUISHING FEATURES: stately form; lobed leaves with attractive fall coloring; distinctive acorns
LANDSCAPE USE: shade or specimen tree; shelterbelt; wildlife planting; grouping in larger landscapes
PHOTO: page 141

Bad Press for a Good Tree

For years, bur oaks were said to be slow growing and lacking hardiness. In reality, they are extremely hardy and grow rather quickly; they are capable of putting on 30 to 45 cm (12 to 18 in.) per year. They are also exceptionally long lived.

So what is the problem? When nursery stock was still largely bare root, bur oaks were difficult to transplant. A 25-cm (10-in.) seedling came with a 45-cm (18-in.) taproot, much of which might be lost in transplanting. As a result, many of them suffered dieback or death, and a bad reputation was born.

The use of deeper pots and largely container-grown stock within the last two decades has facilitated growing bur oaks, but its reputation lingers. Container-grown bur oaks transplant easily and grow quickly. You won't be disappointed.

On the Edge

🍁 *Rhododendron* spp. (roh-doh-*den*-dron), including both rhododendrons and azaleas, are among the showiest of the spring-flowering shrubs for milder climates. Their requirement for acid soil can be satisfied by developing beds to which generous amounts of acidic peat moss are added. Consistently moist soil is also critical to their success.

Recent developments have given us three groups that are worthy of trial in favorable microclimates on the prairies. Northern Lights azaleas are the result of a plant breeding program led by Dr. Harold Pellett at the University of Minnesota Landscape Arboretum. They are small-to medium-sized shrubs and are generally flower-bud hardy to between -37° and -43°C (-35° to -45°F). The pink-flowered cultivars are the hardiest. The second group, the PJM rhododendrons, were developed in Maine in the 1940s. They are compact, upright, medium-sized shrubs, with elliptical, evergreen foliage. In spring, they produce a spectacular display of flowers in shades of lavender pink. Finally, the Marjatta hybrid rhododendrons are a new group of hybrids developed in Finland. Although they are rated hardy to zone 4, they are worthy of trial in protected sites in the warmer parts of the prairies. Most are flower-bud hardy at between -34° and -37°C (-29° to -34°F).

🍁 *Rhus glabra* (ruce *glab*-rah), smooth sumac, is a large native shrub, 3 to 4 m (10 to 13 ft.) in height, with a spread of 2 to 3 m (6.5 to 10 ft.), which should be used where the going is tough. Extremely drought tolerant once established, it spreads by suckers and is useful in reclamation, on

161

steep slopes, and for naturalizing and wildlife plantings. Place in full sun in poor but well-drained soils. It has large, pinnately compound leaves, and the scarlet fruit, borne in dense, hairy clusters on the female plants, persist into winter. 'Laciniata' has deeply cut and lobed leaflets. 'Morden's' is a more restrained form, only 1.8 m (6 ft.) in height, with bright red fruit. *Rhus glabra* var. *cismontana* (syn. *R. cismontana*), the western smooth sumac, is native to South Dakota, Wyoming, and Montana. Both spread to form large thickets.

* *Rhus trilobata* (ruce try-low-*bah*-tah), lemonade sumac, bore the common name of skunkbush until recently, when commercial interests found that it sold better with a more attractive association. At 1 to 2 m (3 to 6.5 ft.) in height, with a spread of 2 m (6.5 ft.), it is smaller and more mound-like than smooth sumac, but still has the ability to form an impenetrable thicket. 'Autumn Amber' is a non-fruiting, low-growing cultivar, only 0.3 to 0.5 m (1 to 1.5 ft.) in height, also suckering to spread widely if not controlled. It has prostrate branches and yellow-red fall coloration if not killed by frost.

* *Rhus typhina* (ruce teh-*fee*-nah), staghorn sumac, is larger, with a height and spread of 3 m (10 ft.). It has a flat-topped appearance, an antler-like branch structure, and attractive conical, red fruit clusters, but it is not as hardy.

Ribes
rie-beez

Currant, gooseberry

Ribes may be from the Arabic or Persian *ribas*, "acid-tasting," referring to the fruit, or from the Danish *ribs*, for red currant. Over 150 species of currants and gooseberries are found in temperate regions of the northern hemisphere and South America. Some bear prickles or spines, while others are unarmed. Some are dioecious. The alternate leaves are three lobed and palmately veined. Small, yellow flowers are followed by clusters of fruit. Although some species are alternate hosts for white pine blister rust, this is not a problem on the prairies due to the scarcity of white pines.

How to Grow

The *Ribes* species discussed here grow in almost any well-drained soil, in sun or shade, and are drought tolerant once established. They are more susceptible to mildew in shade.

Ribes alpinum
rie-beez al-*pie*-num

Alpine currant

Alpinum, "of the mountains," describes the native habitat of this plant. Native to northern and central Europe, from Wales to Russia, the alpine currant is one of the first woody plants to leaf out in the spring. It forms a dense, erect shrub, with foliage to its base. Young stems are straw colored; older stems are rich brown and shredding.

The glossy, dark green, three-lobed leaves turn a soft yellow in the fall. The inedible, red berries are seldom seen because male clones are thought to be more resistant to rust diseases and are more widely used.

OTHER SPECIES AND HYBRIDS

* *Ribes odoratum* (*rie*-beez oh-doh-*rah*-tum), clove, buffalo, or Missouri currant, forms a loose, open shrub, with a height and spread of 1.5 m (5 ft.). It has arching stems, and its simple, alternate, blue-green, oval leaves have prominent lobes and good gold to red fall color. The small, yellow flowers, produced in early spring, have a clove-like fragrance, hence, the common name. The fruit is black. Extremely drought tolerant and

somewhat suckering, they are useful for naturalization and wildlife plantings. *Ribes aureum* (golden currant), native to the Cypress Hills, is similar. Indeed, it is difficult to distinguish the two, and they are often confused in the horticultural trade.

* *Ribes oxycanthoides* 'Dakota Dwarf' (*rie*-beez ox-ee-ah-can-*thoy*-deez), gooseberry, forms a low, dense, but upright shrub of 1 m (3 ft.) in height, with a spread of 1.2 m (4 ft.). It has thin, wiry, curved stems and dark green, glossy foliage, which turns a rich red-bronze in fall. The greenish purple to white flowers are followed by round, reddish purple fruit. Armed with prickles, it makes an attractive drought-tolerant shrub or impenetrable low hedge. It is resistant to mildew.

Rosa
row-zah

Rose

Rosa is a large and diverse genus with representative species throughout temperate and subtropical regions of the world. Roses have been cultivated for many centuries and are widely loved in gardens for their spectacular flowers, fragrance, and medicinal properties. Thousands of cultivars have been developed, and while most of these are are difficult to grow in our challenging climate, there are still many fine species and cultivars that thrive in prairie gardens.

Pruning Roses in Prairie Gardens

Large, hardy shrub roses that bloom once in early summer should be pruned in early spring to renew the wood. Thin out about a third of the oldest canes at ground level.

Roses in the Parkland Series and the Explorer Series bloom on new growth and will produce more blooms if pruned back hard in early spring before growth starts. When spring cleaning in the garden, evaluate how much wood has survived the winter. Remove all dead wood and any weak canes. Cut back the remaining canes to the first out-facing bud, usually 6 to 15 cm (2.5 to 6 in.) above ground level.

How to Grow

Roses are easy to transplant and can be moved bare root in spring or in containers throughout spring and summer. They prefer well-aerated, well-drained soil, which is rich in organic matter. If your soil is sandy or very heavy, add organic matter to it before planting. Roses grow best in

Native Prairie Roses

Four rose species are native to the prairie region. Although seldom planted in gardens, they are attractive features in the natural landscape, and some have been used in the development of hardier roses.

- *Rosa acicularis* (*row*-zah ah-sick-yew-*lair*-ris), prickly rose, is the provincial floral emblem of Alberta. It is the earliest blooming of our native prairie roses and usually the darkest pink in color. The stems are very prickly. Not usually grown in gardens, it spreads aggressively and is useful in large, naturalized plantings.

- *Rosa arkansana* (*row*-zah are-kan-*sah*-nah), prairie rose, is a short shrub, found in dry, sunny sites. The lowest growing and latest blooming of the native roses, it often flowers until late summer, especially if the tops were pruned back or destroyed the previous summer. It was used as parent material in the development of the Parkland Series of roses.

- *Rosa blanda* (*row*-zah *blan*-dah), smooth rose, is native to eastern Canada, as far west as

164

Manitoba. It is closely related to Wood's rose, but has fewer thorns.

* *Rosa woodsii* (*row*-zah *wood*-zee-eye), Wood's rose, is common in moist sites and is often seen along country roadsides. It is quite variable in color, from near white to rose red, and in form, from spreading to upright. The stems are red and usually prickly near the bottom; there are fewer prickles on the flowering branches.

sunny sites that are open to summer breezes but protected from cold winter winds.

Pruning encourages new growth and optimum bloom. Some roses demand care, while others, such as the rugosas, perform well for years with minimal attention.

Explorer Series

This group of complex hybrids was developed through the plant-breeding work of Dr. Felicitas Svejda at the Central Experimental Farm in Ottawa, Ontario. The first cultivars in this series, hybrids of *Rosa rugosa,* are listed with the *R. rugosa* hybrids. The later cultivars in this series are hybrids of *Rosa* x *kordesii* and have brought significant improvements to the quality and variety of roses that

can be successfully grown on the prairies.

These later cultivars vary in plant habit from compact shrubs to large, arching, or nearly climbing plants. Most are quite disease resistant. Their foliage is shiny and dark green, and the flowers are, with one exception, semi-double to very double and slightly to intensely fragrant. The petals have good substance, with clear colors in various shades of pink to red.

Although most will grow in prairie gardens with little protection, it is best to plant them where they'll be sheltered from winter winds and to mulch their crowns until they are well established. They all bloom on new growth, and hard pruning in spring and maintaining good fertility will encourage new growth and bloom.

PLANT AT A GLANCE

TYPE: small to large, flowering, deciduous shrubs; some nearly climbing

HEIGHT/SPREAD: 0.6 to 2.5 m (2 to 8 ft.)/0.6 to 1.8 m (2 to 6 ft.)

LIGHT: full sun

SOIL: well drained; fertile

DISTINGUISHING FEATURES: showy flowers all summer

LANDSCAPE USE: specimen; in beds; on walls and trellises

PHOTOS: page 142

CULTIVARS

- 'Alexander MacKenzie' has very shapely, pointed buds, which open to very double, medium red flowers that require deadheading. It reaches 1.7 m (6 ft.) in height with a spread of 1.5 m (5 ft.).
- 'Captain Samuel Holland' is an upright, arching shrub, reaching 2 m (7 ft.) with a spread of 1.5 m (5 ft.). It has a climbing habit and clusters of medium red flowers. It is susceptible to mildew where air movement is limited.
- 'Champlain' has clusters of bright red flowers, which are abundantly produced throughout summer on upright stems. It is 0.6 m (2 ft.) in height with an equal spread.
- 'George Vancouver' has abundant medium red flowers throughout summer into early fall. This is one of the most winter hardy of the Explorer roses. It is 0.6 m (2 ft.) in height, with a spreading habit to 1 m (3 ft.).
- 'J. P. Connell,' although not strictly an Explorer Series rose, was developed from Dr. Svejda's breeding program. Flowers open a light lemon yellow, fading to cream. This cultivar has an upright habit, with a height of 1.5 m (5 ft.) and spread of 1.2 m (4 ft.).
- 'John Cabot' has clusters of medium red flowers on a vigorous, arching plant, 1.8 m (6 ft.) in height, with a 1.5-m (5-ft.) spread. It is very winter hardy.
- 'John Davis' offers continual bloom, with clusters of beautiful medium pink flowers. It has a climbing habit, reaching 2 m (6.5 ft.) in height and a spread of 1.5 m (5 ft.). This cultivar requires regular fertilizing to thrive.
- 'Louis Jolliet' has very double, medium pink flowers, with a lavender tone and a button center. It climbs to 1.5 m (5 ft.) with a similar spread.
- 'Marie Victorin' is a compact shrub, 1 m (3 ft.) in height, spreading to 0.8 m (2.5 ft.). Clusters of large, semi-double blooms are an interesting peach pink.
- 'Royal Edward' is a low shrub, 0.3 m (1 ft.) tall and spreading to 1.2 m (4 ft.), with small, double, medium pink flowers. It blooms all summer.
- 'William Baffin' is a tall, upright-type, climbing rose, 2.5 m (8 ft.) tall and spreading to 1.5 m (5 ft.), with continuously blooming clusters of up to thirty semi-double, hot pink flowers.
- 'William Booth' has clusters of single, medium red flowers, with a lighter eye, and a vigorous, trailing habit. It reaches 1.2 m (4 ft.) with a spread of 2 m (7 ft.).

Parkland Series

The Parkland Series of roses are the result of a breeding program that has been ongoing at the Agriculture and Agri-Food Canada Research Centre at Morden, Manitoba, since the late 1960s. They were developed from initial hybrids between *Rosa arkansana* (prairie rose) and floribunda cultivars. The stems often die back over winter, but with hard pruning in spring, they grow back vigorously and bloom on new wood. They combine a compact growth habit with summer-long bloom. Most of the cultivars have dark green, shiny foliage, composed of five to nine leaflets. The flowers are single to double and produced singly or in clusters of up to thirty blooms. Their colors are intense and, in some cultivars, are fade resistant.

CULTIVARS

- 'Adelaide Hoodless' has clusters of up to thirty semi-double, bright red flowers throughout the summer. It is 1.2 m (4 ft.) in height, with a 1-m (3-ft.) spread, and is very reliable.
- 'Assiniboine' is an attractive, but seldom available, compact shrub, 0.6 m (2 ft.) in height, with a 1-m (3-ft.) spread. It has large, semi-double, medium red flowers.
- 'Cuthbert Grant' is 1.5 m (5 ft.) in height, with a spread of 1 m (3 ft.). It has large, double, dark red flowers, which recur through-

out summer. Protect the crown to ensure its winter survival.
- 'Hope for Humanity,' named in honor of the centennial of the Canadian Red Cross, has very dark red buds, which open into blood red, double flowers. It has a height and spread of 0.8 m (2.5 ft.).
- 'Morden Blush' has very pale pink, double flowers, fading to ivory. It is very hardy and blooms through-out summer on an upright shrub, 1.2 m (4 ft.) in height, with a 1-m (3-ft.) spread.
- 'Morden Centennial' has clusters of bright pink flowers on a very sturdy and reliable, upright shrub, 1.5 m (4 ft.) in height, with a 1-m (3-ft.) spread.
- 'Morden Fireglow' is susceptible to black spot, but its attractive long, pointed buds open into unique orange-red flowers. The 1.2-m (4-ft.) high plant spreads to 1-m (3 ft.) and has dull, bluish green foliage.
- 'Morden Snowbeauty' is a vigorous, spreading shrub, 1 m (3 ft.) in height, with a spread of 1.5 m (5 ft.). Clusters of long, pointed buds open to pure white, single to semi-double flowers. It blooms all summer and is very disease resistant.
- 'Morden Sunrise' has single to semi-double, bicolor blooms that are yellow infused with a pink blush at the ends of the petals. It is a compact shrub with a height and spread of 0.8 m (2.5 ft.).
- 'Prairie Joy' is Hugh's favorite Parkland Series rose. It is a very dense shrub, with a height and

spread of 0.8 m (2.5 ft), and is clothed in foliage to the ground. Medium pink flowers are produced throughout summer.

* 'Winnipeg Parks' has medium red flowers of very good form on a compact shrub, with a height and spread of 0.6 m (2 ft.).

Rosa rugosa

row-zah roo-*goh*-sah

Rugosa rose

The rugosa rose is native to eastern Asia, where it often grows on beaches. It's easy to grow and is well adapted to difficult growing conditions. It is tolerant of drought, poor soil, and salt spray and is much more disease resistant than most of the rose hybrids.

These spreading shrubs have stout, gray stems that are densely covered with bristly prickles. The plants sucker and develop into colonies. The leaves are bright green, wrinkled,

---

PLANT AT A GLANCE

TYPE: medium, flowering, deciduous shrub

HEIGHT AND SPREAD: 1 to 2 m (3 to 6.5 ft.)

LIGHT: full sun

SOIL: well drained; variable

DISTINGUISHING FEATURES: white to dark purple flowers

LANDSCAPE USE: specimen; hedge; border

---

and pinnately compound, with five to nine leaflets. Depending on the cultivar, they turn from yellow to orange in fall.

The flowers of *Rosa rugosa* and its hybrids range from white to dark purple. They are produced from late June through August, with some hybrids flowering until hard fall frost. Most, but not all, produce round hips, which turn red as they ripen. The fruit is very high in vitamin C and can be used to make jelly or tea.

CULTIVARS

* 'Aylsham' is 0.8 m (2.5 ft.) in height with a 1.2-m (4-ft.) spread. It has deep rose red flowers in July, shiny foliage, and red or orange fall color.
* 'Charles Albanel' is 0.6 m (2 ft.) in height and spread. The flowers are mauve-red, with dense, dark green foliage (Explorer Series).
* 'David Thompson' offers continual bloom, with rose red flowers on a compact plant that is up to 1 m (3 ft.) in height with an equal spread (Explorer Series).
* 'Frau Dagmar Hartopp' ('Fru Dagmar Hastrup') is a compact shrub, 0.6 m (2 ft.) in height, spreading to 1 m (3 ft.). With its satiny, light pink, single flowers and orange fall color, it is highly rated as a landscape plant.
* 'Hansa' has highly fragrant, purplish red flowers on a large shrub, 1.5 m (5 ft.) in height and spread, and repeat blooms throughout summer. It is susceptible to chlorosis if grown in heavy soils.

- 'Henry Hudson' has white flowers, tinged pink, on a low, spreading shrub, 0.6 m (2 ft.) in height, with a 1.2-m (4-ft.) spread (Explorer Series).
- 'Jens Munk' is a very prickly, upright shrub, 1.5 m (5 ft.) in height, with a 1.2-m (4-ft.) spread. It has abundant very fragrant, medium pink flowers all summer (Explorer Series).
- 'Marie Bugnet' is a dwarf, upright plant, 0.6 m (2 ft.) in height, with a 0.8-m (2.5-ft.) spread and pure white flowers all summer.
- 'Thérèse Bugnet' is a favorite. It has double, pink flowers all summer, upright, red stems with almost no prickles (a feature inherited from its *Rosa blanda* parent), a height of 1.8 m (6 ft.), and a spread of 1.5 m (5 ft.).
- 'Will Alderman' has large, double, pink flowers that bloom all summer on an upright shrub, 1 m (3 ft.) tall and wide.

OTHER SPECIES AND HYBRIDS

- *Rosa glauca* (*row*-zah *glaw*-kah), syn. *R. rubrifolia* (*row*-zah rube-reh-*foe*-lee-ah), redleaf rose, has interesting reddish purple foliage, which can be a significant asset in a shrub border. The leaf color is muted and combines well with other plants. The upright canes, 1.5 to 2 m (5 to 6.5 ft.) in height, develop an arching habit over time, spreading to 1.5 m (5 ft.). Small, single, pink flowers are followed by dark orange, oblong hips.

- *Rosa pimpinellifolia* var. *altaica* (*row*-zah pim-peh-nel-eh-*fow*-lee-ah al-tie-*ee*-kah), Altai Scotch rose, is native to Siberia. It is a large, freely suckering shrub, with abundant creamy white, single flowers in late spring. It is a beautiful sight when in bloom, but is more significant for its contribution to hardy rose hybrids.

- 'Hazeldean' (photo page 143) has upright growth to 2 m (6.5 ft.) and a spread of 1.5 m (5 ft.). Spectacular in bloom, it has double, deep yellow flowers, which are very freely produced in late June.

- 'Isabella Skinner' usually dies back in prairie gardens, but will grow back to approximately 1.8 m (6 ft.) in height, and a spread of 1.2 m (4 ft.). Medium pink, double flowers appear in clusters throughout summer on new wood.

- 'Prairie Dawn' is an upright, pillar-type rose, with double flowers of intense clear pink, reaching 2 m (7 ft.) in height with a spread of 1.2 m (4 ft.). It is not as winter hardy as 'Prairie Youth' but has larger, more attractive flowers.

- 'Prairie Youth' is a very hardy and attractive, upright shrub, up to 2 m (6.5 ft.) in height and spreading to 1.5 m (5 ft.). Delicate, pale pink flowers bloom all summer.

Salix

say-licks

Willow

Salix is the Latin name for willow. All are moisture-loving, wet-site species. Their natural habitat is near ponds, streams, and rivers and in poorly drained sites. Vigorous and fast growing, they are relatively short-lived. They range from large trees to prostrate shrubs, but share many characteristics.

Young stems tend to be long, unbranched, flexible, and highly colored, which gives willows a pronounced presence in the late winter and early spring landscape. These supple branches have been used in basketry and weaving worldwide, wherever willows are found.

The leaves are alternate, simple, and lance shaped. Male and female flowers are on separate plants. The showier "pussy willows," long catkins produced by male trees in late winter and early spring, are often used in fresh and dried arrangements.

HOW TO GROW

Willows are wet-site species and do best in deep soil and full sun, with even moisture.

Aspirin or Willow?

Willow extracts have long been used to treat pain, fever, and headaches in most regions where willows grow, including the Canadian prairies. Salicin, the glycoside compound responsible for its medicinal properties, was isolated in the 1800s. Although synthesized in a laboratory by 1875, it had the unpleasant and dangerous side effects of stomach pain, bleeding, and nausea.

In 1893, Felix Hoffman, working for the Bayer Company in Germany, produced acetylsalicylic acid. Less acidic than salicylic acid, it was called "aspirin"—a contraction formed by using the "a" from acetyl and "spirin'" from *spirea*, an older name for *Filipendula,* which contains a similar compound.

First sold as a powder, the tablets so familiar today were on the market by 1915. It took the Treaty of Versailles, which ended World War I, to demote aspirin to a generic term for acetylsalicylic acid. But it all began with willow.

Salix alba

say-licks *al*-bah

White willow

Alba, "white," refers to the whiteness of the wood. The species forms a broad, low-headed, dense, "billowing" silvery tree. The blue-gray, lance-shaped leaves are pointed, with finely toothed margins and a silky pubescence on both sides. The yellow male catkins emerge with the leaves.

Native to Europe and western Asia, the species is seldom seen on the prairie landscape, but several cultivars are well represented. Used extensively for wicker work in Europe, its bright new growth signals the approach of spring on western farmsteads.

🍁

PLANT AT A GLANCE

TYPE: large deciduous tree
HEIGHT/SPREAD: 15 m (50 ft.)/ 12 m (40 ft.)
LIGHT: full sun to partial shade
SOIL: moist; deep
DISTINGUISHING FEATURES: billowy form; red or yellow stems in spring; attractive foliage
LANDSCAPE USE: shade or specimen tree where space permits; shelterbelt

---

CULTIVARS

🍁 'Chermesina' (syn. 'Britzensis'), sometimes called the red-barked white willow, is an upright tree, 15 m (50 ft.) in height, with a spread of 6 m (20 ft.). Its brilliant red, new growth becomes golden with age.

🍁 'Sericea,' called silver willow or Siberian silky white willow, is somewhat smaller and slower growing than the species. Tough

and hardy, it is thought to be more drought tolerant and less prone to littering than other willows. It forms an upright, spreading to rounded tree, 12 m (40 ft.) in height, with a spread of 10 m (33 ft.). It has bright silver-white foliage and yellow to brown bark. The long, narrow leaves are covered with silky, white hairs and remain silvery in the fall.

🍁 'Vitellina,' golden willow, is known for its distinct, egg-yolk yellow twigs and stems in late winter and early spring. It grows quickly into a large tree, 15 m (50 ft.) in height, with a round crown that spreads to 12 m (40 ft.). It is ideal for a large landscape or for an irrigated shelterbelt. The foliage turns yellow in the fall.

Salix pentandra
say-licks pen-*tan*-drah
Laurel leaf willow

Broad, low headed, and dense, laurel-leaf willow has glossy, reddish brown twigs, a short, stout trunk, and deeply furrowed, gray-brown bark. The leaves resemble bay leaves and are aromatic when crushed. They are a lustrous, leathery, dark green, oval to elliptical, and pointed, with a very distinct yellow mid-rib. *Pentandra*, "five stamens," describes the minute, bright yellow male flowers, which appear in late spring.

Perhaps the most commonly planted willow on the prairies, it is highly susceptible to storm damage and was once advertised as "self-pruning."

Unfortunately, it's not self-raking. In spite of its brittleness, it makes a wonderful shade tree and is unbeatable as a climbing/tree-house tree.

🍁

PLANT AT A GLANCE

TYPE: large deciduous tree

HEIGHT AND SPREAD: 8 to 14 m (26 to 45 ft.)

LIGHT: full sun

SOIL: moist

DISTINGUISHING FEATURES: rounded, somewhat weeping form; glossy foliage

LANDSCAPE USE: shade; specimen; shelterbelt

OTHER SPECIES AND HYBRIDS

🍁 *Salix exigua* (*say*-licks eks-*zig*-yew-ah), coyote willow, (photo on page 144) is a native plant that forms an erect shrub or small tree, 3 to 5 m (10 to 16 ft.) in height, with a 2-m (6.5-ft.) spread. It colonizes recently formed sandbars in rivers and streams, quickly forming thickets and stabilizing soil. The silky, silver leaves are long, narrow, and minutely toothed. Slender catkins emerge with the leaves and persist for much of summer. Given sandy soil, full sun, and adequate moisture, it suckers quickly to form a bamboo-like thicket, so give thought to its placement.

🍁 *Salix fragilis* (*say*-licks frah-*gill*-lis), bullata willow, has a spherical form, with a height and spread of 12 m (40 ft.). It resembles a huge cumulus cloud. Native to northern Asia, it has lance-shaped, glossy, dark green leaves. It has performed well in various parts of the prairies, and although it is not readily available, it should be tried much more extensively.

🍁 *Salix integra* 'Hakuro Nishiki' (*say*-licks in-*teg*-rah), Japanese willow, is native to Japan and Korea. A dwarf willow, with a height and spread of only 1 to 1.5 m (3 to 5 ft.), it has striking green, white, and pink variegated young foliage. It is very attractive, but unless it is in an extremely sheltered site, it's liable to die back (or die outright) in most parts of the prairies.

🍁 *Salix lanata* (*say*-licks lah-*not*-tah), woolly willow, is a woolly, gray groundcover, only 30 cm (12 in.) in height, spreading to 1 m (3 ft.), with tiny, felt-like leaves. It is perfectly hardy and useful in a mixed or perennial border, for edging, or in a rock garden, but it may not be readily available.

🍁 *Salix* x 'Prairie Cascade,' is a hybrid of laurel leaf willow and white weeping willow, introduced by the Morden Research Station in Manitoba. With a height and spread of only 10 m (30 ft.), it has a distinctive weeping habit and is ideal for a smaller landscape.

One year it was observed to suffer tip kill in a zone 2 rural garden, perhaps due to wet fall weather, which postponed hardening off.

* *Salix purpurea* (*say*-licks purr-purr-*ree*-ah), purple osier willow, forms a large, fan-like shrub, 1 to 2 m (3 to 6.5 ft.) in height, with a spread of 1 to 2 m (3 to 6.5 ft.). Its long, pliable, arching branches are a distinct purple when young, but become gray with age. The leaves are small, narrowly oblong, and blue-green. The cultivar 'Nana' (syn. 'Gracilis'), or dwarf arctic willow, is a compact selection that makes a low hedge in a damp site. Smaller (1 m/3 ft. in height and spread) and of finer texture than the species, it has purple stems and narrow, blue-green leaves, which turn yellow in fall.

* *Salix silicicola* 'Polar Bear' (*say*-licks si-lee-seh-*coh*-lah), is a selection found on the Athabasca Sand Dunes. A large, upright shrub or small tree, 3 m (10 ft.) in height, with a spread of 2 m (6.5 ft.), it has silver-gray foliage. It is an outstanding accent within a shrub or mixed border. Older stems die out for no apparent reason, but are replaced by newer ones.

Sambucus racemosa
sam-*bew*-kus
rah-seh-*mow*-sah

European red elder

Sambucus is from the Greek *sambuke*, a musical instrument resembling a harp that was originally made from elder wood. There are more than twenty species of elders distributed in temperate and subtropical regions worldwide. Leaves are opposite and pinnately compound, with serrated leaflets. The stems are pithy. Small, white flowers are borne in large terminal clusters, followed by fleshy berries, which are well loved and generously distributed by birds. With the exception of the cultivar 'Goldenlocks,'

PLANT AT A GLANCE

TYPE: large, flowering, deciduous shrub

HEIGHT AND SPREAD: 3 m (10 ft.)

LIGHT: full sun to shade

SOIL: well drained; variable

DISTINGUISHING FEATURES: large, pinnately compound leaves; white flowers; red fruit

LANDSCAPE USE: shrub or mixed border; naturalization; wildlife planting

PHOTO: page 144

these are not plants for a small garden.

Native to Europe and western Asia, red elder has been cultivated since 1597. Welsh women once used crushed elder leaves to make green patterns on their freshly washed stone floors in the belief that this practice would keep evil at bay.

Red elders are large, upright shrubs, with arching branches and a loose, open habit. They can be pruned to a single trunk to form a small tree. The stems are stout and pithy, are easily broken, and contain prominent lenticels. The wood burns and polishes well.

The large, green leaves are alternate, pinnately compound, composed of five to seven leaflets, and turn yellow in the fall. Small, creamy white flowers are formed in large, round or cone-shaped terminal clusters—*racemosa* means "with flowers in racemes." The dense clusters of red fruit are much loved and freely distributed by birds. Parts of this plant are believed to be poisonous, although the ripe fruit is considered harmless once cooked.

How to Grow

Elders will grow almost anywhere (as witnessed by seeds that have germinated after passage through avian digestive tracts). They are shade tolerant, but prefer well-drained soil in full sun. Those with golden foliage are not as bright in shade. Fast growing and pest and disease free, elders are exceptionally drought tolerant once established. They generally require spring pruning to remove dead branches.

Cultivars

* 'Dropmore Fernleaf,' a Frank Skinner (Manitoba) introduction, with a height and spread of 1.5 m (5 ft.), has finely dissected foliage that is tinged purple in spring and fall.
* 'Goldenlocks,' is a Les Kerr (Saskatchewan) introduction, dwarf, with a height and spread of only 1 m (3 ft.) and finely dissected golden leaves.
* 'Sutherland Golden' is a large, dense shrub, with a height and spread of 2 to 3 m (6.5 to 10 ft.). Selected at the Sutherland PFRA tree nursery near Saskatoon, it has bright golden, finely dissected foliage and creamy flowers. Place in full sun for the best color.

On the Edge

* *Shepherdia*, buffaloberry, are native shrubs in the Russian olive family. *Shepherdia argentea* (shep-*purr*-dee-ah are-*gen*-tee-ah), silverleaf buffaloberry, is a large, upright shrub, 3 to 5 m (10 to 16 ft.) in height, with an indefinite spread if not controlled. Its opposite, small, strap-shaped leaves are covered with silvery scales. It is dioecious, with female plants producing small, red berries in the fall. The berries were used to flavor buffalo meat, hence, the common name. *Shepherdia canadensis* (shep-*purr*-dee-ah cah-nah-*den*-sis), russet buffaloberry, is a dense, round, upright shrub of 1 to 2 m (3 to 6.5 ft.) in height with an equal spread. The small, yellow flowers are without petals and produce red

berries on the female plants. Buffaloberries are very tolerant of dry, alkaline soils and do best in full sun. They are useful for naturalization, reclamation, wildlife plantings, and shelterbelts.

Sorbaria sorbifolia

sore-*bare*-ree-ah

sor-bi-*fow*-lee-ah

Ural false spirea

False spireas are vigorous shrubs that spread quickly by suckering, making them particularly suitable for massing or for stabilizing banks. Panicles of white flowers are produced in mid-

summer. The pinnately compound leaves resemble those of a mountain ash. The botanical name emphasizes its similarity to mountain ash: *Sorbaria* is from the Latin *sorbum*, "resembling *Sorbus.*"

Ural false spirea is a suckering shrub, which develops a great mass of upright stems. The bark is green to pinkish on new growth and later becomes brown to gray-brown and peels in strips. The leaves, which resemble those of mountain ash, are pinnately compound, with thirteen to twenty-five lance-shaped, doubly toothed leaflets. *Sorbifolia* means "with leaves like *Sorbus.*"

The creamy white flowers are held in plume-shaped panicles, which open in early summer. Flower panicles develop at the ends of the current season's growth. It is very attractive in bloom when grown as a mass planting. As the flowers fade, they turn brown, and less-attractive dry seed capsules develop. 'Aurora' false spirea is a Skinner hybrid that is taller than Ural false spirea and has a cleaner look because its flowers drop completely and do not produce seed.

How to Grow

Sorbaria is easy to transplant from bare-root plants when dormant or from container-grown plants at any time. It will grow in full sun, but is also quite shade tolerant. It prefers well-drained, moist soils and will become dwarfed in dry soils. It suckers freely to form thickets. Flowers are produced on the current year's growth, so early spring pruning encourages more prolific bloom.

PLANT AT A GLANCE

TYPE: large, flowering, deciduous shrub

HEIGHT AND SPREAD: 1 to 2 m (3 to 6.5 ft.)

LIGHT: full sun to shade

SOIL: well drained; rich

DISTINGUISHING FEATURES: creamy white flowers; large, pinnately compound leaves

LANDSCAPE USE: shrubby groundcover; bank stabilization; reclamation

PHOTO: page 145

Sorbus

sor-bus

Mountain ash, rowan

The British common name, rowan, is from the Swedish word *ron*, which is related to the English word *rune*, "having magical significance." The rowan is widely associated with magic and was once frequently planted by cottage doors to ward off evil. In parts of the British Isles, it is called the wiggentree or witchen, and it was greatly venerated by the Druids. *Sorbus* is the classical Latin name for this tree and means "stop," perhaps another reference to warding off evil. Mountain ash, the common name in North America, is derived from the resemblance of its leaves to those of ash (*Fraxinus*).

Mountain ash, which range from shrubs to medium-sized trees, are noted for their clusters of orange-red fruit in the fall. Some types are edible, but usually these fruit are food for the birds. The American species are generally better adapted to our area than the European mountain ash. Although a few species have simple leaves, all those grown on the prairies have pinnately compound leaves. The clusters of small, white flowers are showy in the spring.

How to Grow

Buy balled and burlapped or container-grown plants. Mountain ash grow best in moist, rich, neutral to slightly acidic soils, which are well drained and well aerated. They also do well in partial shade, in association with other trees. Prune in winter or early spring when the trees are dormant.

Mountain ash require little cultural attention when established in favorable environments. They are more susceptible to fireblight, canker, and borers if they are stressed by drought, sunscald, or excess nitrogen. The best defence is to maintain them in a vigorous, healthy condition and to grow winter-hardy species and cultivars. Avoid planting mountain ash in high stress (dry or wind-exposed) environments.

Sorbus americana

sor-bus ah-meh-ri-*kah*-nah

American mountain ash

American mountain ash is native to eastern North America, as far west as the southeast corner of Manitoba.

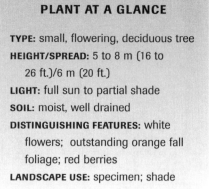

PLANT AT A GLANCE

TYPE: small, flowering, deciduous tree
HEIGHT/SPREAD: 5 to 8 m (16 to 26 ft.)/6 m (20 ft.)
LIGHT: full sun to partial shade
SOIL: moist, well drained
DISTINGUISHING FEATURES: white flowers; outstanding orange fall foliage; red berries
LANDSCAPE USE: specimen; shade

In its natural form, it is a low-branched or multiple-stemmed, small tree, with slender, upright branches and an open, rounded crown. The bark is smooth, shiny, and dark reddish brown. The dark green leaves are pinnately compound, with eleven to seventeen leaflets, and turn an attractive orange in fall. Winter buds are black, sharply pointed, and sticky. Numerous very showy, small, white flowers are borne in flat-topped clusters after the leaves have fully emerged in spring. The orange-red to scarlet berries are a favorite of waxwings and robins.

Sorbus aucuparia

sor-bus ah-kew-*pare*-ree-ah

European mountain ash, rowan

European mountain ash are native over a wide area of northern Europe and Asia. Upright and oval when young, they become open and round headed at maturity. The smooth bark is light gray to reddish brown. The alternate leaves are pinnately compound, with nine to fifteen leaflets. Each leaflet is oblong, pointed, dull dark green, and smooth. The white flowers are produced in terminal clusters after the leaves emerge in spring. The clusters of small, orange-red berries that follow may be used to make juice, vinegar, tea, or an alcoholic beverage, but most are eaten by birds. *Aucuparia* is derived from the Latin *avis*, "bird," and *capere*, "to catch." The fruit is often cleaned up in short order by migrating robins and waxwings. *Sorbus aucuparia* var. *rossica* (*raw*-sik-ah), Russian mountain ash, is

PLANT AT A GLANCE

TYPE: small, flowering, deciduous tree
HEIGHT/SPREAD: 8 m (26 ft.)/5 m (16 ft.)
LIGHT: full sun to partial shade
SOIL: moist, well drained; average to fertile
DISTINGUISHING FEATURES: white flowers; orange-red berries
LANDSCAPE USE: specimen; border feature
PHOTO: page 145

a columnar form, with sharply angled, upright branching.

OTHER SPECIES AND HYBRIDS

- *Sorbus decora* (*sor*-bus deh-*cor*-ah), showy mountain ash, (photo on page 145) is a northern species that is native from southern Greenland to Manitoba. It is the hardiest of the mountain ash and a very attractive small tree, 4 to 8 m (13 to 26 ft.) in height, spreading to 4 m (13 ft.). The berries are larger and showier than those of *S. americana*.

- *Sorbus scopulina* (*sor*-bus skop-pew-*lee*-nah), Rocky, western, or Greene's mountain ash, usually forms a multi-stemmed, small, shrubby tree, 4 to 6 m (13 to 20 ft.) in height, with a spread of 4 m (13 ft.). The stems are upright and stiff, and the fruit clusters are large and showy. It is native to Alberta and British Columbia.

177

✦ ✦ ✦ ✦ ✦ ✦

Spiraea
spy-*ree*-ah

Spirea

Mounded or vase-shaped, flowering shrubs ranging from 0.6 to 2 m (2 to 6.5 ft.) in height, spireas are native to Asia and North America. They have alternate, simple leaves and white to pink flowers. Some species have small umbels of flowers along the branches, which bloom early on the previous season's wood. Others have larger terminal clusters of flowers in mid-summer on the current season's wood. *Spirea*, from the Greek *speiraira*, means "a plant used as a garland," which in turn is derived from *speria*, "twist" or "spiral." Flowering branches were often used in a tiara-fashion for ceremonial purposes.

How to Grow

Spireas grow best in full sun, but tolerate partial shade. They also perform best in soils amended with organic matter that have good drainage but are evenly moist. Although they are largely pest and disease free, they may suffer from lime-induced chlorosis in soils with a high pH.

Spiraea x *bumalda*
spy-*ree*-ah bew-*mal*-dah

Dwarf bumalda spirea

Bumalda spireas are dwarf, flowering shrubs, with coarsely toothed, oval, pointed leaves. The foliage is pink-red when young, matures to blue-green, and often becomes red in fall. The white to pink to reddish flowers, produced on the current season's wood, are in broad, flattened corymbs and bloom from mid-summer to fall, longer if deadheaded.

✦

PLANT AT A GLANCE

TYPE: small, flowering, deciduous shrub

HEIGHT AND SPREAD: 0.6 m (2 ft.)

LIGHT: full sun to partial shade

SOIL: moist, well drained

DISTINGUISHING FEATURES: pink to white flowers; attractive foliage

LANDSCAPE USE: mixed or shrub border; mass planting; rock garden

PHOTO: page 146

Cultivars

✦ 'Anthony Waterer' is one of the oldest bumalda cultivars (dating from 1890) and is often considered the standard against which others are compared. It produces flat clusters of small, carmine red flowers through June and July, on dwarf plants, 0.6- to 1-m (2- to 3-ft.) tall, with a 1- to 1.5-m (3- to 6-ft.) spread. It has bronze stems, with

Spiraea Nomenclature and History

Spiraea x *bumalda* is a hybrid of *S. japonica*, which has pink flowers, and *S. albiflora*, which has white flowers. It originated not in the wild but in cultivation in Switzerland. First described in 1891, Karl Froebel of Zurich sent it to Kew Gardens in England in 1885.

Spiraea japonica, native to Japan, China, and the Himalayas, was introduced to cultivation in 1870 and is amazingly variable. *Spiraea albiflora* is also native to Japan. The chance union of these two species in the Swiss Alps has resulted in a great number of selections, almost all of which have arisen as branch sports, or mutations, on parts of the parent plant.

In Europe, these cultivars are generally listed as *S. japonica*; in North America, they are classified as cultivars of the hybrid *S.* x *bumalda*. Regardless of how you find them in catalogues and nurseries, they form an integral part of our present prairie landscape. A toast to Mr. Froebel!

bronzy green foliage throughout summer, which becomes red in fall.

* 'Crispa' was selected for its deeply toothed (almost cutleaf), twisted, and somewhat puckered or fluted foliage. The leaves are reddish purple when young, maturing to dark green. The plant is compact and rounded, 0.6 m (2 ft.) in height, with a 1-m (3-ft.) spread. It has reddish rose flowers in flat clusters in June. Otherwise, it is very similar to 'Anthony Waterer.'

* 'Froebelli' is a tall, vigorous selection, with a height and spread of 1 m (3 ft.). It has deep carmine-pink flowers from June until fall. It is similar to 'Anthony Waterer,' but has broader leaves (often green with red tips), which, as they develop, effectively hide the seed heads of the first flush of flowers, greater drought tolerance, and smaller but brighter flowers. It is considered one of the hardiest and best adapted of the dwarf spireas.

* 'Goldflame' is a dwarf, compact, densely mounded shrub, 0.8 m (2 ft.) in height, with a 1-m (3-ft.) spread. The young growth emerges reddish orange, becoming soft yellow (with better coloration in cooler summers), then green, with intense red fall color. The flowers are pink and smaller than those of 'Anthony Waterer.'

* 'Gumball' is only 0.6 m (2 ft.) in height, with a 1-m (3-ft.) spread, and has a compact form, which is smaller and neater than 'Froebelli.' It has pink flowers from summer to fall and dark green reddish

foliage in spring, which matures to green by summer.

* 'Magic Carpet' is a compact plant, with a height and spread of 0.6 to 0.8 m (2 to 2.5 ft.). Considered a groundcover version of 'Gold-flame,' it is ideal for smaller land-scapes. It has deep, dark pink flowers from late spring to early summer, and the foliage, bronze-green to russet-red and often red tipped, turns red in fall.

* 'Mini Sunglow' is a very dense, dwarf, and mounding spirea of 0.8 m (2.5 ft.), with a 1-m (3-ft.) spread. It has pink flowers and brilliant yellow foliage.

* 'Rosebella,' a Skinner introduction, is smaller but hardier than 'Froebelli'—only 0.5 m (1.5 ft.) in height. It has large clusters of dusty rose flowers continually throughout summer.

OTHER SPECIES AND HYBRIDS

* *Spiraea japonica* (spy-*ree*-ah jah-*pon*-i-kah), Japanese spirea, is a variable species native to Japan, China, and Korea. Mostly small, mound-forming shrubs, the numerous cultivars, some of which are described here, are grown for both their flowers and foliage. The dark green foliage of the species is similar to that of the bumalda spirea. The white, pink, and red flowers are in large, flattened heads on new wood. 'Goldmound' forms a low mound, 0.5 m (1.5 ft.) in height, spreading to 1 m (3 ft.). The gold foliage may fade to yellow-green during prolonged heat. It has small heads of light pink

flowers in May and June. 'Little Princess' is a dwarf, rounded plant of 0.3 m (1 ft.), with a 1 m (3 ft.) spread; it has pink flowers all summer and blue-green foliage that turns red in fall. 'Shirobana' ('Shibori') is unique because of the mixture of deep pink, light pink, and white flowers on a single plant. It has handsome dark green foliage on dwarf, mounded plants, 0.8 to 1 m (2.5 to 3 ft.) in height, with a spread of 1 m (3 ft.). It is not reliably hardy in all parts of the prairies and may revert to mostly pink flowers.

* *Spiraea nipponica* 'Halward's Silver' (spy-*ree*-ah ni-*pon*-i-kah), 1 m (3 ft.) in height with an equal spread, is denser and more compact than the species. It is covered with white flowers in early June, which are borne on last year's wood. Prune after flowering.

* 'Fairy Queen' is a Frank Skinner introduction, a hybrid between *S. trilobata* and *S. trichocarpa*. It has dark green foliage and masses of white flowers in early spring. Although similar to Vanhoutte spirea, it is hardier and more compact, with a height and spread of 1.5 m (5 ft.).

* 'Summersnow,' another Skinner introduction, produces terminal clusters of white flowers in July. The long stamens are thought by some to be untidy. It is 0.6 to 0.8 m (2 to 2.5 ft.) in height, spreading to 2 to 3 m (6.5 to

10 ft.). It is a hybrid between *S. betulaefolia* and *S. media*.

🍁 *Spiraea trilobata* (spy-*ree*-ah try-low-*bah*-tah), three-lobed spirea, is native to northern China, Siberia, and Turkestan and was introduced in 1801. It is similar but superior to and hardier than either *S.* x *arguta* (garland spirea) or *S.* x *vanhouttei* (bridalwreath spirea). Globe shaped and compact, with dark blue-green foliage to its base, it is a medium-sized, dense shrub, with a height and spread of 1 m (3 ft.). The slender, arching stems are covered with a profusion of single, white flowers, which arise on the previous season's growth, so prune after flowering rather than in early spring.

🍁 *Spiraea trichocarpa* 'Density' (spy-*ree*-ah try-coe-*car*-pah), Korean spirea, is a compact form of the species that originated at the PFRA Tree Nursery in Indian Head, Saskatchewan. Only 0.6 to 1 m (2 to 3 ft.) in height, spreading to 1 m (3 ft.), it is a very dense, stiff, upright plant, with bright green foliage. Large, rounded, terminal clusters of snow white flowers are produced in June on old wood. Prune after flowering.

🍁 'Snowwhite,' sometimes listed as a cultivar of *S.* x *vanhouttei*, is arching and compact, with a height and spread of 1.5 m (5 ft.). It has white flowers in very early spring.

🍁

Chlorosis

Iron deficiency, or "lime-induced" chlorosis, occurs when plants are unable to absorb enough iron from the soil. They need iron to produce chlorophyll. Without adequate iron, the newest leaves turn yellow, with only the veins remaining green. (Nitrogen deficiency can also cause yellowing, but it appears in the oldest leaves first.) In extreme cases, the tips and margins of the leaf brown or the entire leaf becomes brown and brittle. Susceptible trees and shrubs include spirea, ginnala maple, rose, mountain ash, apple, crabapple, highbush cranberry, and elder.

Although most prairie soils have plenty of iron, they also have a high lime content and a high pH (7.0 or higher). These conditions make iron less soluble and less available to plants. Iron may also become unavailable in cases where there are excess phosphates (be cautious when adding phosphate fertilizers!), low organic matter, or excess moisture (low oxygen) combined with a low soil temperature.

Successful treatment often requires a combination of strategies. Plants respond quickly to foliar and soil applications of chelated iron, but for lasting effect, combine this treatment with improved soil drainage, the incorporation of organic matter, and acidification of the soil by the addition of peat moss and acidic fertilizers, such as elemental sulfur or ammonium sulfate. In soils that are high in lime, you may need to add large quantities or make regular applications of chelated iron combined with peat moss and acidic fertilizers for the desired effect.

On the Edge

❧ **Symphoricarpos albus** (sim-for-i-*kar*-pus *al*-bus), snowberry, is a bushy native shrub, with many slender, upright stems and a 1-m (3-ft.) height and spread. It suckers freely to form thickets. The small, oval leaves are opposite on the stem and are bluish green and hairy on the underside. The tiny, pinkish flowers are produced in terminal spikes and are followed by white berries, which persist into winter. Snowberry is a valuable groundcover, particularly on difficult dry, sunny, or shaded sites. It suckers freely; use with caution in small spaces.

Syringa
sir-*ring*-gah

Lilac

The genus *Syringa* derives its name from the Greek myth of the nymph Syrinx. She was pursued by the god Pan and turned into a hollow reed, from which Pan made his flute or pan-pipe. Like a syringe, the hollow stem is typical of the genus.

Syringa is a genus of shrubs and small trees that are native to eastern Europe and Asia. Most of the species that are native to northern China are known for their spectacular displays of flowers in late spring and early summer. Plant breeders have been working to improve lilacs for 150 years and have developed many cultivars with attractive blooms and more-compact plant forms.

Lilacs have opposite, simple leaves. Their small, tubular flowers, in densely packed panicles, are spectacular due to the size of the panicles, the subtle variety of colors, and the intense scent of many species and cultivars.

How to Grow

Lilacs growing around long-abandoned homesteads are a testament to their adaptability to prairie conditions. Once established, they need little attention. They prefer lime-based soils and grow best in near-neutral soils that are well supplied with organic matter. Well-drained soil is the key to success—lilacs will not survive if they are flooded in spring. They will grow on wet sites with heavy soil if they are planted in beds raised above ground level.

Pruning faded flower trusses prevents seed formation and encourages maximum growth and flower production. Additional pruning may be required to control suckering and to maintain their shape. If you wish to cut back branches, do it immediately after bloom in the spring. This will give the plant time to develop flower buds for the following year.

Syringa meyeri 'Palibin'
sir-*ring*-gah *my*-er-eye
Dwarf Korean lilac, Meyer lilac, littleleaf lilac

The Meyer lilac, a very attractive shrub, was originally collected in northern China, where it is known only in gardens. Although it produces seedlings, it should be grown from cuttings, layers, or sucker shoots, as the seedlings are not uniform or as compact as the cultivar.

Meyer lilac is a very dense shrub, with many fine, twiggy branches. The gray bark has numerous small, round lenticels. It maintains its dense form without pruning, but adapts very well to pruning to control size. It is one of very few lilacs that never shows mildew. The leaves are opposite, round, and dark green, with slightly wavy margins and a leathery appearance. The small panicles of deep purple flower buds burst into pinkish lavender blooms in spring, and the plant often produces a lighter crop of blooms in late summer.

OTHER SPECIES AND HYBRIDS

❀ *Syringa* x 'Bailbelle,' Tinkerbelle™ lilac, is a new, more upright hybrid of Meyer lilac, with a height of 1.5 m (5 ft.) and a spread of 1 m (3 ft.). Wine red flower buds give rise to pink flowers. Marginally hardy in colder locations, it should be planted in a sheltered spot.

❀ *Syringa patula* 'Miss Kim' (sir-*ring*-gah pah-*tew*-lah) is similar to Meyer lilac but at 2 m (6.5 ft.) in height and a 1.5-m (5-ft.) spread, it is more upright in habit. It has oval leaves a bit larger than those of *S. meyeri* 'Palibin,' and they turn burgundy to purple in fall.

PLANT AT A GLANCE

TYPE: medium, flowering, deciduous shrub

HEIGHT/SPREAD: 1.5 to 2 m (5 to 6.5 ft.)/2 to 2.5 m (6.5 to 8 ft.)

LIGHT: full sun

SOIL: well drained; average to fertile

DISTINGUISHING FEATURES: miniature in overall size, foliage and flowers; a lilac for smaller spaces

LANDSCAPE USE: specimen; hedge; mass planting

PHOTO: page 146

Syringa reticulata

sir-*ring*-gah reh-tick-yew-*lah*-tah

Japanese tree lilac

Tree lilacs are lovely small trees that are native to northern China and Japan. The best form is the Japanese tree lilac described here. It is well adapted to prairie gardens and requires a minimum of maintenance once established.

The Japanese tree lilac has one or multiple trunks, which develop a number of large, ascending branches and a round head. The bark is an exquisite dark reddish brown, peeling as it ages, and it is a delightful feature in the winter landscape. *Reticulata*, "netted" or with a "net-like pattern," describes the leaves, which are dark green, simple, entire, and broadly oval, with a sharp point. They emerge early in spring and do not color appreciably in the fall.

The last of the lilacs to bloom,

♣

PLANT AT A GLANCE

TYPE: small to medium, flowering, deciduous tree

HEIGHT/SPREAD: 6 to 8 m (20 to 26 ft.)/5 m (16 ft.)

LIGHT: full sun to partial shade

SOIL: well drained; average to fertile

DISTINGUISHING FEATURES: large panicles of creamy white flowers in late June

LANDSCAPE USE: specimen; accent

PHOTO: page 147

---

from late June to early July, the Japanese tree lilac has large, loose, triangular terminal panicles. The white flowers have protruding, yellow anthers, which give them a fuzzy, ivory appearance. Their fragrance has been described as *exhalant une odeur de miel,* "exhaling the fragrance of honey." For some, it may be so sweet it is objectionable.

As a specimen, it should either be pruned to a single stem or reduced to three stems, with the branches pruned from the lower part of the stem to display the attractive bark. 'Ivory Silk' is a cultivar selected for its single-stemmed tree form and dense, round head.

Syringa villosa

sir-*ring*-gah veh-*low*-sah

Late lilac

Late lilac is native to northern China. Dried specimens were collected near Beijing and sent to Paris by Pierre d'Incarville, a Jesuit missionary, about 1750. However, it wasn't introduced into cultivation in the Western world until 1889.

Late lilac is a large, round-topped shrub, with many upright branches. The bark is gray, with many small, round lenticels. The medium to dark green leaves are oval to oblong and have a row of soft hairs down the midrib on the back of each leaf (*villosa* means "covered with soft hairs"). The impressed veins give the leaves a pleated appearance. It blooms after the common lilac, hence, the common name. The flowers are produced in narrowly triangular panicles at the ends of shoots and vary from pinkish,

with a tinge of lavender, to near
white.

Non-suckering, it is attractive as
a background shrub or in mass plantings in large landscapes. It can also
be used as a tall hedge or shelterbelt
shrub.

CULTIVARS

In the 1920s, Isabella Preston, from
the Central Experimental Farm in
Ottawa, developed *Syringa* x *prestoniae*
hybrids of *S. villosa* and *S. reflexa*.
These have given us a number of
cultivars, which are much like the
S. villosa parent.

* 'Agnes Smith' is an outstanding
  compact, white-flowered cultivar,
  2.5 m (8 ft.) in height, with a
  spread of 2 m (6.5 ft.).
* 'Donald Wyman' has purple buds
  that open to reddish purple flowers. Vigorous and hardy, it is an
  excellent specimen or hedge plant,
  which reaches 3 m (10 ft.) in
  height and spreads to 2 m (6.5 ft.).

* 'James MacFarlane' has prolific
  bright pink flowers and grows to
  2.5 m (8 ft.) in height and spreads
  to 3 m (10 ft.).
* 'Minuet' has dense growth and
  very dark, shiny foliage on a 2 m
  (6.5 ft.) tall plant, which spreads
  to 1.5 m (5 ft.). Light purple buds
  open to pale pink.
* 'Miss Canada' (photo on page
  147) has deep reddish buds that
  open to bright pink flowers and a
  large, open form, 2.5 m (8 ft.) in
  height, spreading to 2 m (6.5 ft.).

Syringa vulgaris
sir-*ring*-gah vul-*gare*-ris
Common lilac

Vulgaris means common. The common lilac has given rise to a large
group of cultivars known as the
French hybrids. Beginning in 1878,
Victor Lemoine introduced his first
lilac hybrid. From then until 1950,
lilacs in an incredible variety of colors
and forms came from the nursery of
Victor Lemoine *et fils* in France.
Others took up this hybridizing work
and there continues to be a stream of
new hybrid cultivars. The colors range
from white to pink, to blue and dark
purple. Newer cultivars have exceptional colors, flower forms, and more
compact habits. Plantings expand over
time by suckering. Only a few of the
hundreds of named cultivars are
described here.

♦

Where to See Lilacs

There are exceptional collections
of lilacs at:

* Agriculture and Agri-Food
Canada, Research Centre,
Morden, Manitoba
* Arnold Arboretum, Jamaica
Plain, Massachusetts
* Devonian Botanical Garden,
University of Alberta, near
Edmonton
* Jardin Botanique de
Montreal, Montreal, Quebec
* Royal Botanical Gardens,
Hamilton, Ontario
* University of Minnesota
Landscape Arboretum,
Minneapolis

CULTIVARS

* 'Agincourt Beauty' has outstanding
deep purple, single flowers, with
exceptionally large individual
florets. It reaches 2.5 m (8 ft.)
in height with a spread of 2 m
(6.5 ft.).
* 'Beauty of Moscow' ('Krasavitsa
Moskovy') has double flowers,
white tinged with lavender-rose,
and is a heavy bloomer. It is one of
the finest white lilacs, 4 m (13 ft.)
tall and 3 m (10 ft.) wide.
* 'Charles Joly' has double, dark purple flowers and is a very good older
cultivar, reaching 3 m (10 ft.) in
height with a spread of 2 m
(6.5 ft.).
* 'Katherine Havemeyer' has double,
lavender-pink flowers, with large,
heavy flower panicles. It is 3 m
(10 ft.) tall with a spread of 2 m
(6.5 ft.).
* 'President Grevy' is 3 m (10 ft.)
in height with a spread of 2 m
(6.5 ft.). It is over one hundred
years old but still one of the finest
double blue lilacs.
* 'Primrose' has unique pale yellow,
single flowers and reaches 3 m
(10 ft.) in height with a 2-m
(6.5-ft.) spread.
* 'Sarah Sands' has large, single, dark
purple flowers. It grows to 2.5 m
(8 ft.) in height with an equal
spread.
* 'Sensation' has very beautiful single, deep purple flowers, edged in
white. It is 3 m (10 ft.) tall with a
2-m (6.5-ft.) spread.
* 'Wedgewood Blue' has lilac-purple
buds, which open to blue, single
flowers; it is lower growing to

1.8 m (6 ft.), with a 2-m (6.5-ft.) spread.

🍁 'Dappled Dawn' is interesting for its variegated foliage and its double, bluish flowers. It is 3 m (10 ft.) in height with a 2-m (6.5-ft.) spread.

Syringa x *hyacinthiflora*

sir-*ring*-gah hy-ah-sin-thah-*flor*-ah

Early flowering lilac, American hybrid lilac, hyacinth flowering lilac

The early flowering lilacs are hybrids of French hybrid cultivars and the Korean *Syringa oblata* var. *dilitata*. The Korean lilac has contributed earlier bloom, better winter hardiness, less suckering, a more-compact habit, and purple fall foliage color to these hybrids in varying degrees.

Many outstanding cultivars in this group were developed by Frank Skinner of Manitoba. They are among the most highly rated lilacs, with newer cultivars becoming available from the breeding work of the late Father Fiala of Ohio.

CULTIVARS

🍁 'Asessippi,' with a height and spread of 3 m (10 ft.), has abundant single, lavender-lilac flowers.

🍁 'Blanche Sweet' is a Father Fiala introduction with single, pale whitish blue flowers. It has a height and spread of 1 m (3 ft.).

🍁 'Excel' is a tall, upright shrub, 4 m (13 ft.) in height and spread. It is a very prolific bloomer, with single, lilac flowers.

🍁 'Maiden's Blush' is an outstanding single-flowered, compact shrub, with a height and spread of 2.5 m (8 ft.). The flower color varies, from pale to medium pink, depending on the soil.

🍁 'Mount Baker' is a taller, single, white-flowered shrub, 3 m (10 ft.) in height and spread. It is a profuse bloomer from an early age.

🍁 'Pocahontas' has single, dark purple flowers, with an exceptionally profuse bloom. It has a height and spread of 1 m (3 ft.).

🍁 'Sister Justina' is a more compact shrub, 2 m (6.5 ft.) in height, with a spread of 3 m (10 ft.) and outstanding single, white flowers.

🍁

PLANT AT A GLANCE

TYPE: large, flowering, deciduous shrub

HEIGHT AND SPREAD: 2 to 4 m (6.5 to 13 ft.)

LIGHT: full sun

SOIL: well drained; variable

DISTINGUISHING FEATURES: colorful, fragrant flowers in June

LANDSCAPE USE: border; specimen in large landscape area

PHOTOS: pages 147, 148

Disease and Insect Problems of Lilacs

Bacterial blight and *Phytophthora* blight cause lilac foliage to wilt and turn brown or black, with bacterial ooze in the former and brown lesions in the latter case. Control these diseases by pruning to remove affected branches.

Verticillium wilt is a fungal disease in which leaves lose their glossiness, turn pale, and wilt. Remove and burn infected plants and do not replant lilacs in the affected soil.

Mildew appears in late summer or fall as a white, powdery coating on the leaves. Generally, it is more disfiguring than lethal. Common lilac is most susceptible, and some cultivars are more susceptible than others. Improve air circulation and water the soil, not the foliage. Meyer lilac is immune to mildew.

Oyster scale and San Jose scale are lilacs' number one problem. They are difficult to control because the insects are protected by shells during much of their life cycle. If few in number, rub scale insects off. For serious infestations, try insecticidal soap or dormant oil.

Lilac borer is characterized by a bit of sawdust on the ground next to small holes in older trunks. Most lilacs can withstand a few borers, but if the population increases, it might be necessary to control them with pheromone traps.

Lilac leaf miner is the larvae of a moth that feeds between the upper and lower layers of lilac leaves. They emerge, roll up within the leaves, and remain there until they mature. They fall to the ground to pupate, emerging in about fourteen days to start the cycle over again. Remove mined leaves and burn them, and clear fallen leaves in autumn. If the infestation is severe, try spraying with insecticidal soap during the larval stage in July.

Thuja occidentalis
thoo-yah ok-ceh-den-*tah*-lis

Cedar, eastern white cedar

Thuja, a Greek word meaning "odorous tree" or "scented gum," refers to the resin that was once used as incense in religious ceremonies. *Occidentalis*, "of the west," distinguishes it from *T. orientalis*, an Asian species. The French explorer Jacques Cartier referred to cedar as *arborvitae*, "tree of life." He credits it with saving his life and the lives of his crew during the winter of 1535. Iroquois people living along the St. Lawrence River gave them a tea made of cedar, and the

high vitamin C content cured them of scurvy. Cedar was introduced to Europe the following year.

Cedars vary from narrow and conical to broad and pyramidal. Some are 10 m (33 ft.) in height; others form neat little buns of less than 0.3 m (1 ft.). They may be multi-stemmed or single trunked. Most are dense, with a relatively shallow root system and grayish brown to reddish brown bark, which shreds vertically once mature. Slow to moderate in growth, they are long-lived.

The alternate, compressed branchlets hold tiny leaves, which are soft and scale-like, overlapping like the scales of a fish and forming feathery, flat sprays. Usually bright green, all are aromatic when crushed because of the presence of volatile oils, which have long been used medicinally. French settlers made brooms from the fragrant boughs, which deodorized as they swept. Today, cedar wood, soft but resistant to decay, is used for shingles, shakes, siding, fences, and fence posts.

The inconspicuous, pollen-bearing male flowers are yellow. The female flowers, which are on the same plant, develop into clusters of small, light brown, four-sided cones, erect when young, pendant when mature.

HOW TO GROW

Cedars do best in sheltered locations, protected from wind, in full sun or partial shade. In deep shade, they become thin, loose, and open. Because they are shallow rooted, they need even moisture throughout the growing season and benefit from mulch. A deep, fertile, well-drained soil is recommended.

Deer love their soft foliage, and male dogs have a compelling social need to urinate on their lower branches. Animal repellents may deter both. Scale insects (see p. 188) can also be a problem.

During winter, screen young plants from the wind and reflected light off the snow to prevent dessication during the first few years of growth.

CULTIVARS

* 'Brandon' is a fast-growing, upright, narrow, columnar selection, 8 m (26 ft.) in height, with a spread of 1.5 m (5 ft.). The soft, dark green foliage is resistant to winter burn. It was introduced by the Brandon, Manitoba, Experimental Station in the early 1900s.
* 'Danica' is a slow-growing, dwarf, globe-shaped cultivar of 0.6 to 0.8 m (2 to 2.5 ft.) in height and spread. Its glossy, emerald green foliage is held in a vertical plane and may become bronze tinged in winter. Place in a sheltered location.
* 'Holmstrup' is very dense, compact, and slow growing, reaching 2.5 m (8 ft.) in height, with a spread of 1 m (3 ft.) and a narrow, pyramidal form. The foliage is vertical and slightly curved, bright green in summer, bronze tinged in winter. Plant it in a protected location with north or east exposure.
* 'Little Gem,' introduced in 1891, is slow growing, small, dense, and globe shaped, reaching 0.6 m

(2 ft.) in height and width. It has glossy, dark green foliage in slightly twisted sprays.
* 'Little Giant' is very hardy and slow growing. This small, dense, globe shaped cultivar, 0.5 m (1.5 ft.) in height, with an equal spread, has soft, rich green foliage.
* 'Robusta' (syn. 'Wareana'), Ware's cedar, was raised by Thomas Ware of Coventry, England, around 1827. It forms a broad, dense pyramid, 3 m (10 ft.) in height, with a 1.5-m (5-ft.) spread. One of the toughest and hardiest cultivars, it seldom suffers from winter dieback.
* 'Skybound,' introduced by Boughen's Nurseries of Valley River, Manitoba, is, as its name suggests, tall, narrow, and columnar, reaching 8 m (26 ft.) in height with a spread of 2 m (6.5 ft.). The foliage is a rich green.
* 'Smaragd' (syn. 'Emerald') is a narrow, columnar cedar of 3 to 4 m (10 to 13 ft.), with a spread of only 1 to 1.2 m (3 to 4 ft.). It has a tapered tip and lacy, dark green foliage in flat, upright sprays. It has experienced winter burn in some parts of the prairies and is best planted in a sheltered location.
* 'Techny' is broadly pyramidal in form with dark green foliage. It is very hardy, with a height of 4 m (13 ft.) and a spread of 1.5 m (5 ft.), and is used for hedging on large properties.
* 'Umbraculifera' is dwarf and compact, reaching just 0.8 m (2.5 ft.) in height and a spread of 1 to 1.2 m (3 to 4 ft.). It has dark blue-

green foliage and is considered by some to be one of the best of the globe-shaped conifers.

* 'Woodwardii' is a larger, globe-shaped cedar, 2 m (6.5 ft.) in height and spread. Vertical sprays of medium green foliage appear to radiate out from its center.

Tilia
til-ee-ah

Linden, basswood

The genus *Tilia* is a group of highly ornamental, flowering shade trees, many of which reach stately proportions. They have a moderate growth rate and are long-lived. No landscape should be without one.

Pyramidal and often symmetrical while young, they become slightly open with age, but remain dense and low headed. Leaves are alternate, simple, heart shaped, and toothed. Their root systems deep and wide spreading.

Botanist Carolus Linnaeus, also know as Carl von Linne, took his name from this genus, which is called *linn* in southern Sweden. *Tilia* is the Latin name for linden, from the Greek *ptilon*, "winged," which describes its distinctive bracts, below which are suspended pendulous clusters of fragrant, yellow flowers in mid-summer, followed by pea-sized nutlets. These are covered by a thin, green husk and contain a single seed.

HOW TO GROW

Although *Tilia* do best in full sun, young plants are very shade tolerant. This makes them a good choice for planting near declining older trees as eventual replacements. Plant them in well-drained, deep, fertile soil, amended with organic matter, and provide even moisture.

Tilia americana
til-ee-ah ah-meh-ri-*kah*-nah
American basswood

Basswoods are native to eastern and central North America, from Manitoba to Texas, but remember provenance. Trees from seed sources of its most northwestern range (Manitoba) will be the hardiest.

A large, pyramidal tree, it forms a dense, low canopy, with a tapered trunk. The bark is thick, smooth, and silver. Fiber from its stem and bark were once used for rope, nets, clothing, shoes, and mats. Plant stem fibers are called bast fibers, hence, the

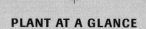

PLANT AT A GLANCE

TYPE: large, flowering, deciduous tree
HEIGHT/SPREAD: 15 to 20 m (50 to 65 ft.)/12 m (40 ft.)
LIGHT: full sun to partial shade
SOIL: deep; fertile
DISTINGUISHING FEATURES: pyramidal form; distinctive bracts with flowers and later fruit
LANDSCAPE USE: shade; specimen

common name, basswood. Twigs are yellow-brown. The large leaves are a lustrous, dark green, heart shaped but asymmetrical at the base, with toothed margins and a pointed tip. They turn pale yellow in fall. The fragrant, yellow flowers hang in clusters. Basswood honey is exceptionally flavorful, and perfume is made from oil distilled from the flowers.

Tilia cordata
til-ee-ah kor-*dah*-tah
Little leaf linden

Swedish strains have proven hardier on the prairies than those originating farther south in Europe. Lindens form a symmetrical, low-headed tree, pyramidal to oval in shape, with a moderately slow growth rate. The bark is an attractive cinnamon color when young, becoming gray-brown with shallow plates when older.

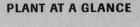

PLANT AT A GLANCE

TYPE: medium, flowering, deciduous tree
HEIGHT/SPREAD: 10 to 12 m (33 to 40 ft.)/8 m (26 ft.)
LIGHT: full sun to partial shade
SOIL: well drained; fertile
DISTINGUISHING FEATURES: symmetrical form; fragrant flowers; red bark
LANDSCAPE USE: shade; boulevard tree
PHOTO: page 149

Cordata, "heart-shaped," refers to the shape of the leaves. The leaves are a shiny, dark green, generally smaller than those of the basswood but otherwise similar. They turn a clear yellow in autumn. The flowers are pale yellow, fragrant, and suspended below a narrow bract that is characteristic of *Tilia.*

CULTIVARS
* 'Golden Cascade' is 12 m (40 ft.) in height, with an 8-m (26-ft.) spread. It has cascading branches, a globe-shaped crown, and consistent golden fall color.
* 'Morden,' at 10 m (33 ft.) in height with an 8-m (26-ft.) spread, is slightly smaller than the species. Although slow growing, it is hardy, dense, and pyramidal.
* Norlin™ is fast growing and broadly pyramidal, reaching 10 to 14 m (33 to 45 ft.) in height, with a spread of 7.5 m (25 ft.). It has strong branches and a low seed set.

OTHER SPECIES AND HYBRIDS
* *Tilia* x *flavescens* 'Dropmore' (*til*-ee-ah flah-*veh*-senz), is a hybrid of American basswood and little leaf linden, which was introduced by Frank Skinner in 1955. It is long-lived, resistant to linden mite and leaf spot, faster growing than either parent, and better adapted to drier soils. Pyramidal and upright, with a dense, compact crown, it reaches 10 to 20 m (33 to 65 ft.), with a 5- to 7- m (16- to 23-ft.) spread, making it ideal for the smaller home landscape.

Elms Not an Option—Yet

* *Ulmus americana* (*ul*-mus ah-meh-ri-*kah*-nah), American elm, is native to riverbank areas of the eastern prairies and was once the preeminent shade and street tree of twentieth-century North America. The devastating effect of Dutch elm disease has made it a symbol of a bygone era. Planting of elms has been largely curtailed and is no longer recommended.

   Large, vase-shaped trees, with narrow-angled crotches, elms are prone to wind damage and breakage and are susceptible to aphids and canker-worms, as well as fungal and bacterial diseases. Their wide-spreading, shallow root systems are highly competitive to plants beneath their canopy. Yet, they're dearly loved.

   Young American elms remain healthy until their bark is furrowed enough to provide habitat for the bark beetles that carry Dutch elm disease. There are, however, some alternative species to American elms as well as disease-resistant elm cultivars, but not all of these cultivars are hardy across the prairies.

* *Ulmus davidiana* var. *japonica* (syn. *U. japonica*) 'Discovery' (*ul*-mus dah-vid-ee-*ah*-nah jah-*pon*-i-kah), Japanese elm, selected by Rick Durand from seed collected at the Morden Research Station in Manitoba, is resistant to Dutch elm disease. It is compact and about a third smaller than an American elm, reaching 10 to 13 m (33 to 43 ft.) in height, with a 10-m (33-ft.) spread. It may suffer some dieback in zone 2. Almost seedless, it has yellow fall foliage. *Ulmus davidiana* var. *japonica* 'Jacan' (photo on page 42), a 1977 Morden selection, is a compact version of the American elm, reaching 11 to 13 m (36 to 43 ft.) in height, with a spread of 10 m (33 ft.). It is hardy to zone 3, has little seed production, and is resistant to Dutch elm disease. Unfortunately, it is seldom available.

* *Ulmus pumila* (*ul*-mus pooh-*mil*-lah), Siberian elm, is native to eastern Siberia, China, and Korea. It has been the mainstay of prairie shelter-belts for decades. It grows quickly where few other trees survive, is adaptable to various soils, and is drought tolerant. However, the wood is brittle and easily broken; its roots are wide spreading, shallow, and high-ly competitive with nearby plants; it is susceptible to a number of fungal and bacterial diseases; and it seeds prolifically, with a 100 percent germination rate. Better trees are now available.

🍁 *Tilia mongolica* (*til*-ee-ah mon-*gol*-i-kah), Mongolian linden, (photo on page 42) is native to China and eastern Russia. At 8 to 10 m (26 to 33 ft.) in height, and a spread of 5 m (16 ft.), it is smaller than other species and the best of the genus for smaller yards. It is broadly pyramidal and round headed, and it has a graceful, somewhat weeping appearance at maturity. New growth is reddish and the bark is attractive and exfoliating. The lustrous, dark leaves turn bright yellow in fall. 'Harvest Gold' is larger, reaching 12 m (40 ft.) in height, with an 8-m (26-ft.) spread. It has an upright habit, a strong central leader, exfoliating bark, and consistent, golden yellow fall color.

Viburnum

vy-*bur*-num

Viburnum, cranberry

Viburnum was originally the Latin name for the Eurasian species, but now applies to the North American species as well. It comes from *viburna*, the term once applied to shrubs that were used for binding or tying.

Prairie-hardy viburnums range from dwarf shrubs to small trees. As a genus, they provide some of our best four-season landscape value: spring flowers, attractive foliage, good fall color, and fruit that are often retained well into winter, if not consumed by birds. No garden should be without at least one, and prefer-ably several, species or cultivars of *Viburnum*.

HOW TO GROW

Viburnum adapt to a wide range of soils, in full sun or partial shade, although most are more compact, more floriferous and fruitful, and have better fall color when in full sun. Nannyberry and the wayfaring tree are very drought tolerant once established. Arrowwood and the American and European highbush cranberries fare better with even moisture.

Viburnum lantana

vy-*bur*-num lan-*tah*-nah

Wayfaring tree

Native to central and southern Europe and to northern Asia Minor, the way-faring tree has been cultivated for centuries. The common name arose from its appearance in odd places, as the seed is widely dispersed by birds. It was once planted near cow sheds to protect animals from evil.

Although multi-stemmed, the way-faring tree appears more tree-like than shrubby. Its stout branches give it a globe-shaped appearance. New stems are light gray-brown and older branches are gray, with many lenticels.

Opposite and simple, the oval, gray-green leaves are fuzzy, wrinkled, and strongly pubescent. The purplish red fall color seldom develops on the prairies.

White flowers with yellow stamens are produced in showy flat-topped clusters in mid-May. The small fruit, well appreciated by birds, change from yellow to red to black as summer progresses, with all colors present in the same cluster during mid-summer.

CULTIVARS

* 'Aureum,' with a height and spread of 2.5 m (8 ft.), has golden yellow young shoots, which later become green. Not widely available, it is worthy of trial.

* 'Mohican' is more compact and globe shaped than the species, with a height and spread of 2 to 3 m (6.5 to 10 ft.). It has thick, dark green leaves, creamy white flowers, and a heavy and highly colored, orange-red fruit set.

* 'Variegatum' has cream and gray-green variegated leaves and a height and spread of 2.5 to 3 m (8 to 10 ft.). Not widely available, it has succeeded in some locations in zone 2 and is worthy of trial.

Viburnum lentago
vy-*bur*-num len-*tah*-goh

Nannyberry

Native to Manitoba and eastward, nannyberry forms a large shrub or small, upright tree, with slender, arching branches. It becomes more open with maturity. *Lentago*, "flexible," refers to the supple nature of the twigs of the species. It suckers moderately if the roots are disturbed.

The leaves are opposite, simple, oval, finely toothed, and pointed. Glossy, dark green through summer, they turn brilliant orange-red-purple in fall if grown in full sun, and they are one of the first to change color. The white flowers, with prominent yellow stamens, are produced in large, showy clusters. Edible berries emerge green and gradually change to yellow, pink, and finally black, with a blue, waxy bloom, persisting throughout

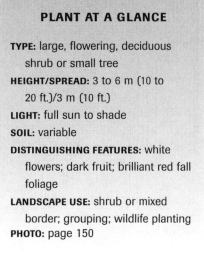

PLANT AT A GLANCE

TYPE: large, flowering, deciduous shrub or small tree

HEIGHT/SPREAD: 3 to 6 m (10 to 20 ft.)/3 m (10 ft.)

LIGHT: full sun to shade

SOIL: variable

DISTINGUISHING FEATURES: white flowers; dark fruit; brilliant red fall foliage

LANDSCAPE USE: shrub or mixed border; grouping; wildlife planting

PHOTO: page 150

winter until consumed by birds.

This is an outstanding plant for four-season ornamental value: flowers, foliage, fall color, and fruit. It deserves far greater use than it generally gets.

Viburnum trilobum

(syn. *V. opulus* var. *americanum*)

vy-*bur*-num try-*low*-bum

American highbush cranberry

American highbush cranberry, native to the prairie woodlands, is a large, upright, spreading shrub, with smooth, gray-brown stems. The species name, *trilobum*, "three lobed," describes the handsome leaves, which are opposite, simple, and palmately veined. Although some viburnum have simple, oval-shaped leaves, *Viburnum trilobum* is one of three species (along with *V. opulus* and *V. sargentii)* with these distinctly and attractively lobed leaves. New leaves

PLANT AT A GLANCE

TYPE: large, flowering, deciduous shrub

HEIGHT/SPREAD: 1 to 4 m (3 to 13 ft.)/3 to 4 m (10 to 13 ft.)

LIGHT: full sun to partial shade

SOIL: adaptable

DISTINGUISHING FEATURES: white flowers; red fruit; handsome three-lobed leaves that turn red in fall

LANDSCAPE USE: shrub or mixed border; wildlife planting

PHOTO: page 150

emerge with a reddish tinge, are dark green throughout summer, and turn a brilliant red-purple in autumn. Fall color is more intense in full sun and can be quite spectacular.

The flowers are in large clusters. The very showy, but sterile, white flowers form an outer ring, which attracts insects to pollinate the inconspicuous, but perfect, flowers of the inner ring. Edible fruit develop from the perfect flowers. Once widely used for pemmican, the fruit produce brilliant clear jelly and persist throughout winter, if not consumed by birds.

CULTIVARS

* 'Andrews,' a compact form similar in size to 'Compactum,' was selected for its superior and early fruit. It has a height and spread of 1.5 m (5 ft.).
* 'Compactum' is a dwarf, compact, upright, and spreading shrub, with a height and spread of 1.5 m (5 ft.). It has white flowers and good fall color, and it is useful for mass planting.
* 'Garry Pink' is 3 m (10 ft.) in height, with a 1.5-m (5-ft.) spread. It is similar to the species, but has very light shell pink, sterile flowers the size of a quarter.
* 'Wentworth' was selected for its fall color and large, edible fruit, which are later ripening, changing from yellow-red to bright red. It has a height and spread of 3 m (10 ft.).

OTHER SPECIES AND HYBRIDS

* *Viburnum opulus* (vy-*bur*-num *op*-yew-lus), European cranberry, is native from Europe to northern

196

Asia and has been cultivated for centuries. Only the cultivars are now found in gardens. The large, white, lace-cap flowers consist of an outer ring of showy, sterile petals and a center of fertile, inconspicuous flowers. The bright red fruit are not palatable and persist throughout winter until consumed by birds. The smaller cultivars, with their uniform shape and foliage, are useful in more-formal situations, such as edging.

* 'Compactum' is a small, dense cultivar, with a height and spread of 1.5 m (5 ft.), which is suited to a smaller landscape. Although it flowers and fruits freely, it develops no fall color.
* 'Nanum' is a dwarf, juvenile cultivar, with a height and spread of 0.6 to 0.8 m (2 to 2.5 ft.). It neither fruits nor flowers. It is grown for its compact, uniform habit, unique tufted appearance, and attractive foliage, which turns a dull purple in autumn. It is useful in formal settings and may do better in partial shade. It needs reliable and deep snow cover in zone 2.
* 'Roseum' (syn. 'Sterile'), often called the snowball bush or guelder rose, has white, sterile flowers in large, globular heads and produces no fruit. It has a height and spread of 2 to 3 m (6.5 to 10 ft.). It is not fully hardy and requires a very sheltered location.

* 'Xanthocarpum' has clear yellow-gold fruit at all stages of development, but no fall color. It has a height and spread of 3 m (10 ft.).

* *Viburnum sargentii* (vy-*bur*-num sar-*gen*-tee-eye), Sargent's viburnum, is native to Siberia, China, and Japan. It forms a large, vigorous shrub, with a height and spread of 4 to 5 m (13 to 16 ft.). It has white, lace-cap flowers, with conspicuous, purple stamens, followed by persistent but not plentiful red fruit. 'Onondaga,' the most common cultivar, has a more compact, rounded form of 2.5 m (8 ft.). Its velvety, dark maroon young foliage retains a maroon tinge, even when mature. Red buds open to pale purple flowers, with darker centers. The red fruit are sparse. It is not widely tested on the prairies, so place it in a sheltered location.

* *Viburnum rafinesquianum* (vy-*bur*-num rah-fin-ess-kee-*ah*-num), arrowwood, is native to the eastern boreal forest of Manitoba. It is a dense shrub, with an upright, oval form, reaching 2 m (6.5 ft.) in height, a spread of 1.2 m (4 ft.), and slender, gray branches. The oval leaves are coarsely toothed and dull green above, with a velvet pubescence below. Large, white, perfect flowers are followed by large clusters of shiny, black fruit.

On the Edge

❀ *Weigela florida* (why-*gee*-lah flo-*ree*-dah), weigela, are small to medium-sized shrubs noted for their showy, tubular flowers, which are produced in late spring and sporadically throughout summer. Only the hardiest of cultivars will survive in protected sites. The most flower-bud hardy are 'Dropmore Pink,' 'Centennial,' and 'Minuet.' Some of the newer cultivars, including 'Alexandra,' 'Red Prince,' and 'Rumba,' with burgundy-purple foliage and repeat-blooming tendencies (which partly compensate for the lack of flower-bud hardiness), are worthy of trial. Plant weigela in a protected, sunny location, with good drainage. Spring pruning is required to remove dead wood and to encourage summer bloom on repeat-blooming cultivars.

Glossary

❦

alternate leaves–leaves that are not opposite each other on a stem

anther–the part of a stamen that bears the pollen (male reproductive cells)

apical dominance–the suppression of the growth of lateral buds by the apical bud

apical meristem–an area of cell division and active growth at the tip of a plant stem

axis–lengthwise support or stem on which leaves, leaflets, flower buds, or other parts are arranged

branch collar–a layer of cambium tissue at the base of a branch; when a branch is removed, the collar can grow to heal the cut

cambium layer–an area of cell division and growth between the bark and the wood; it produces bark to the outside and wood and conducting vessels to the inside

candle–the elongated new growth of a conifer branch that has not yet become woody

conifer–belonging to the *Coniferales*, a group of trees and shrubs characterized by needle-like leaves and seeds borne in cones

coniferous–of the conifers

corymb–a flat-topped or convex flower cluster in which the outer flowers open first

cultivar–a variety developed in cultivation that has stable characteristics which can be maintained when the cultivar is propagated

deciduous–a tree or shrub that drops its leaves for part of the year

dioecious–the male and female flowers are on separate plants

dormant–a resting or non-vegetative state, especially in winter

entire–leaf margins without teeth or divisions

genus–a group of plants or animals with common structural characteristics distinct from all others, usually encompassing several similar species, or occasionally a single species with uncommon differentiation

inflorescence–stem or axis along which all buds are flower buds

lateral bud–an inactive lateral meristem that can grow into a branch

lateral meristem–an area of cell division and growth that gives rise to a branch in a tree or shrub

leaflet–the leaf-like part of a compound leaf

monoecious–male and female flowers are separate but on the same plant

ovary–the part of a pistil that contains the ovules (female reproductive cells); as it ripens, it encloses the seed or seeds and becomes the fruit

palmately compound–a compound leaf in which the leaflets radiate from one point

palmately veined–a leaf in which the veins arise from one point in a way that is similar to the fingers of a hand

panicle–a compound inflorescence formed along a central stem or rachis

perfect flower–a flower with both female (pistil) and male (stamen) parts

petiole–the leaf stalk

pinnately compound–a compound leaf with leaflets coming off either side of a central stem or rachis

pistil–the seed-bearing (female) organ of a flower, normally consisting of the ovary, style, and stigma

provenance–the origin, documented source, of a plant

pubescent–covered with short, soft hairs

rachis–an axis bearing flowers or leaflets

samara–a one-seeded fruit with a membrane or wing

sessile– without stalks

simple leaf–not compound, with a single blade

specific epithet–the second tern of the Latin name of a plant that combined with the genus name designates a species

sport–a spontaneous mutation of a single branch

stamen–the pollen-producing (male) organ of a flower, normally consisting of the anthers and the filament

stigma–top part of the pistil, which receives the pollen

stomata–the specialized cells in the epidermis of a leaf that open and close to regulate gas exchange between the leaf's cells and the air

style–stem-like part of the pistil joining the stigma to the ovary

suckers–shoots arising from a below-ground portion of a stem or a root near, or at a distance from, the trunk of a tree or the main stem of a shrub

water sprouts–succulent and weak shoots arising due to dieback or the severe pruning of a tree

whip–a young tree with one stem and no side branches

References

✦

Bailey, L. H., *Hortus Third*. New York, NY: MacMillan Publishing Co., 1976.

Bailey, L. H., *Manual of Cultivated Plants*, revised edition. New York, NY: Macmillan Publishing Co., Inc., 1949.

Bailey, L. H., *The Standard Cyclopedia of Horticulture, second edition*. New York, NY: The Macmillan Company, 1917.

Bean, W. J., *Trees and Shrubs Hardy in the British Isles, third edition*. London, England: John Murray, 1921.

Bloom Adrian, *Gardening with Conifers*. New York: Firefly Books, 2002.

Brickell, Christopher, editor-in-chief, *American Horticultural Society Pruning and Training , 1st American edition*. New York, NY: DK Publishing, Inc., 1996.

Britton, L. N. and Hon. Addison Brown. *An Illustrated Flora of the Northern United States, Canada and the British Possessions, second edition*. New York, NY: Charles Scribner's Sons, 1913.

Budd, Archibald C. and Keith F. Best, *Wild Plants of the Canadian Prairies*. Ottawa, ON: Information Canada, 1964.

Coates, Alice M., *Garden Shrubs and Their Histories*. New York, NY: Simon and Schuster, 1992.

Coombes, Allen J., *Dictionary of Plant Names*. Portland, OR: Timber Press, 1985.

Den Ouden, P. and Dr. B. K. Boom, *Manual of Cultivated Conifers Hardy in the Cold- and Warm-Temperate Zone*. The Hague, Netherlands: Martinus Nijhoff, 1965.

Dirr, Michael A., *Dirr's Hardy Trees and Shrubs*. Portland, OR: Timber Press, 1997.

Dirr, Michael A., *Manual of Woody Landscape Plants, Their Identification, Ornamental Characteristics, Culture, Propagation and Uses, fifth edition*. Champaign, IL: Stipes Publishing L.L.C., revised 1998.

Fiala, John L., *Flowering Crabapples, The Genus Malus*. Portland, OR: Timber Press, 1994.

Fiala, John L., *Lilacs, the Genus Syringa*. Portland, OR: Timber Press, 1988.

Filmore, Roscoe A., *Roses for Canadian Gardens*. Toronto, ON: The Ryerson Press, 1959.

Frère Marie-Victorin, D Sc., *Flore Laurentienne*. Montreal, QC Imprimerie de la Salle, 1935.

Grace, Julie, editor, *Ornamental Conifers*. Portland, OR: Timber Press, 1983.

Hillier Nurseries, *The Hillier Manual of Trees and Shrubs*. Newton Abbot, England: David & Charles, 1998.

Hosie, R. C., *Native Trees of Canada, eighth edition*. Don Mills, ON: Fitzhenry & Whiteside Limited, 1979.

Hoag, Donald G., *Trees and Shrubs for the Northern Plains*. Minneapolis, MN: Lund Press, 1965.

Kingsbury, John M., *Poisonous Plants of the United States and Canada*. Englewood Cliffs, NJ: Prentice-Hall, Inc., 1964.

Knowles, Hugh, *Woody Ornamentals for the Prairies*. Edmonton, AB: University of Alberta, Faculty of Extension, 1995.

Krussmann, Gerd, *Manual of Cultivated*

Conifers. Portland, OR: Timber Press, 1985.

Lampke, Kenneth F. and Mary Ann McCann, *Handbook of Poisonous and Injurious Plants.* Chicago, IL: American Medical Association, 1985.

Leatherbarrow, Liesbeth and Lesley Reynolds, *101 Best Plants for the Prairies.* Calgary, AB: Fifth House Ltd., 1999.

Macoun, John, *Catalogue of Canadian Plants.* Montreal, QC: Dawson Brothers, 1883.

Marles, Robin J. et al., *Aboriginal Plant Use in Canada's Northwest Boreal Forest.* Vancouver, BC: UBC Press, 2000.

Marshall, H. H., *Pembina Hills Flora,* Morden, MB: Morden and District Museum (1971) Inc., 1989.

Merriam-Webster's Geographical Dictionary, third edition. Springfield, MA: Merriam-Webster, 1997.

Osborne, Robert, *Roses for Canadian Gardens.* Toronto, ON: Key Porter Books, 1991.

Pirone, P. P., *Tree Maintenance, fourth edition,* New York, NY: Oxford University Press, 1972.

Rheder, Alfred, *Manual of Cultivated Trees and Shrubs Hardy in North America, second edition.* New York, NY: The Macmillan Company, 1940.

Rose, Nancy, Don Selinger and John Whitman, *Growing Shrubs and Small Trees in Cold Climates.* Chicago, IL: Contemporary Books, 2001.

Rydberg, P. A., *Flora of the Prairies and Plains of Central North America.* New York, NY: The New York Botanical Garden, 1932.

Shosteck, Robert, *Flowers and Plants, An International Lexicon with Biographical Notes.* New York, NY: Quadrangle/The New York Times Book Company, 1974.

Skinner, Frank Leith, *Horticultural Horizons.* Winnipeg, MB: The Manitoba Department of Agriculture and Conservation, 1966.

Stary, Frantisek, *Poisonous Plants.* London, England: Hamlyn, 1983.

Stearn, William T., *Stearn's Dictionary of Plant Names for Gardeners.* London, England: Cassell Publishers Limited, 1996.

Summer, Judith, *The Natural History of Medicinal Plants.* Portland, OR: Timber Press, 2000.

Williams, Sara. *Creating the Prairie Xeriscape.* Saskatoon, SK: University Extension Press, University of Saskatchewan, 1997.

Wyman, Donald, *Wyman's Gardening Encyclopedia.* New York, NY: The Macmillan Company, 1972.

Index

❦

In this index, numbers appearing in Roman bold type indicate main entries in the book; italic bold type indicates photographs.

Bacteria 20, 55, 57, 76, 188, 193

Balled and burlapped plants 24, 26, 59, 83, 89, 107, 115, 119, 176

Balsam fir (*Abies balsamea*) 11, *43*, **59–60**

Barberry (see *Berberis*)

Bare-root plants 24, 25, 27, 107, 130, 175

Bark beetles 55, 57, 193

Basswood (see *Tilia*)

Beaked hazelnut (*Corylus cornuta*) 18, 80

Bearberry (*Arctostaphylos uva-ursi*) 6, 11, 14, 16, 18, **68**

Berberis thunbergii (Japanese barberry) 6, 14, 16, **69–70**, 'Golden Nugget' 69, 'Rose Glow' *46*, 69, 'Royal Burgundy' ('Gentry') 69, 'Royal Cloak' 69, 'Ruby Carousel' ('Bailone') 69

Betula (birch) 35, **70–73**: *B. fontinalis* (water birch) 72; *B. glandulosa* (bog birch, shrubby birch) 72; *B. papyrifera* (paper birch) 18, *45*, *46*, **70–71**, 120; *B. pendula* (European birch, silver birch), **71–72**, 'Fastigiata' 71, 'Gracilis' 72, 'Lacinata' 72, Purple Rain™ ('Monte') 72, 'Youngii' 72

Big sagebrush (*Artemesia tridentata*) 3, 5, 7, 68

Bigtooth aspen (*Populus grandidentata*) 132

Birch (see *Betula*)

Bird/birds 1, 6, 10, 56, 57, 62, 63, 76, 83, 87, 111, 112, 123, 153, 159, 173, 174, 176, 177, 194, 195, 196, 197

Black ash (*Fraxinus nigra*) 19, 93, 95

Black Hills spruce (*Picea glauca* 'Densata') *42*, 120

Black knot 154, 157

Black spot 57, 58, 167

Black walnut (*Juglans nigra*) **101**

Blight 84, 188

Bog birch (*Betula glandulosa*) 72

Bog rosemary (*Andromeda polifolia*) 12, 18, **68**

Borer 14, 70, 72, 73, 176, 188

Box elder (*Acer negundo*) 6, 8, 9, 14, 16, 18, 23, 24, *44*, 61, 63

Box elder bug 63

Bracted honeysuckle (*Lonicera involucrata*) 19, 111

Bristlecone pine (*Pinus aristata*) 125

Bronze birch borer 73

Broom (see *Cytisus, Genista*)

Buffaloberry (see *Shepherdia*)

Buffalo currant (*Ribes odoratum*) 163

Bullata willow (*Salix fragilis*) 172

Bumalda spirea (*Spiraea* x *bumalda*) 4, *146*, 176, **178–180**

Bur oak (*Quercus macrocarpa*) 6, 7, 9, 15, 19, *141*, **160–161**

Burkwood daphne (*Daphne burkwoodii*) *48*, 86

Burning bush (see *Euonymus*)

Butternut (*Juglans cinerea*) 9, 11, 100, **101**

Buxus microphylla var. *koreana* (Korean boxwood) 73

Canada plum (*Prunus nigra*) 11, **153**

Canker 131, 176

Canker worms 1, 56, 93, 193

Caragana (caragana) **73–75**: *C. arborescens* (common caragana, Siberian pea shrub) 6, 14, **74–75**, 'Lorbergii' 74, 'Pendula' (weeping caragana) *46*, 74, 'Sutherland' 75, 'Tidy' 75, 'Walker' 75; *C. frutex* 'Globosa' (globe caragana) 4, 8, 75; *C. pygmaea* (pygmy caragana) 3, 4, 75; *C. rosea* (rose flowered caragana) 75

Cedar (*Thuja occidentalis*) 1, 2, 6, 8, 13, 19, 37, *43*, 56, 114, 127, 128, *148*, *149*, **189–191**

Celtis occidentalis (common hackberry) 6, 7, 14, 18, **75–76**

Chelated iron 181, 182

Cherry (see *Prunus*)

Cherry prinsepia (*Prinsepia sinensis*) 4, 5, 6, 11, 15, *134*, *139*, 151

Chinese golden pfitzer juniper (*Juniperus* x *media* 'Pfitzeriana Aurea') 106

Chinook 23, 36

Chlorosis/lime-induced chlorosis 61, 65, 168, 178, 181

Chocolate hawthorn (*Crataegus cerronis*) 84

Chokeberry (*Aronia melanocarpa*) 6, 7, 8, 10, 11, 14, **68**

Chokecherry (*Prunus virginiana*) 3, 7, 8, 9, 11, 12, 16, 19, *141*, 154, **157–158**

The Best Books for Prairie Gardeners
from Fifth House Publishers

❦